DEEP MEMOIR

Also by Jennifer Leigh Selig

Reimagining Education: Essays on Reviving the Soul of Learning (2009)
The Soul Does Not Specialize: Revaluing the Humanities and the Polyvalent Imagination (2012/2019)
A Tribute to James Hillman: Renegade Psychologist (2014)
Integration: The Psychology and Mythology of Martin Luther King, Jr. and His (Unfinished) Therapy With the Soul of America (2012)
Deep Creativity: Seven Ways to Spark Your Creative Spirit (2019)
Everyday Reverence: A Hundred Ways to Kneel and Kiss the Ground (2019)
The Writer's Block Workbook: A Psychologist's Guide for Working With and Through Writer's Block (2022)

DEEP MEMOIR

An Archetypal Approach to Deepen Your Story and Broaden Its Appeal

Jennifer Leigh Selig, Ph.D.

With gratitude for "Sometimes" by Mary Oliver
Reprinted by the permission of The Charlotte Sheedy Literary Agency as agent for the author. Copyright © 2008, 2017 by Mary Oliver with permission of Bill Reichblum

Excerpts from SOMEBODY'S DAUGHTER by Ashley C. Ford. Copyright © 2021 by Ashley Ford. Reprinted by permission of Flatiron Books, a division of Macmillan Publishing Group, LLC. All Rights Reserved

And "The Alchemy of Writing," by Leslie Caplan
Writer, Writing Coach, and Trauma-informed Somatic Practitioner, Ashland, Oregon

Author photo by Stephanie Mohan, Fairfax, California @ Creative Portraiture.

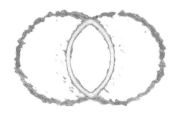

MANDORLA BOOKS
WWW.MANDORLABOOKS.COM

Dedicated and devoted to my beloved Lori Richards
and the mandorla that is our love

Because memoir brought you to me one fateful day
and because your love brings me to my knees every fricking day

Ani L'dodi V'dodi Li
I am my beloved's, and my beloved is mine

TABLE OF CONTENTS

PREFACE

Do We Really Need Another Craft Book About Writing Memoir?

The answer is yes—and no.

No, no we don't need another book on the basics of memoir writing. That's been done and done well by the likes of folks like Mary Karr (*The Art of Memoir*), Beth Kephart (*Handling the Truth: On the Writing of Memoir*) and Judith Barrington (*Writing the Memoir: From Truth to Art*). I know these books well. I assign all three of them to my memoir students. They're good, very good, at covering the basics: how to write good scenes, how to incorporate dialogue, the inclusion of sensory details, the importance of voice, the thorny issues surrounding writing about other people, etc. We have enough of these books—I mean, look, we even have *Memoir Writing For Dummies* now.

No, the problem isn't that we don't have enough books about memoir writing—it's that none of them go very deep.

This is not a criticism. We all need a map of memoir's landscape, a discussion of the important elements of the genre. All these books till the same ground, important ground for a memoir writer for sure. We all need books that help us answer the question, how do I write my story and write it well?

But that's not the question this book asks. Instead it asks, how do I deepen my story in order to broaden its appeal to readers? And to answer that, then yes, we need another craft book about writing memoir.

All the good memoir books worth their salt will mention the importance of connecting with the reader. And they all tip their hats to the importance of seeing the universal in your particular story as a way of doing so. But they don't cover these things in much depth. They're not devoted to exploring and expanding on these like I am with this book.

For example, in Beth Kephart's book, she states, "Some of the best memoirs are built . . . from the contemplation of universal questions within a framed perspective." She gives four examples in three pages. That's it.

Many memoir teachers and books will talk about finding the universal themes in your story. In Marion Roach Smith's book *The Memoir Project*, she asks writers to identify what their story is about. She suggests an algorithm: "This is an (x) and the illustration is (y)." X is the theme of the story, the universal, and y is your particular story intended to illustrate the theme, as in, "This is a story about revenge, and the illustration is my sister's engagement party." This algorithm decenters the author and centers the archetypal theme, and she argues, "Understanding this essential shift is the difference between writing good memoir and boring our socks off." While I appreciate her sensitivity to the needs of the reader "whose hunger for truth is enormous and whose thirst for understanding this life is unquenchable," I think identifying a theme is pretty low-hanging, albeit juicy fruit as a strategy for writing something that will resonate with readers.

Two of my favorite writers and teachers of memoir, Linda Joy Myers and Brooke Warner, are also sensitive to the needs of the reader, and emphasize the importance of what they call takeaways. A takeaway is your take on a theme, your philosophy or your stance, the wisdom you've garnered from your life's journey that you offer the reader for theirs. If we added takeaways to Smith's algorithm, we might say, "This is a story about (x) about which I believe or have learned from experience (y) and the illustration is (z)." To expand on the example above, we could write, "This is a story about revenge, which I believe always comes back to bite us in the end, and the illustration is my sister's engagement party."

Yes, all of this is essential, and we'll explore it in this book—the contemplation of universal questions, the importance of not only knowing but foregrounding your theme, and the value-added nature of takeaways. Yes, yes, and yes. But more yesses too. Yes, to archetypal structure. Yes, to archetypal values. Yes, to archetypal emotions. Yes, to archetypal characters. Yes, to memoir writing as an archetypal process. Yes, to using an archetypal lens to explore memory itself.

The answer to the question about whether we need another book about writing memoir is yes.

This Book's Guiding Symbol or Key Image

I've long been drawn to the symbol of the mandorla, the almond-shaped middle of what looks like a Venn diagram—I consider it a key image that unlocks the passion and purpose of my life. The mandorla is a feminine symbol of connection, the womb of the world, a place where opposites unite, and the bridge between heaven and earth, masculine and feminine, and self and other. It is the latter bridge that I'm most interested in with this book, the place where the self of the author reaches out to connect with the self of the reader and finds common ground. Inside the mandorla is where we search for universality, where we say this is an experience that happens to *us*, this is a feeling common to *us*, this is a value *we* share, this is a journey *we* both recognize, this is a human trait *we* both know.

I have read memoirs that are not mandorlas but are singular, self-contained circles where an author seemingly has no sense of a reader, no sense of a "you," an "us," or a "we," no sense of anything other than the "I" who's telling the story. I'm not going to name names, though I could, and if you're a voracious reader of memoir, you probably could too.

Let me state emphatically that there's nothing wrong with these kinds of memoirs. Some of them spin fabulous yarns. Some of them captivate with language so cultivated that it's wild. Some of them are laugh-out-loud funny. Sometimes we don't care about connection—sometimes the story is enough. Sometimes we're happy just being in the darkened audience, watching a one-person performance under a singular spotlight.

If you want to write that kind of memoir and have the skill and the story, go for it. If you scoff and snort "Reader, Smeader, I just want to tell my story," this book is not for you.

This book is for those memoir writers who want to connect with readers. This book is for anyone who wants to write memoir, not just as art for my sake or art for art's sake, but art for the reader's sake. It's for those who want to write a memoir-song that resounds with others, a song that others can hum along with you, a bird-song that cries, "You too? You too?" It's for memoir writers who want to be generous, à la author Rebecca Solnit when she writes, "The act of widening one's focus is itself an act of generosity . . . not as a way of ignoring one's own life but as a means for connecting it with others' lives."

This book is for those memoir writers who agree with Jerry Waxler in *Memoir Revolution*: "Writing a memoir builds a bridge and reading a memoir crosses that bridge." The bridge connects writer and reader, and as Marina Aris shares in *The Magic of Memoir*:

> Reading and writing a memoir is about only one thing: human connection. And as a writer, I can't think of any greater reward than to know my words have connected me to another human being. To know that my thoughts have traveled the wire of transcendence and rested in the heart and mind of someone who might, just might, understand me, if only a little.

This truly is the magic of memoir. But let's not leave this transcendence one-directional, a reader understanding the writer. This book is for those memoir writers who want to offer their stories as a way to say to the reader, "I understand you, if only a little. And I hope my humble story will help you understand yourself a little more too."

This book is for you.

A Little Bit About Me

I began teaching memoir when two of my academic interests collided—literature and depth psychology. Since I was young, I've been avid reader, so earning a master's degree in literature was a natural for me—my focus was on multicultural literature because I've always been interested in self and other and the connections between us. Since I was young, I've been asking "why," so earning a doctoral degree in depth psychology was also a natural, since it's a psychology concerned in part with understanding the role of the unconscious and its motivations, in addition to what connects us as human beings through the collective unconscious.

While teaching at Pacifica Graduate Institute, a school dedicated to the study of depth psychology, a course on memoir writing opened up. I had read memoirs before, of course, but I had never studied the genre. Geeky researcher that I am—think Brené Brown, without the Texas twang and Oprah as her bestie—I began reading every book on the topic I could get my hungry little hands on, teaching myself the basics. I designed and taught the 10-week course, and I fell. I fell hard.

When the course was over, I still had the jitters, still jonesing for more. That course became a gateway drug, and I was hooked. The problem was, the course was discontinued, and I was left with all this material and a concomitant desire to delve deeper into it. Within a couple of years, when my schedule allowed for more flexibility, I pitched a certificate program in memoir writing called "Writing Down the Soul" to Pacifica's public programs department. I invited my Pacifica colleague, Dr. Maureen Murdock, to teach the course with me. Maureen wrote her dissertation on memoir, and her book *Unreliable Truth: On Memoir and Memory* was required reading in my course. The program was wildly popular, and we've been teaching it together since 2017.

In the decade since I got my first taste of the power and pleasure of teaching memoir, I've read voraciously in the field. I've studied the how-to books, I've read widely across all sub-genres of memoir, I've taught hundreds of students, and I've read and given feedback on countless pages of memoir writing. I've studied *The New York Times* bestseller list, reading the memoirs that find their way onto the list to discern their secrets. I've studied book reviews by trained professionals and I've read lay reviews on sites like Goodreads. I've watched countless hours of YouTube videos of memoirists reading from their books and watched their interviews. The same goes for memoir podcasts. For my students, I've hosted over a hundred "memoir of the month" book club Zooms where we meet to discuss a memoir of interest, and I've listened carefully to them as they've noted what worked for them—or not—in any given memoir. I'm writing a full-length memoir myself, and I've written and had published my own memoir-adjacent pieces, most notably in the book *Deep Creativity: Seven Ways to Spark Your Creative Spirit*.

Ah, there's that word "deep" again. I can't get away from it. *Deep Creativity* is a book about using the principles of depth psychology to enhance your creativity. *Deep Memoir* is a book about using the principles of depth psychology to enhance your memoir, in particular, through an understanding of how archetypal patterning acts as a bridge between "I" and "we," from the sterility of the circle enclosing "me" to the embrace of the mandorla inviting "us."

"The stories we create influence the stories of other people, those stories give rise to still others, and soon we find meaning and connection within a web of story making and story living."

~Dan P. McAdams, *The Stories We Live By*

INTRODUCTION

The Potential and Promise of an Archetypal Approach to Writing Memoir

We are living in the golden age of memoir. While critics once dismissed the genre as an exercise in self-important navel-gazing (and it often still is), memoir writing as a genre has been elevated, not only in popularity (there are often several memoirs on *The New York Times* bestseller list in any given week) but also in status. Memoirist Annie Ernaux received the 2022 Nobel Prize in Literature "for the courage and clinical acuity with which she uncovers the roots, estrangements and collective restraints of personal memory." In her acceptance speech, Ernaux acknowledged that although memoir is written "in the individual mode—'it is to me this is happening,'" memoir also has a transpersonal dimension, when the "I" of the writer reaches across to the "I" of the reader and connects through the universal. Memoir writing is a paradox then—memoirs are written by an "I" to the "you" of the reader in order to say something about "we the people."

I expand upon that paradox in this book, that we are each incredibly particular human beings with life stories as unique as our fingerprints, *and* that there is nothing new under the sun. All life experiences we've had (at least on the archetypal level) have also been experienced by multitudes of others before us and others who will come after us. We share a story with no one and we share a story with everyone. And that leads to the premise of this book—to write a memoir that strikes the most resonant chord possible in your readers, it's important to know that your story is entirely personal and specific to you, *and* your story shares something in common with the stories of others—a place where you and your readers meet in the middle of the mandorla.

Ralph Waldo Emerson wrote, "The good writer seems to be writing about himself, but has his eye always on that thread of the universe which runs through himself and all things." We can take Emerson's quote and make it specific to memoir: good memoirists seem to be writing about themselves, but they have their eye always on that thread of the universe that runs through themselves and all readers.

And what is that thread of the universe? The answer is simple, yet amazingly powerful: *the archetypes that live in our collective unconscious.* They are the raison d'être for this book, the throughline for every chapter, and my goal for the book, which is also simple, yet amazingly powerful: to help memoir writers become more conscious of the archetypal dimensions of their story, and of the memoir writing venture itself, the process we go through as we shape our stories first for ourselves, then for our readers.

What is an Archetype?

If archetype is an unfamiliar word for you, you'll be pleased to know that the definition is easy to grok. Archetypes are universal patterns that live in the psyche—the Greek word for soul—or in the mind, if you prefer that word. In calling them universal, I mean that all people in all cultures in all time periods recognize these patterns, though they may live in the unconscious or run like a script in the background of which we're unaware. In fact, the computer analogy is a good one. We can imagine archetypes as the software that comes preloaded on every computer. The neurotypical brain is wired, so to speak, for pattern recognition.

We see this illustrated in even the youngest of children who recognize archetypal patterns in the stories they love. Take *The Lion King* for example. Children recognize **archetypal characters**, like the orphan and hero (Simba), the fool (Timon and Pumba), and the guardian (Zazu). They recognize **archetypal themes**, like the fall from innocence (when Mufasa is killed and Simba is exiled) and good versus evil (Simba and Mufasa versus Scar). They recognize **archetypal values** like friendship and love (Simba and Nala) and harmony (the state of the Pride Lands before Mufasa's murder and after Simba takes the throne back). They recognize **archetypal feelings** like anticipation (Simba just can't wait to be king!) and guilt and grief (when Simba thinks he's killed his father).

They recognize **archetypal structures** like the hero's journey that Simba embarks upon, beginning with the call to adventure when an exiled Simba returns to the Pride Lands and, with the help of allies like Zazu, Nala, Timon, and Pumba, defeats Scar in a final battle on Pride Rock. They don't just recognize them in *The Lion King*–they recognize them in other books and movies as well, without anyone having to sit them down and point them out.

Of course, a memoir is a true story and not a piece of art like a film that's easy to pepper with archetypal patterns writ large. Alfred North Whitehead said that "art is the imposing of a pattern on experience," and while that may be true, you can't impose a pattern upon your past in the art of memoir–you can't simply create a character in order to impose the pattern of a ruler upon it, or create a theme like the healing power of love. No, you can't create a pattern out of whole cloth, but you can *discover* or *uncover* the patterns that are already there in your story as you lived it in the past, and you can *deepen* and *enhance* the patterns on the page as you write them in the present. And your future readers will thank you for it, because in memoir, the connection between the writer and the reader is key, and what connects us is the archetypal screen upon which our stories are projected. While our fingerprints are uniquely ours, we all have fingers upon which those prints rest. This book will show you how to give your readers the finger (so to speak!) *and* the fingerprint, the universal transpersonal *and* the uniquely personal.

The Universal Transpersonal and the Uniquely Personal Aspects of Memoir

While the metaphor of giving your readers the finger may be original to me, this idea that great memoirists combine the unique with the universal is, *well*, rather universal among teachers and critics of memoir. Cheryl Strayed, author of the immensely popular memoir *Wild: From Lost to Found on the Pacific Crest Trail*, writes, "The most powerful strand in memoir is not expressing your originality. It's tapping into your universality. This isn't to say you shouldn't be original in your writing– you are the only one who can write that universal experience in just that way." Other people steeped in the genre may reverse the formula and argue that the most powerful strand is the originality, and indeed, I've seen the argument made time and time again by memoir teachers—if you go deep enough into your own originality, if you tell your own story in all its unique glory, you'll automatically tap into the universal. No matter which side of the equation you give more weight to, there is consensus in the memoir world that stories need to be both personal and transpersonal.

It's the people in the latter camp to whom I take exception, those who think that if you just dig deep enough into your personal story, you'll automatically strike a universal vein and mine memoir gold, connecting with masses of readers who will resonate with your story. I've read many memoirs, *few of them memorable*, where I never sensed a writer trying to connect with the reader, trying to throw out a universal thread that weaves us both together. Indeed, it's partly why memoir still carries some stigma around navel-gazing—there are plenty of memoirs and memoirists who focus exclusively on their navels, who never seem to look up and notice their readers have navels too. Their memoirs scream *me me me* and *mine mine mine*. So no, I don't think universality comes automatically with the telling of a uniquely personal story.

Nor do I think it's as easy as "tapping" into universality. That implies too easy a process, a mere *tap tap tap* on the keyboard and *voilà*! Out comes a universal story! Emerson said we have to keep our eye *always* on the thread of the universe, implying a certain requirement to pay attention, to stay awake and alert for insight into the collective nature of our personal story. Just as a relationship takes hard work, forging a relationship with our readers also takes hard work, a conscious commitment to connect deeply. This book offers archetypal sites of connection, places we can *tap tap tap* to connect with our reader.

In *The Art of Time in Memoir*, Sven Birkerts writes, "The search for patterns and connections is the real point—and glory—of the genre" of memoir. Kate Christensen shares about the searching she did in her two memoirs, *Blue Plate Special* and *How to Cook a Moose*: "I wanted to connect with readers in the course of figuring out, in writing, how my own life was both singular and universal." She also writes, "Finding the universal in the singular, and vice versa, is a challenge and a thrill and, ultimately, a source of tremendous peace." Why peace? If I had to answer for Christensen, I'd say it's because in writing with an eye to the universal aspects of your story, you discover you're not alone. Because you're connected to the web of human experience. Because you're living well-worn patterns that others have lived before you and will live after you. Because what happened to you is yours, yes, but it's also ours.

Maureen Murdock writes, "That's what we do when we write memoir: We put back together fragments of our life and the lives of our loved ones in a way that reflects the universal experience of being human. In doing so, we become a part of each other." She also speaks of a connection with the reader that memoir makes possible. "If I write about some experience in my life and reflect on it in such a way that it touches your experience of your life, then we have made a connection, regardless of our difference in class, ethnicity, or gender. We may not be aware of it at the time, but something happens on a deep level to both of us." She attributes this to the current popularity of memoir, how "we all search for a way to express our lives and we yearn for an experience of the commonality of our human existence." Expressing our lives equals the uniquely personal aspect of memoir writing. Experiencing the commonality of our human experience is the universal, transpersonal aspect of memoir writing.

Yes, to both. And yes to doing both, not by stumbling into universal territory unconsciously, but by mining our stories consciously, with an Emersonian eye on the threads that connect us.

Archetypes Meet Neuroscience

If neuroscience intimidates or overwhelms you, I've got your back. Give me eight paragraphs to make a connection here, or you can skip to the end of this section for the money shot and still write a damn fine memoir. I just want to offer a little theory on why an archetypal approach to writing memoir is a good idea, brain-wise.

The Swiss psychiatrist C.G. Jung is credited with bringing archetypal theory into the mainstream in the first half of the 20th century, though the idea of archetypal or universal forms is certainly as old as the fourth century BCE and Plato. In the Platonic view, archetypes or universal forms are "absolute essences that transcend the empirical world yet give the world its form and meaning. They are timeless universals that serve as the fundamental reality informing every concrete particular" (Richard Tarnas). Sensing a theme here?

Jung was, of course, exploring and writing about archetypes before technology allowed us to spy inside the brain, so he could only speculate about where archetypal pattern recognition comes from. He acknowledged pattern recognition could be taught, but he ultimately believed it was "inherited," that "endless repetition has engraved" the archetypes into our minds. He wrote, "It seems to me that their origin can only be explained by assuming them to be deposits of the constantly repeated experiences of humanity." For example, people experience enough orphans over time, and through evolution, the brain develops to recognize the orphan archetype without needing to be taught it. Jung called the recognition of archetypes "inborn, shared, collective."

Jung was quick to point out, like Plato, that the archetypes we inherit are merely ideas and forms without specific content attached—it's up to us to fill in the content later, in the same way that the writers of *The Lion King* took the form of the orphan and filled it with Simba, and the writers of *Frozen* filled it with Elsa and Anna, and the writers of *Moana* filled it with Maui. Think of the orphan archetype like an empty glass, and Simba, Elsa, Anna, and Maui are what these screenwriters poured into it.

Let me extend the metaphor. Jung would say we're all born with a bunch of empty glasses (the archetypes) that we will eventually, when it's developmentally appropriate, begin to fill with content. Take the example of two baby girls born around the same time to mothers who are best friends. Their mothers share the fantasy that these girls will grow up to be best friends as well. For the first two or three years of those girls' lives, though their brains are hardwired to recognize friendship, they're not developmentally ready for it yet. What they are developmentally ready for is the archetype of play, which they do side-by-side, together but not really together-together. The archetype of friendship will eventually awaken, with all its recognizable traits such as interest in and enjoyment of the other person, trust and loyalty, support and nurturing. Then, both girls will decide if they want to fill the glass of best-friendship with the content of the other, or if there's someone else better suited to their unique characters and temperaments to fill the role.

Of course, they'll also absorb what their family and their culture teaches them about friendship. There's a nature aspect to archetypes—our brains are wired to recognize these forms—but there's also a nurture aspect, a way that we're taught *how* to fill the forms. If I can offer another analogy, we can compare the archetype to the body. If we're born healthy, we're all born with the same basic skeletal and organ structure, but how we come to flesh out that body will vary and is culturally signified. What clothes are deemed appropriate for our gender or age, whether we mark our bodies with tattoos or piercings, how we wear the hair on our heads or groom the hair on our bodies—there's no cross-cultural agreement on any of this. Plus, it often changes over time (just look at those wigs on America's founding fathers!).

In *Metaphors of Self*, James Olney also offers the analogy of the human body to describe the archetypes, writing that they are "like the human body, given to us at birth to be lived into." We don't *choose* them (in the same way we don't choose to come into the world with five fingers or seven), and we *don't* make them (in the same way we can't make another finger), but we *experience* them.

Jung was often critiqued for his theory of inherited archetypes, and he died in 1961 before the advent of MRI and fMRI machines that could actually scan the brain and tell us what's going on inside. However, current neuroscience is proving him right. Let me just quote a few authors and researchers to make this point quickly because it's so important for memoir writers and the premise of this book.

Nobel Prize-winner Gerald Edelman, in his book *Second Nature: Brain Science and Human Knowledge*, discusses how pattern recognition is the basis for all thinking: "Brains operate . . . not by logic but by pattern recognition." In *I Is An Other*, author James Geary's book on metaphor (a form of pattern recognition we'll discuss in Chapter VII), he picks up on this idea and writes, "Our brains are always prospecting for pattern." Infants as young as two months old know how to shift their eyes in response to expected patterns. Research shows that adults, "when presented with random stimuli and explicitly informed that the stimuli are random . . . still claim to be able to find patterns in the sequences. The brain is so fanatical about patterns that it will gladly generate patterns even where none exist." Evolution has played an important role here. Geary writes, "From an evolutionary perspective, pattern recognition is essential. The brain's pattern recognition circuits take raw data from the senses, sort through it for apparent patterns, and use those patterns to determine a response." That's how we learned to survive dangers, forage for safe food and water sources, protect our tribe, and find a mate and procreate.

In *Wired for Story*, Lisa Cron quotes neuroscientist Anthony Damasio who states, "The brain is a born cartographer." Cron adds, "From the moment we leave the womb, [the brain] begins charting the patterns around us." James Geary writes, "Pattern recognition is so basic that the brain's pattern detection modules and its reward circuitry became inextricably linked. Whenever we successfully detect a pattern—or think we detect a pattern—the neurotransmitters responsible for sensations of pleasure squire through our brains." Our brains love to map, it appears. Our brains love to see patterns, to seek patterns, and to think through patterns. And here's the money shot—if memoir writers want to send sensations of pleasure squiring through the brains of their readers (and what memoir writer wouldn't?!), we can do so by keeping our eyes trained toward archetypal patterns.

Four Pieces of Good News About Archetypes for Memoir Writers

First, let me assure you, you've got this. Even if you've never heard the word archetype before, you came hardwired just like all of us to recognize them, and with some conscious attention, you can work them into your writing. That's what this book is for, to bring what you already know in the back of your mind to its front and center.

Let me give you an example of just how easy it is. Let's return to the archetypal theme of friendship. Every friendship memoir will be particular because the two friends are particular—they have their own individual fingerprints, after all. Gail Caldwell's story of her friendship with Caroline Knapp in *Let's Take the Long Way Home: A Memoir of Friendship* tells an entirely different story than Hua Hsu's story of his friendship with Ken in *Stay True*. But friendship itself? That's the finger, and you know a lot about that finger already. So when you sit down to write a memoir about friendship, you think deeply about who your friend is and what they mean to you—the "me" of the story—but you also think broadly about friendship in general, what friendship means to us as human beings, its archetypal nature. What are the qualities of a good friend? What do people value about friendship? What are some of the hallmarks of friendship? What draws people to each other? What causes them to move apart? How are friendships tried and tested and found true? If friendship follows patterns, what might those patterns look like?

And you don't have to think alone. Maybe you'll read and reference a few books on friendship, the psychology and philosophy of it. Maybe you'll include quotations about friendship. Maybe you'll refer to famous friends over the ages, like Ralph Waldo Emerson and Henry David Thoreau, or Susan B. Anthony and Elizabeth Cady Stanton. Maybe you'll do some research on friendship in different cultures, searching out what's universal. Maybe you'll reference movies and music about friendship, or popular children's books on the topic. You'll go deep, and you'll go wide—remember Rebecca Solnit's quote in the preface: "The act of widening one's focus is itself an act of generosity . . . not as a way of ignoring one's own life but as a means for connecting it with others' lives." That's what it means to keep friendship as an archetype front and center in your memoir writing, as an act of generosity to your reader with whom you want to connect. Not only is it not difficult, but it can be a lot of fun to gaze, not only at the navel of your own friendship, but at the navel of friendship itself. Hua Hsu did that in his friendship memoir, and it won the Pulitzer Prize. Just sayin'.

A second piece of good news addresses a worry many memoir writers share—the old "does the world really need another memoir about _____?" Fill in the blank here—friendship, coming out, grief, illness, difficult childhoods, addiction, etc.—they've all been done already. But that's the thing about archetypes—they've all been done already too! There's nothing new about addiction as an archetype. Sure, there may be new drugs to get addicted to and new treatments for addiction, but addictive substances have always existed and people have always tried to curb addiction. Saying the reading world doesn't need another memoir about addiction is like saying the music world doesn't need another song about love. No, there's always going to be an audience for songs about love and memoirs about addiction because love and addiction are archetypal experiences. In any given maternity ward in any given place in the world, there are babies being born who will fall under the spell of love and who will succumb to the siren song of addiction.

Leslie Jamison, author of *The Recovering: Intoxication and Its Aftermath*, writes about the bias the publishing industry has against memoirs in fields they find saturated.

> Googling the phrase "just another addiction memoir" yields several pages of results, mostly blurbs insisting that a certain book isn't "just another addiction memoir," an author insisting his book isn't "just another addiction memoir," or an editor insisting she didn't acquire "just another addiction memoir." This insistent chorus reflects a broader disdain for the already-told story, and a cynical take on interchangeability: the idea that if we've heard this story before, we won't want to hear it again. But the accusation of sameness, just another addiction memoir, gets turned on its head by recovery—where a story's sameness is precisely why it should be told. Your story is only useful because others have lived it and will live it again.

I think she's spot on here, and the comparison to the stories told in recovery is apropos. "In recovery," she writes, "I found a community that resisted what I'd always been told about stories—that they had to be unique—suggesting instead that a story was most useful when it wasn't unique at all, when it understood itself as something that had been lived before and would be lived again. Our stories were valuable because of this redundancy, not despite it." Archetypal experiences, by their very nature, *are* redundant. Leslie Jamison's recovery shares patterns with Mary Karr's recovery in *Lit*, Caroline Knapp's recovery in *Drinking: A Love Story*, and Augusten Burroughs' recovery in *Dry*. Though they are all "already-told stories," they are in no way interchangeable and the value of one does not take away from the value of another.

In other words, we need your story too. Just because someone filled a glass with their story doesn't mean there's not a glass for you as well.

Cheers!

The third piece of good news about archetypes for memoir writers is right there in the subtitle of this book: writing into the archetypal dimensions of your story will broaden your audience and deepen your memoir's appeal. Now, I'm not promising that if you write more explicit archetypal patterns into your story, it will become an instant bestseller.

I'm not saying if you write about the archetypes of eating, praying, and loving, that you'll sell millions of books like Elizabeth Gilbert, or if you write about the archetypes of being lost and found, you'll sell millions of books like Cheryl Strayed (*Wild: From Lost to Found on the Pacific Crest Trail*), or if you write about the archetype of the student/mentor relationship, you'll sell millions of books like Mitch Albom (*Tuesdays With Morrie*). Even if your story is universal, the particulars need to be interesting and your voice and skill as a writer matter. But what I can say with absolute confidence is you'll connect more with your readers–and your readers will connect more with you–if you invite a "we" and an "us" into your story.

The book summary for Mitch Albom's *Tuesdays With Morrie* offers an instructive example of this. Listen to the way the summary reaches out to connect with the reader.

Maybe it was a grandparent, or a teacher, or a colleague. Someone older, patient and wise, who understood you when you were young and searching, helped you see the world as a more profound place, gave you sound advice to help you make your way through it.

For Mitch Albom, that person was Morrie Schwartz, his college professor from nearly twenty years ago.

Maybe, like Mitch, you lost track of this mentor as you made your way, and the insights faded, and the world seemed colder. Wouldn't you like to see that person again, ask the bigger questions that still haunt you, receive wisdom for your busy life today the way you once did when you were younger?

Mitch Albom had that second chance. He rediscovered Morrie in the last months of the older man's life. Knowing he was dying, Morrie visited with Mitch in his study every Tuesday, just as they used to back in college. Their rekindled relationship turned into one final "class": lessons in how to live.

Tuesdays with Morrie is a magical chronicle of their time

together, through which Mitch shares Morrie's lasting gift with the world.

This bit of marketing text shows a publisher highly aware of the archetypal relationship at the core of the story. The description doesn't focus on the particulars of the characters of Mitch and Morrie—we'll come to know them in more detail once we enter the pages of the story. Instead, it wraps itself around the universal, cozying up to its potential audience through a shared connection, cooing the bird-song of "You too? You too?"

We'll study these memoirs and scores more to see how their authors successfully use archetypal patterns. I'll give you example after example in every chapter as we focus on the following archetypes—the storyteller, structure, the journey, character, meaning, truth, image, transformation, and community—taking a 360-degree circle around the components of the genre. In doing so, I see myself in the archetype of the host. Anne Lamott writes in *Bird by Bird: Some Instructions on Writing and Life*: "It is one of the greatest feelings known to humans, the feeling of being the host, of hosting people, of being the person to whom they come for food and drink and company. This is what the writer has to offer." This is my hope as well. In the end, I hope this banquet table I've laid out for you will provide plenty of food for thought and fuel for the journey of deepening and broadening your memoir.

And finally, the fourth piece of good news is that even if you never publish your memoir, even if you never finish it, taking an archetypal approach can help you deepen your own story and broaden your connection to humanity and its ageless patterns. It can help you feel less alone, and it can offer you the companionship of others who have danced to similar music, sung similar songs, wrestled with similar questions, stared down similar challenges, and traveled similar journeys. Writing is such a solitary task, but in consciously writing a memoir from an archetypal perspective, you'll know you're not alone—you're a thread in the warp and woof of the universe, woven with everyone else into the pattern of time.

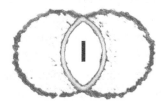

THE ARCHETYPE OF THE STORYTELLER
Reading and Writing the Human Instruction Manual

When I was younger, I loved to get on my yellow banana seat bicycle and cruise the neighborhood at night, looking into the soft-lit windows of other people's homes, imagining their lives, imagining alternative lives to my own, alternative homes not laden with addiction where the children felt safe.

So I loved coming across this line by Meredith Maran in her book *Why We Write About Ourselves*: "Is the urge to read memoirs the same urge that makes us peek into strange, undraped windows at night–not *just* because we're nosy, but to learn something from how other people live, in order to live better lives ourselves?"

I didn't have memoir then, but I wish I did. It would take a dozen-ish years until I ran across memoirs by others who had grown up in alcoholic homes. Reading these stories showed me the resilience of the human spirit, taught me that people could survive anything, in most cases childhoods much worse than mine. Not only did reading these memoirs help me to *relativize* my pain, it helped me to *normalize* my pain, showing me how others had suffered as well. Reading memoirs by alcoholics gave me a sense of compassion for my stepfather as I realized just how strong and thirsty the demon of drink really is. When I was younger and he would come into my room after a drinking binge and promise never to drink again, I would think, in my naiveté, *then just don't*. It took finding the genre of memoir (coupled with Al-Anon and my own research) to realize just how difficult it is for addicts to quench the thirst for self-destruction.

And this is the interesting part about memoir to me—that in order to understand ourselves and our experiences, we often turn to the stories of others, though no two stories are ever the same. No two alcoholic families, no two illnesses, no two coming-out stories will share the same details, and yet, we still find ourselves in these stories. What does this reveal about the human condition?

I believe it speaks to the archetypal nature of storytelling, how we're literally, to borrow the title from Lisa Cron's book, *Wired for Story*. Cron writes, "Story originated as a method of bringing us together to share specific information that might be lifesaving. *Let me tell you a story about what happens to children who disobey their parents*, a storyteller might begin. *Let me tell you the story of a man filled with too much pride.*" Cron argues, "Story, as it turns out, was crucial to our evolution—more so than opposable thumbs. Opposable thumbs let us hang on; story told us what to hang on to. Story is what enabled us to imagine what might happen in the future, and so prepare for it—a feat no other species can lay claim to, opposable thumbs or not. Story is what makes us human, not just metaphorically but literally. Recent breakthroughs in neuroscience reveal that our brain is hardwired to respond to story; the pleasure we derive from a tale well told is nature's way of seducing us into paying attention to it."

"Story is the human instruction manual," as my friend and screenwriting consultant Dara Marks is fond of saying. "Stories teach us through symbolic experiences *how* to be human." We can change the language a bit here and say memoir teaches us through literal experiences *how* to be human. I can learn facts about the human condition of addiction through reading medical websites—I *feel* the lived experience of addiction in reading memoir. I can learn stats on the prevalence of addiction, but through memoir, I better understand the phenomenon of addiction.

James Olney calls autobiography and memoir "the literature that most immediately and deeply engages our interest and holds it and that in the end seems to mean the most to us because it brings an increased awareness, through an understanding of another life in another time and place, of the nature of our own selves and our share in the human condition."

So I think we're drawn to memoir as a genre to read about others' experiences and see something there of our own. But many of us don't just read memoirs about those who share our particular stories. Many of us are drawn to the genre of memoir in general. Here's where my addictive personality comes in—I'm not just drawn to memoir, I'm addicted. I'll read stories that parallel my experiences, and I'll read stories of experiences I'll never have and people I'll never be and places I'll never go. Why is that? Outside of escapism, outside of the pleasure of a novel story, is there an archetype that unites all memoirs and offers instructions for living that apply to everyone?

The Archetype of Transition

I've come to believe that the vast majority of memoirs are built around one archetypal theme—the theme of transition, or change. That's not to say it's the only theme, but I think it's one inherent to the genre (with some exceptions I'll discuss later at the end of this section). For example, a memoir can be focused on the theme of betrayal, but it's also about how experiencing betrayal changes us, about how we transition from being a trusting person to one who's suspicious of others, and maybe transition in the end into someone who trusts again, but with eyes wider open. In *The Emotional Craft of Fiction*, Donald Maass speaks to the archetypal nature of change. "Change is a universal experience. We've all gone through it. We cannot avoid it. The passages of life guarantee it. Change is necessary, difficult, wrenching, and individual. When a character in a story changes, we are reminded of the emotional earthquakes of our own lives. We feel for characters, or so we say. We're really feeling for ourselves."

So one of the reasons we read memoirs, even about experiences we're never likely to have, is to learn how others have gone through life's transitions, have navigated necessary changes, and have weathered the emotional earthquakes of their lives. In the end, memoirs may point to the transformation of a person, but the way I see it, transition is a process, and transformation is a product of the process, the outcome of a transition. I'll discuss this distinction in more detail in Chapter VIII on the archetype of transformation, but for now, I want to explore how the archetype of transition is at the core of the genre of memoir.

I came to this insight when I was teaching my first class on memoir. I was writing down categories or what we might call sub-genres of memoir like **addiction memoirs, coming-out memoirs, illness memoirs, relationship memoirs, loss and grief memoirs, vocation memoirs, coming-of-age memoirs, sudden accident memoirs, travel memoirs, self-help memoirs,** and **spiritual memoirs,** to name a few—and I realized their commonality. They all tell the story of transition.

For example, the arc of most **addiction memoirs** is the transition from being substance-free to substance-using to substance-addicted, and almost invariably end with the transition back to substance-free. The pattern is *I didn't use, I used, I no longer use.* Sometimes the addiction creeps up on people, as Mary Karr explores in her memoir *Lit,* or sometimes it's a pretty instantaneous change, like the sudden onset of an eating disorder explored in all three of Glennon Doyle's memoirs, *Carry On, Warrior, Love Warrior,* and *Untamed.*

Coming-out memoirs are obviously transition memoirs, showing the journey from being closeted to opening the door and coming out. They also chronicle the transitions that occur in our relationships with others when we do so. In his memoir *Mama's Boy,* Dustin Lance Black tells the story of coming out to his conservative Mormon mother when he was 21 years old, and how their relationship changed over time, as she moves from seeing gays as "sinners" and "sickos" to accepting and embracing her son's community.

Illness memoirs, a very popular sub-genre of memoir, tell the transition from health to sickness. Sometimes, if grace descends upon the person, their story chronicles the transition back to health again. There are so many examples, but I'll just mention Eve Ensler's memoir, *In the Body of the World: A Memoir of Cancer and Connection,* which tells the compelling story of Ensler's cancer journey. It's about much more than this—it's also the story of how she disconnected from her body and then became connected to it through cancer—making it a memoir about both physical and psychological change.

Sometimes in **illness memoirs**, the author doesn't survive. Paul Kalanithi's *When Breath Becomes Air* tells about his transition from health to sickness—in his case, lung cancer—and then his transition to death. It also tells of the transition from being a neurosurgeon to being a writer, from being a doctor to being a patient, and from being a career-driven single man to being a devoted husband and father.

Another sub-genre of memoir is **relationship memoirs**, which chronicle how our lives are changed through our relationships. Sometimes the transitions here are quite literal, as in Kalanithi's transition from being single to being married and a father after he meets and marries his wife Lucy. The transitions are always psychological, where a relationship with another changes our lives, like *In the Dream House* by Carmen Maria Machado, which tells of her abusive relationship with her lover—how she got into that relationship, how she struggled within it, and how she got out.

Relationship memoirs are often closely tied, most unfortunately, to **loss and grief memoirs.** This combination documents the loss of a loved one and tells us why the relationship mattered. I mention two friendship memoirs in the introduction, *Let's Take the Long Way Home* by Gail Caldwell and *Stay True* by Hua Hsu, where the beloved friend dies. Another memoir in this combined category is the poet Gregory Orr's memoir *The Blessing*, which tells the tragic story of how 12-year-old Orr accidentally shot and killed his younger brother. These memoirs ask and answer the question, "They were here and I cared for them and now they're gone, and how do I survive the transition?" In Orr's memoir, it's also ultimately about how he became a poet, making it also a **vocation memoir**, which answers the question, "How did I come to this particular occupation?" The memoir *Bone Black* by bell hooks is also a **vocation memoir**, a **coming-of-age memoir** that ends with the discovery of her destiny: "I am a young poet, a writer. I am here to make words."

Coming-of-age memoirs are about the transition from childhood or youth typically into young adulthood, and all the attendant psychological changes. *Lipstick Jihad: A Memoir of Growing Up Iranian in America and American in Iran* by Azadeh Moaveni is another example of this category. You can see by the title that it's layered with transitions—the transition inherent in the words "growing up," but also the transition from one culture to the other. *Lipstick Jihad, Bone Black, The Blessing, Stay True*, and *Let's Take the Long Way Home* illustrate that not only are the majority of full-length memoirs transition memoirs, but they often describe more than one transition—it makes sense that the events in our lives that are most "memoir worthy" are those when we're going through the biggest changes, plural.

Let me offer a few more examples, not to belabor my point, but to give you some other categories of memoir to consider for yourself as well, because I believe we all have multiple memoirs within our life's story, since life is a chef who's constantly serving up change. **Sudden accident memoirs** are all about transition—who I was before the accident or before someone else's accident, and who I am after the accident. Two examples are Gregory Orr's memoir about how his life cleaved in two the moment he killed his brother, and Darin Strauss' memoir *Half a Life* about the similar cleave that occurred when he accidentally killed a high school classmate in a car accident.

I also use the term "sudden accidents" to refer to accidents that occur to us internally, inside our bodies. *The Diving Bell and the Butterfly: A Memoir of Life in Death* by Jean-Dominique Bauby is one such memoir about a man who suffered a tragic stroke and was left with only his brain and his left eye intact. He dictated his memoir by blinking the letters of the alphabet with only that one eye (a human instruction manual I suggest anyone suffering from writer's block should read to relativize their pain). Another memoir in this sudden accident genre is Jill Bolte Taylor's stroke story called *My Stroke of Insight: A Brain Scientist's Personal Journey*, made immensely popular by her TED Talk of the same name.

And speaking of immensely popular, there's Elizabeth Gilbert's *Eat, Pray, Love*, which falls into the category of a **travel memoir**. Travel memoirs tell the story of the literal transition from one place to another, and the way new experiences change us. *Eat, Pray, Love* is also a **relationship memoir**. Gilbert transitions from being a single divorcee to being coupled in a romantic relationship with Philipe in Bali. She later marries him in another transition chronicled in *Committed: A Love Story*, which I would classify as being in the sub-genre of **self-help memoirs**, along with Glennon Doyle's three memoirs I mentioned earlier.

Another popular sub-genre is the **spiritual memoir**, which, in the case of Sue Monk Kidd's *The Dance of the Dissident Daughter: A Woman's Journey from Christian Tradition to the Sacred Feminine*, is also a kind of coming-out story. It's about her transition from being a serious Christian with a career writing for Christian publications to becoming spiritual, not religious, in love with the divine feminine. *Eat, Pray, Love* is also a bit of a **spiritual memoir**, at least the pray part in India.

Finally, let's talk about the **transition memoir** itself, and by that, I mean the literal transition of people who are transgender. Jennifer Finney Boylan's memoir *She's Not There: A Life in Two Genders* was one of the earliest books to gain popularity. It tells of her transition from James to Jenny, and the transitions in all of her relationships that followed, including with her wife and children, and with her students and colleagues at the college where she was teaching. Elliot Page's memoir *Pageboy* chronicles her transition from Ellen to Elliot, from actress to actor, which is also a **celebrity memoir**.

If you're an avid memoir reader like me, you'll be able to add many more examples of memoirs in each of these sub-genres. Of course, this list is not exhaustive, but rather, suggestive. And what I suggest is this— make a list of all the transitions you've been through in your life. List the external transitions that come with age, body changes, accidents, illnesses, relocations, vocations, relationships, travel, etc., but also list the internal transitions and transformations that accompanied the external change. (For those of you who like lines, draw two columns, one with the external change on the left, accompanied by the internal changes on the right). This should give you plenty of material for either more full-length memoirs or standalone shorter pieces.

In Chapter VII, you're going to see how in love I am with image and metaphor as archetypal ways to connect with your reader. Just a hint of it here. Joy Harjo gives us the doorway as a metaphor for transition in her **coming-of-age** and **vocation memoir** *Crazy Brave*. She shares how she became a poet on the other end of a difficult childhood, writing, "It was the spirit of poetry who reached out and found me as I stood there at the doorway between panic and love. There are many such doorways in our lives. Some are small and hidden in the ordinary. Others are gaping and obvious, like the car wreck we walk away from, meeting someone and falling in love, or an earthquake followed by a tsunami. When we walk through them to the other side, everything changes." It's a helpful metaphor—as memoir readers, we need brave storytellers as guides to help us walk through the doorways in our lives, and as memoir writers, we can mine our own doorways for material, for the times we walked through one to the other side.

Memoirs, both those we read and those we write, allow us to slow down time and reflect upon our transitions. Often when we're living through them, especially the sudden ones, we don't have the luxury of time to reflect upon them, and we certainly don't have the clarity that hindsight affords. Transition memoirs can model for us how to be more reflective. Sven Birkerts, author of *The Art of Time in Memoir*, calls this "one of the signal uses of the memoir. For whatever story the memoirist may tell, he or she is also at the same time modeling a way to reflectively make sense of experience—using hindsight to follow the thread back into the labyrinth. Reading their work, we borrow their investigative energy and contemplate similar ways of accessing our own lives." Perhaps through reading memoirs that parallel our experiences, we can actually speed up our hindsight process, allowing us to live more consciously through our own transitions in life as they are occurring.

Now I mentioned earlier that while transition is at the core of the majority of memoirs, there are some exceptions. **Slice-of-life memoirs** may fall into this category. Wikipedia defines slice-of-life as a literary technique "in which a seemingly arbitrary sequence of events in a character's life is presented, often lacking plot development, conflict and exposition" and "the depiction of mundane experiences." A classic example is *Safekeeping: Some True Stories From a Life* by Abigail Thomas. The book is a collection of vignettes from different periods in Thomas' life (what reviewer Elizabeth Andrew calls "tiny windows onto tiny moments"), with no particular theme other than *these things happened to me*, and told in first person, third person, whatever suits the particular vignette. **Humorous memoirs** may also fall in the non-transition category, especially those which focus on funny anecdotes or laugh-out-loud moments in life, though even then, some of those moments are bound to occur during transitions, because it's true what Heraclitus said—the only constant in life is change.

Why Write a Memoir When There Are So Many Good Ones to Read?

I'm channeling my inner Mary Karr with that maybe-only-slightly sarcastic question. She's unsentimental and unsparing and a real straight-shooter, and since she's published three highly successful memoirs, she's got a lot to teach us about writing in the genre.

In the preface to *The Art of Memoir*, she shares, "In some ways, writing a memoir is knocking yourself out with your own fist, if it's done right. . . . The form *always* has profound psychological consequences on its author." She calls writing memoir "a major league shit-eating contest. Any time you try to collapse the distance between your delusions about the past and what really happened, there's suffering involved." And who wants that, right? Who wants to confront their delusions? Who wants to knock themselves out with their own fist? Who wants to suffer? Who wants to devote month after month to a shit-eating contest?

You and me, friend. You and me both.

But why?

Why write a memoir when there are so many good ones to read?

Mary Karr believes that the best memoirs "come from the soul of a human unit oddly compelled to root out the past's truth for his own deeply felt reasons." That's her answer—we write memoir for our own deeply felt reasons. But I think there's more to say than that, and I'm gonna say it because I paid a ton of money for a degree in a field that's always trying to get to the "why" of human behavior.

Be serious, Jennifer. You're no Mary Karr.

Okay then.

I have a deeply felt reason for offering you the following 12 reasons why we write memoir. I believe that the strength of our reason or reasons (because we may have more than one) will strengthen our resolve and sustain us when the going gets tough.

And the going will get tough.

Stephanie Foo knows something about how tough it is. Writing her memoir, *What My Bones Know: A Memoir of Healing From Complex Trauma,* required her to revisit and relive her abusive childhood and confront her parents' actions on the page. In an interview, she shared how knowing her "why" helped get her through it. "I don't think it was really that important to tell this story until I understood my 'why,' which was understanding that there needed to be a story about Complex PTSD told, like somebody just had to tell it, and I didn't see anybody else telling it so I had to be the one to tell it. And the good outweighed the bad. The potential good in many many people's lives that this book could do outweighed the bad."

Putting a sticky note on your computer screen with your reasons may motivate you to keep your proverbial butt in that proverbial chair and muddle your way through writing your memoir. Even better, tell your friends, all your friends, so they can remind you of your reasons when you're pounding your head and repeating, "Why? Why? Why?"

So should we start with what motivated Mary Karr to write her first memoir? **Reason number one** is money, fame, acclaim, credentials–the worldly reasons. Karr needed the money. Her marriage was ending, she had a son to raise, and she didn't have a car. She was willing to knock herself out with her own fist to buy a Toyota. She struck gold, quite literally, with her massively popular (and lucrative) memoir, *The Liar's Club*.

Now Mary Karr had three things going for her: she had a great story to tell, she's a fantastic storyteller, and she had literary connections. While it's great to dream about being a bestselling memoirist, most of us have more realistic expectations and need other less materialistic and more humanistic reasons to sustain us.

A second reason (these are in no particular order, but this one is so important that I'll only briefly discuss it here and give it more of its due in Chapter V and touch on it again in Chapter IX) is our hunger to discover meaning. Sir Laurens van der Post, in the documentary film about his life, *Hasten Slowly*, shares:

> The Bushman in the Kalahari Desert talk about two "hungers." There is the Great Hunger and there is the Little Hunger. The Little Hunger wants food for the belly; but the Great Hunger, the greatest hunger of all, is the hunger for meaning. . . . There's ultimately only one thing that makes human beings deeply and profoundly bitter, and that is to have thrust upon them a life without meaning. . . . There is nothing wrong in searching for happiness. . . but of far more comfort to the soul . . . is something greater than happiness or unhappiness, and that is meaning. Because meaning transfigures all . . . once what you are doing has for you meaning, it is irrelevant whether you're happy or

unhappy. You are content—you are not alone in your Spirit—you belong.

Meaning transfigures all, he writes. To transfigure means to transform, especially to elevate, even to make beautiful. Next to the word transfigure in the dictionary should be the Italian film *Life is Beautiful*. I can barely even write about it without crying. In the film, a father uses his imagination to transfigure the events happening inside a Holocaust concentration camp to entertain and protect the psyche of his young son. Viktor Frankl, the Holocaust survivor who wrote the book *Man's Search for Meaning*, wrote, "Ultimately, man should not ask what the meaning of his life is, but rather must recognize that it is he who is asked. In a word, each man is questioned by life; and he can only answer to life by answering for his own life; to life he can only respond by being responsible." In other words, he's arguing that it's less about *uncovering* the meaning of our lives and what befalls us, but more about *assigning* meaning, answering for ourselves, "What did this mean to me? What meaning do I assign to this event?" This is what the father does in *Life is Beautiful*—he assigns another meaning to the events in the concentration camp for his son.

Eve Ensler answers for her own life in her cancer memoir *In the Body of the World*: "My job was to survive and find a way of imagining all this so that I could transform and tolerate it. My job was to find the poetry." She wanted, perhaps needed, to transfigure her cancer experience by imagining it as meaningful, even poetic. Otherwise, she might succumb to the profound bitterness we may feel when something meaningless has been thrust upon us. "Meaning makes a great many things endurable—perhaps everything," C.G. Jung wrote in his memoir, *Memory, Dreams, Reflections*. So we write memoir to find the meaning of, or assign meaning to, what we've endured in the past.

Reason three is to discover "the hidden narrative of the past," in Sven Birkerts's words in *The Art of Time in Memoir*. "They all [great memoirs], to greater or lesser degree, use the vantage point of the present to gain access to what might be called the hidden narrative of the past." He calls these memoirs "an account of detection, a realized effort to assemble the puzzle of what happened in the light of subsequent realization." We're not in the archetypal role of the storyteller-as-reporter, simply describing what happened in the past, but rather, we're the storyteller-as-detective, sniffing the past for clues about who we are in the present. Writing for this reason suggests, Birkerts notes, that "life can be figured on the page as a destiny, a filling out of a meaningful design by circumstance, and that this happens once events and situations are understood not just in themselves but as stages *en route* to decisive self-recognition."

This was one reason why Natasha Trethewey wrote *Memorial Drive: A Daughter's Memoir*, about her mother's tragic murder by her stepfather when Trethewey was 19. In the beginning of the book, she shares, "I need now to make sense of our history, to understand the tragic course upon which my mother's life was set and the way my own life has been shaped by that legacy." By the end of the book, she has a realization: it was that tragedy that lead her to become a poet. She writes, "This is how the past fits into the narrative of our lives, gives meaning and purpose. Even my mother's death is redeemed in the story of my calling, made meaningful rather than merely senseless. It is the story I tell myself to survive."

This was one of the reasons why A. M. Homes wrote her memoir, *The Mistress's Daughter,* which tells the story of how Homes was given up for adoption at birth, then meets her birth parents for the first time when she's in her thirties. "A big piece of my motivation was to research my history, both my adoptive and biological relatives whose lives I didn't know. I wanted to achieve some kind of understanding of them, and the kinds of decisions they'd made, and the time period in which my adoption happened." Understanding their story allows her to understand more of her story, and while I'm not sure she'd claim Birkerts' promise of "decisive self-recognition," she did come to know herself better. She writes, "You think you know who you are, [and then] the reveal of a piece of information, an addition or subtraction to your known narrative, can yank it all out from under you."

Sometimes information comes to us, and then we put on our detective hats, like Homes did when her birth mother contacted her out of the blue, or like Dani Shapiro did when a DNA test she had "whimsically" taken revealed that the man she thought was her father, was, in fact, decidedly not. *Inheritance: A Memoir of Genealogy, Paternity, and Love* is her account of finding the hidden narrative of her past, including trying to understand why her mother and the man she thought was her father kept her true paternity a secret from her, and searching for the man who was her biological father. But other times we put on our detective hats first, and go out in search of information. Piece by piece, we both collect and recollect information in order to understand, as Birkerts writes, "how I came to be who I am now. Here were the influences, the choices: these were the paths taken, these the ones refused."

Koren Zailckas names this as her reason for writing *Smashed: Story of a Drunken Girlhood*. In the preface, she writes, "My alcohol abuse was a seed that fell at just the right time, in just the right place, when all the conditions were just right to nurture it. To understand the outgrowth, I have to go back to the first bottle that fell out of the liquor chest and into my ready hands. I have to go back to the beginning."

Memoir doesn't demand we arrive at one definitive and perhaps too facile understanding of our beginnings. In *Writing the Memoir: From Truth to Art,* Judith Barrington tells us:

> If the charm of memoir is that we, the readers, see the author struggling to understand her past, then we must also see the author trying out opinions she may later shoot down, only to try out others as she takes a position about the meaning of her story. The memoirist need not necessarily know what she thinks about her subject but she must be trying to find out; she may never arrive at a definitive verdict, but she must be willing to share her intellectual and emotional quest for answers.

Mary Karr refers to this as "the sheer, convincing poetry of a single person trying to make sense of the past."

Koren Zailckas' preface points toward a **fourth reason** we write memoir: to normalize our lives. She clearly views her alcohol abuse as a teenager and young adult as normal for a large swath of girls. In her words: "I wrote this book knowing that my alcohol abuse, though dangerous, was not unprecedented. Nor were the aftereffects I experienced as a result of it. Mine are ordinary experiences among girls and young women in both the United States and abroad, and I believe that very commonness makes them noteworthy."

Another example comes from Ishmael Beah, author of *A Long Way Gone: Memoirs of a Boy Soldier*. His memoir recounts his conscription into the army in Sierra Leone at age 13, where he begins to abuse drugs and commit violent murders. He writes, "My aspiration was to show how everyone is capable of violence if you happen to find yourself in circumstances that propel you toward violence as a way to live." Both he and Zailckas are not necessarily normalizing alcohol and drug abuse or violent crime per se, but their memoirs normalize these things as a response to familial and cultural circumstances. You could do this too if you were me and in these circumstances, their memoirs suggest.

A **fifth reason** we write memoir is to "restory" our lives. The archetypal psychologist James Hillman, in his book *The Soul's Code: In Search of Character and Calling*, writes, "Our lives may be determined less by our childhoods than by the way we have learned to imagine our childhoods. We are . . . less damaged by the traumas of childhood than by the traumatic way we remember childhood as a time of unnecessary and externally caused calamities that wrongly shaped us." The events of our life remain the same, but how we imagine and interpret those events can change—that's what it means to restory or reimagine our lives.

For example, I can imagine myself as a victim of my stepfather's alcoholism, but I can restory that narrative. I can shift my point of view and see my stepfather as a victim himself of his own father-line of alcoholism. I can see my story from another angle and view myself not as a victim but as a victor, the woman who arose from troubled beginnings to become the survivor I am today. I can change my focus away from my stepfather as the source of all things wrong in my life, and look at all the right he did. Through writing memoir, I can restore him as a full human being and not just an alcoholic, and thus restory my life.

bell hooks clearly resonated with this theory of Hillman's. She used the first sentence in his quote as one of the epigraphs for her memoir of childhood, *Bone Black*. hooks shares how she began writing her memoir in order to kill off the child she was. She wants to get rid of her, and rid herself from the past, to break the hold the past had on her, to liberate herself from herself. Instead, she shares that "in writing about her, I reclaimed that part of myself I had long ago rejected, left uncared for, just as she had often felt alone and uncared for as a child. Remembering was part of a cycle of reunion, a joining of fragments, 'the bits and pieces of my heart' that the narrative made whole again."

Hillman's quote focuses on reimagining our childhoods, but we can reimagine and restory our lives as adults as well. We can look back on a failed marriage, a difficult experience of parenting, an act of violence perpetrated on us, and instead of imagining that it "wrongly shaped us," we can reimagine that it shaped us just right, spinning straw into gold with the benefit of hindsight that aging offers us.

A **sixth reason** we write memoir is to unburden ourselves of our secrets. In his book *The Divided Self*, psychologist R. D. Laing writes, "We have our secrets and our needs to confess." That's one of the main reasons we go to therapy, or, if you're Catholic, go to the confessional. It's also one of the main reasons we read memoir, to hear other's confessions.

Kiese Laymon's memoir *Heavy: An American Memoir* is written as a direct address to his mother. He writes of childhood physical and sexual abuse and his struggles with his weight, which leads him to obesity and anorexia, and the psychological weight of the abuse and of being a black man in America. He tells us, "I needed to write that book because there were just so many secrets my mother and I kept from each other. And I just wanted to think a lot about the way secrets impact our bodies. Not just in the way they make us eat too much, or not just in the way they make us eat too little, but often in the way they make us hide our bodies from each other." In revealing these secrets, Laymon calls on his mother, and America, to tell the truth and be "radically honest, generous, and tender with each other."

A classic memoir in the secret-revealing category is Katherine Harris' *The Kiss*, which chronicles the four-year-long incestuous relationship she had with her father when she was in her twenties. Why confess that secret? Because her father laid a curse on her, she tells us—tell anyone about their affair, and she's doomed to never find love. In this way, he would own her forever, not just her body, but her heart and soul. And so she confesses the secret and unburdens herself from the curse. She might agree with Pat Conroy, himself the author of several memoirs: "A story untold could be the one that kills you." Or with Audre Lorde, who in her book *Sister Outsider* asks, "What are the words you do not yet have? What do you need to say? What are the tyrannies you swallow day by day and attempt to make your own, until you will sicken and die of them, still in silence?" Or with the author Carlos Fuentes, who wrote, "Writing is a struggle against silence."

Kim Stafford struggled against silence when he wrote his memoir, *100 Tricks Every Boy Can Do*. The memoir is a tribute to his older brother, Bret, who committed suicide as an adult, and a way for Stafford to come to terms with his loss. He writes, "If we are silent about the story of someone dear to us, silence will be the story of that person. . . . I was not willing to let silence be the final story of my brother."

And this leads us into a **seventh reason** we write memoir is to liberate ourselves from our pasts. Mary Karr writes, "A curious mind probing for truth may well set your scribbling ass free." She notes the cathartic and therapeutic aspects of memoir writing (a topic we'll explore more deeply in Chapter VIII), and adds, "Nobody can be autonomous in making choices today unless she grasps how she's being internally yanked around by stuff that came before." So writing memoir can be a way of cutting the chains that bind us or the puppet strings that yank us. We might not set out with that intention, but it can certainly be a byproduct. About her memoir *Whip Smart: The True Story of a Secret Life*, Melissa Febos shares, "I didn't write a memoir to free myself, though in the process I did."

Sue Monk Kidd, author of the memoir *The Dance of the Dissident Daughter*, writes, "I'm cursed—and maybe a little blessed, too—by being very introspective. I'm constantly probing and contemplating my inner life. Oddly enough, I find that the deeper I go into myself, the more I'm freed from myself. When I write about myself, I find release and freedom in the end because I've managed to distill the experience into some sort of meaning that I can integrate into my life, and then move on without all the preoccupation and unconscious pull of it." bell hooks speaks too of the liberating aspect of writing our memories: "It was the act of making it [a childhood memory] present, bringing it into the open, so to speak, that was liberating."

Sometimes it's not just our scribbling ass we want to set free, but someone else's, or a whole lot of someone else's. Memoir writer Sonvy Sammons shares, "I feel powerless to influence the alcohol use of family members of my generation, but my motivation to reach my daughters, nephew, and grandchildren is strong." Many of my memoir students share a similar motivation—to address intergenerational cycles of addiction, abuse, codependency, and violence in order to liberate the next generation.

Sometimes we're motivated by a need to let go of the past, and other times, by a need to hold onto the past. That's the **eighth reason** we write memoir: preservation or memorialization. In William Zinsser's introduction of *Inventing the Truth: The Art and Craft of Memoir*, he shares how he was writing about his childhood house and decided to go visit it again, only to discover that it was gone. He writes, "But the house survived only as an act of writing." Memoir is a way of preserving the past, of making it present again—and if we publish our memoir or share it with our family, it's a way to preserve the past for the future.

This reason motivated Maureen Murdock to write about her mother. In *Unreliable Truth: On Memoir and Memory*, she states, "In writing about my mother, I am trying to put her back together by passing her on to the future in the only way I can—as memory. When I write about her and the complexity of our relationship, I try to bring her alive in the most honest way I can." She quotes Fred Perles, who said that to remember is to put things back together, "to re-attach a lost member." She continues, "The idea of reattaching a lost member of our tribe through memory is a remarkable concept, because, in truth, that may be the most tangible experience we have of one another."

So we write memoir to make sure our house survives, our mothers and our fathers and all the lost members of our tribes survive, our memory survives, our story survives. Paul Kalanithi, the neurosurgeon who wrote about his life and his struggle with lung cancer, had less than a year between diagnosis and death, the year between his 36th and 37th year of life. He lost his struggle, but his story survives, his life preserved for the daughter he left behind. Memoir becomes a form of memorialization, a monument to something monumental that happened to us, a way of inscribing the indelible experiences of our lives in a format that will survive us.

A **ninth reason** we write memoir is to discover or explore the thread or the pattern of our lives. In his book *Metaphors of the Self: The Meaning of Autobiography*, James Olney writes, "One must wonder what there is, if anything, besides the thread of consciousness to connect the various transformations of the self." I'd assert that the thread of consciousness is a patterned thread, our lives being variations on a theme that is uniquely ours and universal at the same time. One of the defining themes of my life is the healing power of love. If I were to write a memoir exploring this thread, it would be full of my own unique experiences, but the healing power of love is universal, broadening the audience for my memoir.

Marlene Schiwy wrote a memoir titled *Gypsy Fugue: An Archetypal Memoir*. Each chapter explores some aspect of her relationship with the archetype of the gypsy. She tells us, "There is a *gypsy* in my soul. I have felt her dark and shimmering presence in my depths for as long as I can remember. Now I want to follow her down the many pathways of my life and see where she will take me. I want to sing her story." She writes, "I have called it an *archetypal memoir* to express my sense of connection with a broader, deeper realm of meaning and significance than my own life could encompass, and to acknowledge the power of mythic patterns and images that shape our lives like invisible magnets, permeating us with particular passions, prejudices, and proclivities."

Schiwy's obvious audience is anyone who's interested in or feels a connection to the gypsy archetype, but broadening out from there, anyone who's interested in the mythic patterns and images that shape *their* lives. There is power in owning our patterns, in pursuing our passions, prejudices, and proclivities on the page—in realizing our lives as ordered, even in their seeming chaos, around thematic threads. Sven Birkerts notes, "The memoirist writes, above all else, to redeem experience, to reawaken the past, and to find its patterns." In large part, that's what *Deep Memoir* is about—finding the patterns in our lives and writing into them to evoke pattern recognition and resonance in our readers.

A **tenth reason** we write memoir is to tell our own story, rather than letting our family or our culture or our world tell us who we are or tell our story for us. Brené Brown tells us, "You either walk inside your story and own it, or you stand outside your story and hustle for your worthiness." Better, methinks, to own our own worthiness ourselves.

I've mentioned *The Diving Bell and the Butterfly* by Jean-Dominique Bauby, the man who could only write by blinking the alphabet with one eye, one letter at a time. Part of his motivation for writing his memoir (200,000 blinks) was to tell his own story of what was going on in his mind and his imagination. He was not what we crudely used to call a "vegetable." He was a man locked into his body while free in his mind, which he said "took flight like a butterfly." We can imagine many memoirs written with the motivation of explanation—*You think you know who I am, but you don't. Sit down, open my memoir. Let me tell you my own story.*

In fact, telling stories is the premise Dorothy Allison's memoir, *Two or Three Things I Know For Sure*—in particular, telling *her* story. She writes, "The stories other people would tell about my life, my mother's life, my sister's, uncles', cousins', and lost girlfriends'—those are the stories that could destroy me, erase me, mock and deny me." And so, she writes, "I tell my stories louder all the time."

In another place in the book, she writes, "Two or three things I know for sure, and one is that I'd rather go naked than wear the coat the world has made for me." That's another way of saying she wants to tell her own story, but this time, she brings the world in, refusing to accept the story the world tells about her. And this is closely tied to an **eleventh reason** we write memoir, which is to resist invisibility, to tell the stories that mainstream culture is not telling. Roxane Gay's motivation to write about her morbidly obese body in *Hunger: A Memoir of (My) Body* combines the tenth and eleventh reasons—she wants to tell her own story, a story that mainstream culture silences. She writes, "More often than not, stories of bodies like mine are ignored or dismissed or derided. People see bodies like mine and make their assumptions. . . . I have been silent about my body in a world where people assume they know the why of my body, or any fat body. And now, I am choosing to no longer be silent."

Rita M. Gardner wrote her memoir *The Coconut Latitudes: Secrets, Storms, and Survival in the Caribbean* about her experience growing up as an expat in the Dominican Republic during the dictatorship of Rafael Trujillo. She describes her "why," which is a combination of this eleventh reason and the eighth, to preserve her story: "In my sixth decade, I realized two things that made me take action: I didn't want this story to disappear, and I didn't want to be invisible anymore."

Many memoirs by writers of color are written against cultural invisibility and ethnic erasure. Jo Harjo's memoir *Crazy Brave* tells the story of a Native American girl growing up dirt poor in Oklahoma, a story most of us have not heard before. *Good Talk: A Memoir in Conversations* takes us inside the conversations Mira Jacob had about race with her Indian parents, her Jewish in-laws and husband, and her biracial son. These are definitely not conversations most of us are privy to. The Nigerian-Finnish-Swedish Faith Adiele, author of *Meeting Faith: The Forest Journals of a Black Buddhist Nun* and the mini-memoir *The Nigerian-Nordic Girl's Guide to Lady Problems* writes, "I am heir to family-group histories that have been at best underrepresented, at worst misrepresented. My job is to wield memoir as the corrective."

All the above reasons, if not done with our eye on the thread of the universal, can risk falling into the naval-gazing category, can risk the accusation of *me me me, art for my sake*. But the **twelfth reason** we write memoir moves us soundly into *us us us, art for the reader's sake*—to make a difference in other people's lives. David Sheff, who wrote *Beautiful Boy: A Father's Journey Through His Son's Addiction*, wasn't planning to write a long-form memoir on this topic, but he wrote a story about his son's meth addiction for *The New York Times Magazine* and was "stunned" by the reaction—thousands of letters poured in from people who saw themselves and their families in the story. He decided to write the memoir for his readers, sharing, "When we suffer trauma, we need to know that we aren't alone."

Ronit Plank wrote her memoir *When She Comes Back* about the childhood trauma she experienced when her mother left her to join a cult. When she was asked what she hoped readers would take out of it, she shared:

> So many memoirs and nonfiction writers have experienced difficult upbringings. Trauma comes in all shapes and at all times. The insecure childhood trauma is the kind that leaves a lasting effect on someone's life. We have to work hard to try to become whole or safe after enduring the relationships or experiences that made us into who we are. I want people to know that it is possible to change and break away. It's really hard, but it is possible to survive and to even have a good life.

While her book is a coming-of-age memoir, Plank does flash forward to weekly Shabbat dinners she has with her mother (she did indeed come back), and a healing conversation they have one night as adults decades after the childhood trauma, leaving the reader with the possibility that transformation can come with time and forgiveness.

Time and transformation also play a role in Peggy Cook's memoir *Released: Walking From Blame and Shame Into Wholeness*. In her author's note, she states her reason for writing her memoir, the story of how she freed herself from Christian Science, which doesn't allow for medical interventions, and had surgery in her late 30s to correct her clubfeet. She writes, "My writings are meant to illustrate how an individual needs agency in following their own truth. Using one's own voice, there are options to gain physical and mental health and wellness. I wrote this memoir to give hope to those seeking a way to be comfortable and belong in this world. It is never too late."

Carol E. Anderson also wrote her memoir, *You Can't Buy Love Like That: Growing Up Gay in the Sixties,* to offer hope—"hope to young people today who are struggling with their sexual identity—to encourage them to believe in their fundamental goodness and to trust worthy friends with the truth about themselves." She sees writing as a form of social activism: "So I write in spite of my fear, because I believe that personal stories are powerful vehicles for social change and my voice can contribute to that change in a positive way." We can see this as a gesture toward literary companionship, a kind of walking beside another to share your experience with them, to assure them they don't walk alone. Author Ariel Gore shares, "I write because I want to tell you that if your life and your grief feel messy and shameful sometimes, too, that maybe it's not just you—you're like me, and we're everybody. That is what it feels like to be human."

In her book on memoir writing, *Old Friend From Far Away: The Practice of Writing Memoir*, Natalie Goldberg offers a metaphor for this sort of literary companionship: "Writing is the act of reaching across the abyss of isolation to share and reflect." It's also a way of freeing other people. In *Bird By Bird: Some Instructions on Writing and Life*, Anne Lamott shares, "Toni Morrison said, 'The function of freedom is to free someone else,' and if you are no longer wracked or in bondage to a person or a way of life, tell your story. Risk freeing someone else."

Contributing to social change, reaching across the abyss of isolation, freeing someone else—I can't think of more beautiful, generous reasons to write memoir.

This is the magic, the potential, and the power of memoir. As archetypal storytellers, we are writing the human instruction manual, one hard-earned lesson at a time. We are assuring our readers, *you are not alone. You can get through this transition. You can tell your secrets and still survive. You can restory your life. You can make this meaningful. You can free yourself and fly. You got this. If I can do it, you can do it too.*

I'm right here with you.

THE ARCHETYPE OF STRUCTURE
Story as Flesh, Structure as Bones

In the introduction, we discussed how our brains are hardwired for pattern recognition. Lisa Cron, the author of *Wired for Story*, writes, "Your brain doesn't like anything that appears random, and it will struggle mightily to impose order." That's what we do when we sit down to write our story—we attempt to impose order and meaning on what might have seemed chaotic when we were living it. Sven Birkerts, in *The Art of Time in Memoir,* calls this "the main incentive for the writing . . . the exploration of discovered themes and connections."

Researcher and neuroscientist Daniel Bor agrees. "Perhaps what most distinguishes us humans from the rest of the animal kingdom is our ravenous desire to find structure in the information we pick up in the world. We cannot help actively searching for patterns." In writing memoir from an archetypal approach, we are actively searching for the patterns in our life, seeking to impose or discover some sort of structure on the lived events of that life.

But once we uncover or discover those themes and connections, once we understand our life's patterns, we face another structural challenge—how do we page our lives as story? How do we ensure we have good bones upon which to flesh out our lives as story? Where do we even begin?

Time and again, my memoir writers come to me, hands thrown up in the air with exasperation, saying something to the effect of, "I know the story I want to tell, I just don't know how to tell it." They don't know where to begin their story. They often don't know where to end. They don't always know what to include, and what to leave out. They don't know how to deal with time in memoir. Should they use flashbacks, flashforwards, linear, present tense, past tense? The more memoirs we read together, the more varied structures they see, the more they are often overwhelmed. It's a particular blessing of the ever-evolving genre that we have so many structures to choose from, but choice can also feel like a curse at times. Which structure is best? How do we choose? How do we know we've made the best choice?

What Other Memoir Books Say About Structure

In Natalie Goldberg's chapter on structure in *Old Friend From Far Away: The Practice of Memoir Writing*, she raises the question, "How do we form our writing into a structure, a book?" and then answers it by saying she simply doesn't know. "Structure is yours to discover," she tells us. She offers three key descriptors: structure should be *dynamic*, meaning it "fits what you are building"; *organic*, meaning it's "natural to what you have to write"; and *authentic* to your voice, which means "finding a container shaped to hold it, not some preconceived form, but something true for what you are saying." She describes structure as the spine of the story, and she argues, "Get a strong spine and you have freedom of movement." She also calls structure as "a frame around your memories."

To the metaphors of structure as a spine and a frame, in *Writing the Memoir*, Judith Barrington adds structure as a pot or vessel to hold the story, and as a skeleton or tree trunk around which the story shapes itself. In *The Memoir Project*, Marion Roach Smith calls structure the frame too, and in a less obvious metaphor, she refers to it as the wrapper around the lozenge inside. She also uses the metaphor of vertebra, back to that spine metaphor, and argues that a single short memoir piece or an essay or blog post may be a single vertebra, but a long-form memoir needs an entire spine where vertebrae are connected to each other.

While Natalie Goldberg lays it squarely on the memoirist to find their own structure, she does say that we need examples of how people have shaped their memories into a cohesive whole. However, she only offers four books as examples, and most how-to memoir books will do the rather skimpy same. While I find specific examples helpful, there's something missing for me that an archetypal approach can offer; namely, if we view structure as an archetypal form, then what are some of the tried-and-true shapes it takes? If structure is a set of bones, what are some common arrangements of bones upon which memoirists have fleshed out their story? If structure is, as Goldberg suggests, a sort of "choose your own adventure," then what are some of the common adventures that memoirists have found useful in their travels toward a completed book?

Brooke Warner and Linda Joy Myers offer some shapes in their slender book, *Breaking Ground On Your Memoir*: they title their structures *linear, framed, circular, braided, associative,* and *experimental,* and they offer one, sometimes two, thin examples per category. I want to name a few other structural shapes as well, and flesh those out with a more robust offering of examples or role models, if you will, for filling in a form with content. These architects who have gone before you have books that offer a blueprint you can follow. In this chapter, I'll offer eight different archetypal structures—*linear, framed, circular, thematic, mosaic, slice-of-life, blended,* and *unconventional*—and offer examples of memoirs within each structure. I'll also look at how *metaphor* can be a very effective way to structure a memoir.

Two caveats before I begin. First, you'll see a bit of overlap in some of the categories, and for this reason, some memoirs resist being placed in just one category, something I'll note in my examples. Still, I believe the effort at categorization is important, not to pin memoirs down with a proper name, but to suggest possible frames for your work. And second, these categories are meant to be suggestive, not exhaustive. Think of them like the pre-set buttons on a car radio—you can still turn the dial and find other channels. (That metaphor will absolutely not work for young memoirists. You'll have to google "old-timey car radios"!)

Linear

The easiest place to begin is with the linear structure, where a memoir is organized chronologically. This one's so obvious that you might think there's nothing more to say about it, but I do want to offer two ways to get clever within this structure.

The first is to break with chronology at the beginning of the memoir. Some writers will open not at the beginning of the story, but in media res, at some place of high drama in the middle or near the end of the story. Mary Karr chose this format for all three of her memoirs. She writes, "I start with a flash forward that shows what's at stake emotionally for me over the course of a book, then tell the story in straightforward, linear time. I wouldn't suggest that shape for everybody but I would say you have to start out setting emotional stakes—why the enterprise is a passionate one for you, what's at risk—early on."

Let's look at how she did this in *Lit*, which she wrote in her early 50s. She chooses to tell the story of her relationship with alcohol, starting at age 17 and ending when she gets sober in her mid-30s. But she opens with a letter to her son, who was a baby and toddler in the book, and at the time of writing, a 20-year-old man. She acknowledges she's "scorched" parts of his childhood and has caused him pain. She makes it clear what's at stake for her—she's writing partially for him, whom she calls both blameless and "the agent of my rescue." She ends the letter: "Maybe by telling you my story, you can better tell yours, which is the only way to get home, by which I mean to get free of us [Karr and her very dysfunctional parents]." It's a brilliant move on her part, to open with that letter, because she shows us 1) that she takes complete responsibility for her alcoholism and its effects on him, 2) she's sober now, and 3) despite the fact that she was drunk much of his early childhood, they are on good terms now, as evidenced by some stories she tells in the letter. As we're cringing our way through those years when she mothers him while drunk, it helps to know that there is redemption.

Meg McGuire's memoir *Blinded by Hope: My Journey Through My Son's Bipolar Illness and Addiction* takes a similar approach with a fast forward in the beginning that she circles back to in the end. The prologue (often where the fast-forward is placed) begins with her son being sentenced to four years in prison. Chapter 1 is titled "How Did It Come to This?" and begins with McGuire's shotgun marriage to her son's father when they were college seniors; the book then moves forward chronologically, ending with a chapter titled "Dawn" when McGuire picks her son up from prison at the end of his sentence, which coincides with the completion of her book. Had she written the book 20 years later as Karr did, she might have added an epilogue that updated us about how her son has fared in the intervening years, something that many memoirists will do when there's a significant gap between the experience narrated in the memoir and its publication.

Another way to get clever within the linear structure is to break the book into meaningful sections. While Joy Harjo's memoir *Crazy Brave* is told chronologically, she doesn't organize her book into chapters, but rather, she uses the four directions as her structure. She begins in the east, writing, "East is the direction of beginnings. It is sunrise. When beloved Sun rises, it is an entrance, a door to fresh knowledge. . . . East is how the plants, animals, and other beings orient themselves for beginnings, to open and blossom. The spirit of the day emerges from the sunrise point. East is also the direction of Oklahoma, where I was born, the direction of the Creek Nation." We turn the page and there she is, telling us about the beginning of her life. Next she moves north, "the direction where the difficult teachers live," and opens that section with her parents' divorce and her mom's subsequent remarriage to a man who is very difficult indeed. Since the four directions are so emphasized in Native American culture, this organizational structure meets Natalie Goldberg's suggestion that whatever structure you choose, it should be dynamic, organic, and authentic to your voice.

Another example of a creative use of sections is Myra Shapiro's *Four Sublets: Becoming a Poet in New York*, who's title says it all—it's organized around the four sublets she rented in New York City in mid-life to fulfill her dream of becoming a poet. The book opens with a section titled "First Sublet: Greenwich Village, 1981" and moves us through her other sublets and subsequent travel in between. The next-to-last section is "Fourth Sublet: The Village, 1983-84" and the last section is simply, "Home," where we find out that Shapiro's husband Harold has relocated from their previous home in Chattanooga, Tennessee, and joined her in making a full-time home in New York.

Even though the linear structure is a natural fit for storytelling, many memoirists struggle with it for a crucial reason—they don't know where to start their stories, or they realize they need a lot of backstory to help the reader make sense of the experience at hand. I worked with one writer who came to my class wanting to tell the story of her marriage and subsequent divorce. She planned to start at the beginning, the moment they first met, and end a year after the divorce, when they met again at her father's funeral and had a meaningful conversation where forgiveness was extended and received, a 12-year time span from meeting to meeting.

But she began to run into some real problems when she realized just how much her parents' marriage really influenced hers. She had married her father, yes, but she had done everything she could to not become her mother, and lost her true self in the process. For a year, she toiled away at writing about her parents and the marriage they modeled for her, and she even began to write about her grandparents, and what they had taught her parents about marriage as well. At the end of the year, she hadn't even graduated from high school, let alone met her future husband during a year abroad after college! But she had over a hundred great pages that illustrated the intergenerational patterns we often inherit in relationships.

She was pretty distraught, as we often are when our writing plans go awry. She didn't know what to do with the pages. She knew she didn't want to start the memoir with her grandparents' marriages, nor did she really want to start with her childhood at all, and she knew she couldn't write a marriage memoir if she didn't meet the man she married until halfway through the book. Necessity declared the linear structure alone wouldn't do, so she decided on the framed structure instead.

Framed

In a framed memoir, there's typically a linear component—the author is telling the story of a time-bound experience from A to Z. In my student's case, the frame is those 12 years between when she met her future husband (A) and when they had closure at the funeral (Z). At 200 pages, her memoir still opens with A and ends with Z, but in between, half of the pages leave the timeline and tell the backstory of her parents' marriage, their parents' marriages, and her childhood. Her challenge, which Brooke Warner and Linda Joy Myers note in their description of a framed memoir, "is to look for entry points along the linear timeline . . . that allow you to jump around in time and shed some light on those past events that have been significant to your life."

Another challenge they don't mention, but that's inherent in this structure, is pacing and timing. How long can you step away from the main narrative without losing your reader's patience to know what happens next? How do you create a propulsive reading experience if you keep going backward in time? And, another challenge—how do you make the backstory as interesting as the main story, the "then" of the story as compelling as the "now"?

A classic example of a memoir that uses a frame so skillfully is Cheryl Strayed's *Wild: From Lost to Found on the Pacific Crest Trail*. The frame for the story, the A through Z, is the time it takes the 26-year-old Strayed to hike 1,100 miles of the Pacific Crest Trail (PCT) through California, Oregon, and Washington. The book opens with a prologue—that dramatic moment when, 38 days into her three-month hike and completely alone, her left boot flies off the edge of a cliff, irretrievable. But then Chapter 1 takes us back to the beginning, which wasn't when she first conceived of the hike or set her first foot on the trail, but over four years earlier, when she received the news that her mother was dying. By Chapter 2, she's on the trail until the very last page, when she reaches her Z, the Bridge of the Gods that crosses the Columbia River. In between, she uses flashbacks to tell us the story of her mother and her death, of her stepfather and siblings, of her husband whom she divorced, of a lover who convinces her to use heroin, of all the ways she was lost before she was found on the PCT.

If you're interested in the framed memoir structure, her book is worth studying, particularly for those entry points Warner and Myers discuss, the places where she's able to jump rather seamlessly out of the frame and into the past. Just one example, an unforgettable one if you've read the memoir or seen the movie. One night on the trail, she's in her tent and plans to read, but her headlamp is dying, so she turns it off. Laying in the dark, she hugs her body, and when she does, she feels the tattoo on her arm—a horse. Not any horse, but Lady, her mother's horse. The next six pages flashback to a horrific scene where her brother shoots Lady in the head four times, and Strayed watches her slowly die. After a section break, she returns us to the tent and the dreams she had that night.

Strayed's time on the PCT makes up a significant proportion of the book, but for an example of the opposite, we have Brian Broome's

Punch Me Up to the Gods. Broome's frame is relatively insignificant in terms of page count, but very significant in terms of storytelling. Broome opens his memoir with "The Initiation of Tuan," the story of a bus ride in Pennsylvania where he watches a young Black father interact with his toddler son. He returns to the bus ride 17 times, but never for more than a few pages, sometimes as few as half a page. In between, Broome writes essays about growing up Black and gay, struggling with his own father's and the Black community's definition of masculinity. While the essays are not always in linear order, the bus ride is, and the book's closing frame returns to Tuan in such an unexpected and moving way that I won't give away here because it is so perfectly satisfying.

Circular

In a circular structure, the writer "keeps coming back to a particular episode or meaningful point in the story," according to Warner and Myers. The writer may tell the story mostly chronologically, or they may go forward and backward, similar to the framed structure, but they keep returning to a central moment, worrying it and working it over and over again. In Mary Karr's *The Liar's Club*, she opens with what she calls her sharpest memory. She's seven years old and a doctor kneels before her and asks her to tell him where it hurts. She writes, "It took three decades for that instant to unfreeze," with the help of neighbors and family members who "turn that one bright slide into a panorama." She doesn't give us all the details of that moment in the chapter—she's setting the stakes, and creating suspense for the reader, writing, "This blank spot in my past, then, spoke most loudly to me by being blank. It was a hole in my life that I both feared and kept coming back to because I couldn't quite fill it in."

About halfway through the book, she circles back to the story, and fills us in on the details, which I will leave a blank spot as well if you haven't read the book. She comes back to the memory in the very last pages, where she asks her mother, on the advice of a therapist, what happened that night. While the book is ostensibly a linear story, with three sections that name the frame—"Texas, 1961," "Colorado, 1963," and "Texas Again, 1980"—it also circles around this central incident from her childhood.

Two other memoirs that fall under the circular structure are both grief memoirs: Joan Didion's *The Year of Magical Thinking* and Elizabeth Alexander's *The Light of the World*, both about the sudden death of their beloved husbands. Both describe the death scenes early on. Both return to the death often. Both go backward and forward in time, cycling rapidly between the death, the aftermath of the death, and what came before the death—both what came immediately before it and what came long before it. This circular structure makes a great deal of sense when writing about traumatic events, particularly those that strike us like sudden shocks that cleave our lives in two, into before and after—it speaks to the repetitive nature of trauma with its tendency toward intrusive memories.

A circular memoir may come back to a meaningful memory, but it also may come back to a meaningful *person* in the writer's life. A whole memoir may circle around this relationship, with a writer trying to come to terms or peace with this person upon whom their energy centers.

I see this structure used quite commonly in memoirs written about a parent. They're typically not presented in a linear fashion, though there may be a time period that demarks the present story's arc, but they tend instead to move deftly through time, dipping into different periods in the author's life, almost like they are spinning around the parent, picking up memories as they go. Sherman Alexie's memoir *You Don't Have to Say You Love Me* takes as its present story arc the year after his mother's death, but most of the real estate of the memoir lies squarely in the past. Alexie refers to himself as "mother-stung," and the book's 160 chapters, some very short, some filled with poetry, feel like his way of itching the scratch of that sting, over and over again, exploring complicated love and complicated grief. Alexie acknowledges his obsession with his mother: "I return to her, my mother, who, in these pages, dies and dies and dies and is continually reborn."

Another mother-stung writer is Ariel Leve, whose memoir *An Abbreviated Life* takes as its present story's arc a time in her mid-40s when she has moved away from her New York-based mother to Bali, where her father has relocated. There she falls in love with a man and becomes the de facto stepmother to his two daughters. Mothering those girls allows her to reflect back on the horrors of the way she was mothered, and by the end of the book, she completely cuts her mother out of her life.

But very little time is spent on that time in Bali, so little that we almost forget it's there. Instead, Leve circles around the previous four decades of her life. Though her chapters are numbered, there's no real sense that this is for any reason other than convention. Even within one chapter, with liberal section breaks, we leap-frog around Leve's mother, landing on a story from when Leve was in her twenties, jumping back to a story from when she was seven, forward to the current moment again, then way back to her mother's childhood, with lots of reflection and meditation and musing and emoting on the page.

Toward the end of the memoir, she writes, "It took a long time. Four decades. To learn the damage was not irreparable. To graduate from childhood, where it is no longer an affliction but part of the story, is scaling the wall. Climbing out of the ruins. We tell our stories to be heard. Sometimes those stories free us. Sometimes they free others. When they are not told, they free no one." So *An Abbreviated Life* reads like one woman's attempt, through writing, to free herself from the gravitational pull of her mother around whom she's been circling her entire life. This is a powerful illustration of the seventh reason we write memoir—to set our scribbling asses free, as Mary Karr says.

Thematic

Another way to structure a memoir is the thematic approach. Here, theme is foregrounded, not plot in the traditional sense. The stories are chosen to illustrate that theme, and the accretion of those stories serves to amplify it—while each story may stand on its own, all the stories taken together add up to a whole larger than its parts.

Take, for example, Maggie O'Farrell's memoir *I Am I Am I Am: Seventeen Brushes with Death*. Each chapter explores a near-death or potentially life-threatening situation O'Farrell faced throughout her life. Sixteen are her own stories, and she names them after the threatened body part and the year of the occurrence, with chapters such as "Neck (1990)," "Whole Body (1993)," and "Cerebellum (1980)." The years are out of order, which disrupts the idea of plot and chronology and keeps us focused on each individual story and its connection to the theme of brushes with death.

In the last story, "Daughter (The present day)," O'Farrell shares her daughter's devastating bouts of anaphylaxis which she suffers 12 to 15 times a year due to severe allergies, an immune system disorder, and chronic eczema that causes agonizing pain as she scratches off her own skin. O'Farrell writes, "The effects of living with a child who has a life-threatening condition, of loving someone who could, at any moment, be snatched from you? I think about this a lot." And then we realize what all these chapters have added up to. O'Farrell had 16 experiences of being a hair's breadth away from her own death, and now she's mothering a child who is constantly herself a hair's breadth away from death. O'Farrell's message? "A near-death experience changes you forever: you come back from the brink altered, wiser, sadder." But as Fiona Sturges writes in her review, this book "isn't purely about peril, it's about the life lived either side of it."

Another thematic memoir is *Abandon Me: Memoirs* by Melissa Febos. The plural word "memoirs" tells us not to expect one story—in this book there are eight, all linked by the theme of abandonment, about what author Jenny Offill calls "the appearance and disappearance of love" in her blurb about the book. People come and go from Febos' life, including the beloved sea captain who raised her, and a married lover who weaves in and out of most of the stories. Febos also explores the way we abandon ourselves. In the first chapter, she writes, "*Abandonment.* What did that really mean? That I was left? That I had learned to leave myself. That I would retell the story until I found a different ending. Until I learned to stay." We imagine then that she'll learn to stay with this new lover who must abandon another woman, her wife, to be with Febos. But she subverts that expectation in the end, choosing to end the relationship, even though her lover had left her wife by then. She refuses to abandon herself any longer, and in doing so, she shows us that sometimes we do need to abandon ourselves—abandon those parts of ourselves that are destroying us.

One variation of the thematic memoir is the **memoir-in-essays**. Beth Kephart's *Into the Tangle of Friendship* is comprised of linked essays on the importance of friendship. Melissa Febos' *Girlhood* explores how women can free themselves from the narratives imposed upon them by patriarchy. Indian-American author Sejal Shah's *This is One Way to Dance* is a series of essays on the complications of race and cultural identity. These books are by single authors, while other memoir-in-essays are compilations such as *Dancing at the Shame Prom: Sharing the Stories That Keep Us Small,* edited by Amy Ferris and Hollye Dexter and containing 26 essays on the importance of letting go of shame.

Mosaic

Like the thematic memoir, mosaic memoirs (also called collage memoirs) are often built around a theme, but the form is different. There may be a lot of white space on the page, with multiple section breaks. The stories—the pieces of the mosaic—may be as short as a sentence or two, or as long as a couple of pages. There may not be chapters at all, or if there are chapters, they may be numbered and not named, because the point of the mosaic is the overall gestalt. There may be a chronology or a sense of moving through time; there may be a loose plot or arc of the story. Mosaic memoirs allow their authors to bring in other material to lie next to their memories—quotations or song lyrics, anecdotes from history or religion or mythology, bits of philosophy or poetry or literature or art, ideas and theories and musings. Anything goes, really, because, like the thematic memoir, mosaic memoirs work by accretion. In my course on mosaic writing, I refer to it as the Miss Congeniality of structures because it's so warm and welcoming.

But the gift of the mosaic structure is also one of its challenges—anything goes can become problematic. The author Dinty W. Moore captures the experience of reading a mosaic memoir for a reader: "There is the gentle roam through a lovely forest on a leaf-strewn path and then there is getting lost, getting annoyed and wondering what the heck you walked into the woods for in the first place." In order not to lose our readers, we have to ask ourselves: What to add in? What to leave out? What's too tangential? What pieces to put next to each other? How to offer the reader a satisfying experience that doesn't feel chaotic but purposeful instead? How not to strain their patience by making them work too hard to stitch together the fragments that make up the bigger picture we're hoping to evoke? How to make sure each little piece stays with the theme of the larger whole?

It's true—readers have to work a little harder to find what Grant Faulkner calls "patterns amid patternlessness" when they read mosaic memoirs. In *The Art of Brevity*, he writes, "Reading is a matter of making synchronic relations. You search for patterns. Some are overt, some are hidden. The juxtaposition of disparate images can serve continuity or discontinuity, but it automatically creates a synthesis of meaning." We'll talk about the importance of mining your memoir for meaning in Chapter V. Meaning is the "so what?" of your memoir. This thing happened to me—so what? So what does it mean?

In mosaic memoirs, we add another level of "so what?" We ask: These pieces are juxtaposed—so what do they add up to? What meaning can we synthesize out of the disparate images? Because meaning is foregrounded while plot may be backgrounded, mosaic memoirs are often quite contemplative or meditative. The phrase "part memoir, part meditation on x" may apply. It's there in the title of Dani Shapiro's mosaic memoir about her long-term marriage, *Hourglass: Time, Memory, Marriage*—the subtitle offers the three topics she's meditating upon. It's there in the subtitle of David Plante's mosaic memoir, *The Pure Lover: A Memoir of Grief*, a meditation upon grief after losing his lover of 40 years.

Meaning is one necessary element of the mosaic memoir, but there are others. Author Theo Pauline Nestor notes that because the mosaic structure "minimizes the impact of plot, the big kahuna of literary elements, the onus of responsibility for creating literary pleasure falls on the other literary elements, namely theme and language." In mosaic memoirs like Shapiro's, the prose is often quite stylized. Some passages may be concise, and others more meandering. Some passages may be quite lyrical, and others more factual. There's tremendous freedom of form, which at worse can make these memoirs feel uneven, and at best, wildly creative and innovative.

Maggie Smith's memoir *The Argonauts* falls into the latter category. It won the National Book Critics Circle Award, and was called by writer Eula Biss "a dazzlingly generous, gloriously unpredictable book!" Smith's book is a meditation on sexuality, gender fluidity, love, and family, of what she calls "genderqueer family making." There is a plot here—she and her gender-fluid partner Harry meet, marry, and have a child together—but there is so much more. The memoir includes art, philosophy, poetry, literature, feminist theory, queer theory, reflections on maternity and motherhood and more; *The San Francisco Chronicle* called it "a lushly poetic intellectual oasis." So the mosaic is a great memoir structure for those writers whose minds resist being placed in a narrow stall, and want the freedom to roam of their own accord instead.

Slice-of-Life

I've mentioned slice-of-life memoirs in Chapter I. These typically contain short tales chronicling the ordinary stuff of life. "Scenes garnered from a life," author Anne Lamott calls *Safekeeping: Some True Stories From a Life* by Abigail Thomas. The memoir is described as "pivotal moments and the tiny incidents" that shaped Thomas' life. Since these memoirs rely less on an over-arching plot, they are typically most successful when they focus on language and voice, the memoirist's storytelling abilities. One reviewer called *Safekeeping* "an artful scatter of snapshot moments . . . revealing a life that's remarkable not for its events but for the way it's recalled, with rue, insight and wit." Those last three adjectives are Thomas' specialties, easily recognizable across her other memoirs, including her other snapshot memoir, *What Comes Next and How To Like It*. Sometimes in slice-of-life memoirs, there is a theme—*What Comes Next* emphasizes the changes that come with aging.

Humorist David Sedaris' slice-of-life story collections, which often take memories as their content, are loosely based on themes sometimes, but the delight of his work isn't in his exploration of ideas or themes but rather, in his keen powers of observation, the way he notices and finds humor in the absurd and the mundane. Slice-of-life memoirs rely on this kind of careful observation of everyday moments which are elevated through a writer's storytelling facility and voice.

Blended

Another memoir structure is the blended memoir, sometimes referred to as a hybrid memoir, where traditional storytelling joins with another genre. I'll mention a few sub-categories here. **The journalistic,** or what's sometimes called the **researched** memoir, combines storytelling with research. One example is *The Family Tree: A Lynching in Georgia, a Legacy of Secrets, and My Search for the Truth* by Karen Branan. Her memoir tells the story of the 1912 lynching of four innocent Black people in Georgia, sanctioned by her great-great-grandfather for reasons revealed in the book. Branan had been researching the story for nearly 20 years, and she is very much a character in her own book, blending her family story with her own journey of racial reconciliation.

Leslie Jamison's memoir *The Recovering: Intoxication and its Aftermath* clocks in at over 500 pages. Jamison blends her experiences with her own addiction and recovery with academic research on addiction studies; her own journalistic endeavors including multiple interviews with other addicts; and literary criticism, blending in parts of her doctoral dissertation on writers who were also addicts. Both books come with an index, a sure sign you're reading a journalistic memoir!

Jill Bolte Taylor's *My Stroke of Insight: A Brain Scientist's Personal Journey* also comes with an index. Taylor tells the story of her massive stroke in the left hemisphere of her brain, and details her recovery, while sharing research about the brain, including pictures of its topography. She writes about the brain in accessible language and grounds the science in her experience, making for a compelling read even for those not really interested in brain science.

Taylor's book crosses into another blended genre, that of the **self-help** memoir. In general, any memoir could be considered self-help if it helps us understand ourselves and our lives better, but the self-help memoir does so overtly, often addressing the reader and offering specific advice for how to live our lives. Taylor does so in her last chapter called "Finding Your Deep Inner Peace," where she offers advice on how to stay present, to slow down our minds, to unhook our brains from any negative scripts, even how to eat and smell and use our senses. She suggests movement practices like yoga and Tai Chi, using a mantra, drawing Angel Cards, using sounding bowls, and having a gratitude practice.

All three of Glennon Doyle's memoirs fall into the self-help sub-category, particularly her memoir, *Untamed*. The "help" she offers is to liberate women from their domestication, to become the wild cheetahs they are born to be. The chapters are brief, following a typical pattern for the self-help memoir structure—Doyle tells a story or recalls a memory, then uses that as a jumping-off place to impart wisdom and inspiration.

She spends a lot of time discussing her decision to divorce her husband and choose love with her wife, Abby Wambach, and how that decision was informed by a new understanding of motherhood—that being a good mother doesn't mean sacrificing your happiness for your children and disappearing into a marriage that's making you miserable. Instead, she writes, "I'd quit using my children as an excuse to not be brave and start seeing them as my reason to be brave. I would leave their father and I would claim friendship-and-fire love, or I would be alone. But I would never again be alone in a relationship and pretend that was love. . . . Because I am a mother. And I have responsibilities." Insights like these fill the pages, and Doyle's voice is spirited and bold.

Another sub-category of the blended memoir is the **graphic** memoir, which tells a story using comic book-like art or sequential images, usually illustrated by the author. *Fun Home: A Family Tragicomic* by Alison Bechdel is a classic and acclaimed example. It tells the story of Bechdel's difficult relationship with her father, and explores themes like creativity, sexuality, secrets, and suicide. It looks like a comic book with its black, white, and gray-blue panels, but the writing is rich and psychologically astute. Since the popularity of *Fun Home*, many other graphic memoirs have been published, including the acclaimed coming-of-age memoir *Gender Queer* by Maia Kobabe.

One of my favorites is Mira Jacob's *Good Talk: A Memoir in Conversations*. The conversations in the subtitle refer to talks Mira has with family and friends in the course of her life around issues of race: I mentioned in Chapter I that Jacob's parents were born in India, Jacob is an Indian-American who married a Jewish man, and they have a mixed-race brown son. Jacob is an accidental memoirist. She didn't set out to write a memoir, let alone a graphic memoir, but after a particularly funny and disturbing conversation with her eight-year-old son about Michael Jackson's desire to be whiter, she drew images of herself and her son, set them on a Michael Jackson album cover, put the dialogue into bubbles and gave the image to a friend at BuzzFeed. After it went viral, she decided to write her book.

Jacob didn't have any experience as an artist, unlike Bechdel who was an established cartoonist with two decades of publication under her belt. She created her book digitally, using black and white cut-out characters, photographs, and a digital font she created just for the book. She made the stylistic choice to have neutral and unchanging ex-pressions on her cut-out characters' faces. She explains her decision: "The discomfort it unleashes when you're reading it was the same dis-comfort I had walking around America watching everything sort of slide into the shitter in 2015. So it felt really freeing for me not to perform the racial pain that Americans, I think, hunger for and then love to dismiss." I mention this feature of the book to highlight the kinds of creative choices graphic memoirs offer that text-only memoirs cannot.

Another creative contribution to the graphic memoir is Kim Krans' *Blossoms and Bones: Drawing a Life Back Together*. Krans is a visionary artist best known for *The Wild Unknown* card decks. In this memoir, Krans enters an ashram to seek healing from an eating disorder, along with other wounds, and chronicles her time there through black and white drawings. From the book's description, "What emerges from Krans' deeply personal undertaking is a raw and beautiful never-before-seen artists' document that explores what it means to prioritize truth and self-discovery in a world of relentless expectations and distractions." We are right there with Krans during her healing journey, along for an inti-mate real-time ride through the depths of her psyche as she's "drawing her feelings."

The **visual** memoir is another form of a blended memoir that can include photographs, images of artifacts like letters or theater stubs or plane tickets or recipe cards, drawings or original artwork, etc. One ex-ample is Sally Mann's *Hold Still: A Memoir With Photographs*. She inher-ited trunks of family papers and photographs, and when she took them down from the attic and sorted through them, she found "deceit and scandal, alcohol, domestic abuse, car crashes, bogeymen, clandestine affairs, dearly loved and disputed family land . . . racial complications, vast sums of money made and lost, the return of the prodigal son, and maybe even bloody murder." While the book is still primarily text-based with chapters-long stories, Mann often has one or two images on a page, sometimes photographs, other times images of things like the clothes she wore, a paragraph from her mother's journal, old report cards, and other memorabilia. In contrast, Cori Crooks' visual memoir *Sweet Charlotte's Seventh Mistake* resembles a scrapbook, with vivid color paper backgrounds and sometimes images collaged onto them. The stories are short and centered on her drug-addicted con-artist mother who had 15 names, seven husbands, and seven children, Cori being sweet Charlotte's seventh. The text is often sparse with creative fonts and formatting, making some pieces read like poetry.

Unconventional

I mentioned in an earlier caveat that some memoirs would fall into over-lapping categories. *Sweet Charlotte's Seventh Mistake* is not only a blended memoir, a visual memoir with text, but it's also what I call an unconventional memoir—the scrapbook format is not one we typically see in the genre. Brooke Warner and Linda Joy Myers label these kinds of memoirs, and *Sweet Charlotte* in particular, as "experimental mem-oirs" which they define as "those that don't follow the rules of conven-tion." But my boots-on-the-ground experience with several hundred writing students is that finding the right format for their memoir feels like a grand experiment, so I'm sticking with "unconventional" for this category.

One of my students, Marsha Rosenzweig Pincus, wrote *Holding Up the Moon: A Memoir in Haiku*. Pincus had joined a Facebook group committed to writing and posting one haiku a day for a year. In that year, she explored the broken container of "wife-mother-teacher" that she found herself confronting in her 60s. Her 365th haiku read:

> who could imagine
> so much could be carried by
> aching syllables

Out of over 2,500 haiku she wrote in the years following the chal-lenge, she selected 90 for her memoir. On the back cover, she issues an invitation: "Part divination, part creative inspiration, part spiritual jour-ney, *Holding Up the Moon* invites readers to engage the slivers of Pincus' story and use the haiku for bibliomancy, writing prompts, or in-spiration for their own self-discovery and creative expression," making her unconventional memoir fit into the self-help category as well.

Sy Montgomery wrote an unconventional memoir in *How to Be a Good Creature: A Memoir in Thirteen Animals*. Each chapter is devoted to an animal that served as her teacher throughout her life, ranging from dogs, gorillas, octopuses, and tigers. The beautiful fairytale-like illustrations by Rebecca Green and the photographs at the end make this a visual memoir as well, and the jacket cover text names its "vast themes: the otherness and sameness of people and animals; the various ways we learn to love and become empathetic; how we find our passion; how we create our families; coping with loss and despair; gratitude; forgiveness; and most of all, how to be a good creature in the world."

Another unconventional structure is Joan Wickersham's *The Suicide Index: Putting My Father's Death in Order*. It's organized like the index of a book, with entries like

Suicide:
>anger about, 35
>attitude toward
>>his, 36-43
>>mine, 43

Wickersham was well aware that her structure needed to be dynamic, organic, and authentic. She shares, "The structure was the last thing. I wanted a structure for comfort, but I couldn't find that structure. I didn't want to impose something gimmicky, so I'm glad I waited and let the index emerge. If I'd started with the index, the book wouldn't have the organic feeling that I hope it has."

A warning label against being gimmicky is something every writer considering an unconventional memoir structure should take to heart. Maggie O'Farrell's book we looked at earlier, *I Am I Am I Am*, a thematic memoir about her 13 brushes with death, is unconventional in how she names chapters after the body parts in peril, and in the jumpy timeline which appears random at first—and I'll admit, upon first glance and a couple of chapters in, I was considering raising the gimmick flag—but in the end, I believe she pulled off the unconventional structure.

Short memoir essays with unconventional structures abound—I wrote one myself, an exploration of my stepfather's drinking through coopting 18 well-known nursery rhymes such as "Mary Had a Little Lamb."

> Daddy had a little drink
> Its ice as cold as snow
> And everywhere that Daddy went
> The drink was sure to go

But unconventional structures like these and many used in shorter memoir pieces risk straining the reader's patience in long-form memoir, as the writer begins to shoehorn content into structure and the reader spies and cries, "Gimmick!"

Metaphor as Structure

Finally, I want to talk about memoirs that rely on metaphor for their structural spine. They typically make use of one or more of the above traditional structures as well, but couple that with a metaphor that holds the work together. Joy Harjo's use of the metaphor of the four directions as headings inside of her linear memoir is one example. Let's look at some others.

Most authors who use this structure will explain their metaphor in a prologue, introduction, or chapter early in the book. bell hooks describes the structure of her memoir in her foreword to *Bone Black: Memories of Girlhood*. She calls it "an unconventional memoir" that "draws together the experiences, dreams, and fantasies that most preoccupied me as a girl." She tells us the book will "bring together fragments to make a whole," and that "bits and pieces connect in a random and playfully irrational way." She reflects on the writing of her memoir in her collection of essays on the writing life, *Remembered Rapture: The Writer at Work*, telling us the metaphor behind the conception of the book is a hope chest. "I remembered my mother's hope chest, with its wonderful odor of cedar, and thought about her taking the most precious items and placing them there for safekeeping. Certain memories were for me a similar treasure. I wanted to place them somewhere for safekeeping." They are there, neatly, if randomly, folded in the pages of *Bone Black*.

Eve Ensler offers her controlling metaphor in the first chapter of her cancer memoir, *In the Body of the World*. "This book is like a CAT scan. A roving examination–capturing images, experiences, ideas and memories, all of which began in my body. Scanning is somehow the only way

THE ARCHETYPE OF STRUCTURE

I could tell this story." This allows her to have chapters that are only one paragraph long, some that are lists, and others that run many pages, a mosaic memoir of sorts, though her journey from diagnosis to cure is told linearly.

Lidia Yuknavitch also explains the choices behind her memoir's structure, *The Chronology of Water*, a book that defies an easy description. We could place it in the category of thematic memoirs, a theme she poetically names as "writing to bring the delicate dream to the tips of words, to kiss them, to rest your cheek on them, to open your mouth and breathe body to body to resuscitate a self." She challenges chronological storytelling in her paragraphs below, offering water as a metaphor for chronology instead.

> I thought about starting this book with my childhood, the beginning of my life. But that's now how I remember it. I remember things in retinal flashes. Without order. Your life doesn't happen in any kind of order. Events don't have cause and effect relationships the way you wish they did. It's all a series of fragments and repetitions and pattern formations. Language and water have this in common.
>
> All the events of my life swim in and out between each other. Without chronology. Like in dreams. So if I am thinking of a memory of a relationship, or one about riding a bike, or about my love for literature and art, or when I first touched my lips to alcohol, or the day my father first touched me—there is no linear sense. Language is a metaphor for experience. It's as arbitrary as the mass of chaotic images we call memory—but we can put it into lines to narrativize over fear.

She builds her table of contents around the water metaphor, with sections like "Holding Breath" and "The Wet" and "The Other Side of Drowning" with their individual chapters containing stories told in those retinal flashes.

In her thematic memoir, *Gypsy Fugue: An Archetypal Memoir*, Marlene Schiwy explains her structure in her first chapter. The book weaves together four of her lifelong passions: life/memoir writing, the work of depth psychologists, the Roma people, and music. It's the metaphor of music that provides the structure of the book. In the first section titled

"Prelude," she explores the gypsy through history, culture, and imagination. In the second section, "Fugue," she offers 26 personal stories and reflections on the gypsy theme in her life, telling us, "There is no linear tale here; these are windows into my soul." The final section, "Coda," brings the book to its conclusion. She reflects there on the archetypal memoir "as a necklace of bead memories around a central image that attracts our life stories to itself." She tells us that her pages are filled with "rambunctious research and treasured quotes from many sources," and that "literary bricolage belongs to the vagabond imagination and mirrors the roving soul of the *gypsy*."

In her linear memoir *Eat, Pray, Love*, Elizabeth Gilbert tells us in her introduction about the metaphor for her structure–the *japa mala*, a necklace of 108 beads that Hindus and Buddhists use for meditation, touching one bead every time they repeat a mantra. She writes about the significance of the number 108–"a perfect three-digit multiple of three, is components adding up to nine, which is three threes"–the number three "representing supreme balance." Since balance was what she was looking for during her year of travel to three different countries, she divided her story into 108 chapters, 36 chapters for each of the three countries.

Did we need to know this in order to enjoy her memoir? Not at all. I'm sure many readers who skipped the introduction didn't notice the structure. But Gilbert needed it. She wrote of the "methodical discipline" that spiritual seeking requires, and the *japa mala* is a tangible symbol of this. "As both a seeker and a writer," she tells us, "I find it helpful to hang onto the beads as much as possible, the better to keep my attention focused on what it is I'm trying to accomplish." So structure may be just as important for the memoir writer as it is for the memoir reader.

Each of these five authors demonstrates Natalie Goldberg's advice about structure: their structures are *dynamic*, meaning they fit what the authors are building; *organic*, meaning it's natural to what they have to write; and *authentic* to their voices, meaning they found or they built a container that can hold their stories and stay true to what they have to say. The content suggested its own container; the story dictated the structure.

Trust—and Play

I offer all these structures, structures-within-a-structure, and examples to suggest ways you can get creative in shaping and crafting your memoir. When my students struggle to find their structure and ask me what to do, I suggest creative play. I agree with Warner and Myers, who write, "Most people who are stuck in their memoir are really just begging for structure and are in need of permission to start mapping out their story—with the understanding that it can change later."

Permission granted to play! Lay out these structures like clothing and try them on. Ask the question, "What if I did it this way—what would that look like?" and sketch out an answer. Then ask the question again, and sketch out another answer. There are no "I shoulds" for memoir structure, not now, when writers are being so inventive with the form. There are only "I coulds" and there's not a limit in the sky to be found. Think of playing with structure like playing jazz music, which is partly defined by its improvisation and its liberal borrowing from other musical genres. The great jazz trumpeter Miles Davis told us, "Sometimes you have to play a long time to be able to play like yourself." Play with structure, and trust that one day you'll find a structure that allows you to play like yourself.

In an interview about *The Color of Water*, Lidia Yuknavitch says, "I did not know that form would emerge when I began. But writing *COW* is where I learned that a writer can FIND the form from the process of writing—a writer can trust the creative process to yield the shape and patterns. I've been trusting that idea ever since." Yes, a form may emerge from the writing process. Be open to receiving a lightning bolt moment where from the sky falls just the right structure for your memoir, but also get active by taking out your index cards, sticky notes, whiteboard, or outlining software, and start pushing the pieces around and imagining how they might be arranged.

And maybe sometimes, get professional help. Even though Yuknavitch knew she wanted her book shaped like the way the brain works, "in the kinds of retinal flashes and layerings and synaptic firings of an actual brain," she actually didn't know how to order the flashes. Rhonda Hughes, her publisher and editor, "literally came up with the order of the fragments. She ordered them on the floor of her house. To be honest, especially then, I would never have put them in the order that they are in now. I couldn't see that. So without Rhonda Hughes, I'd have a pile of mess. Like my life." Hiring a developmental editor at some point, or handing over your manuscript to trusted readers or a writing community, may be just what you need to show you the forest (the structure of your book) when you can only see the trees (your specific scenes).

Until then, keep writing those trees. And check out the next chapter, a companion chapter to this one really, where we'll look at some common archetypal journey structures that may be useful for organizing your scenes into story.

THE ARCHETYPE OF THE JOURNEY

Nine Archetypal Maps to Understand, Organize, and Convey Your Life's Journey

We've explored how the majority of memoirs center around the archetype of transition. I defined transition as the *process* of change, and transformation as the *product* of the process, the outcome of a transition. Transition memoirs are inherently about a journey—the journey from one place to another, whether that's from one psychological place to another, à la Elisabeth Kübler-Ross' stages of grief, or one physical place to another, à la Cheryl Strayed's *Wild* (of course her physical journey was accompanied by a psychological journey as well).

When you think about it, the archetype of the journey is the primal archetype. A sperm journeys to find an egg; the zygote journeys to become an embryo and then a fetus; the fetus journeys out of the womb to become a baby; and then that baby journeys through life and ends up at its final destination, death (or whatever journey you believe comes after death). All people walking this planet today or any day—which means all your readers present and future—have experienced the archetype of the journey. It's simply hardwired into the human experience. So it makes sense that the majority of memoirs center around transition. In the human instruction manual, we need stories about how to navigate life's vicissitudes.

The Three Basic Stages of Every Journey

The mythologist Joseph Campbell is renowned for mapping out 17 stages of the hero's journey using his vast knowledge of cross-cultural mythology, but he also offered a simpler version, with three main stages: departure, initiation, and return. Something happens to set us off on a journey, some things happen to us while we're on our journey, then we return from our journey. The sperm departs the body and inseminates the egg; the zygote becomes the baby becomes the person who ages and experiences various initiations; the aged person returns to the world beyond the world upon death. We know this story well—we live it every day. Birth. Life. Death.

So how does this translate to memoir writing? How do these three stages of the journey apply to the journey we're preparing to take our readers on? I find when I work with my memoir students, the second stage is the most obvious—they know the story from their lives they want to tell, the events they want to cover, the experiences they want to give words to. It's usually not the middle of their memoir that gives them trouble, it's often the beginning and the end. Where is the story born (begin), and where does it die (end)? Let's look at a classic journey memoir, *Eat, Pray, Love: One Woman's Search for Everything Across Italy, India and Indonesia*, and see how Elizabeth Gilbert framed her story.

This is the basic story Gilbert tells: she journeys to Italy for pleasure (eating), to India for devotion (praying), and to Indonesia for "the art of balancing the two" (loving). Her trip takes a year and is filled with many initiations, including all the trials and tribulations and tests inherent in international travel and cultural challenges. Because of the time-bound nature of this journey, she has a natural framing device for the middle of her story—the initiation stage will be that entire year.

But where to start the story? What is the departure? Is it the minute she gets on the plane to Italy? Is it earlier than that, when she receives the book deal that will pay for her year abroad? Is it earlier than that, when her marriage falls apart and she becomes a spiritual seeker? Is it earlier than that, when she first meets her husband, or when she becomes a published author, or when she writes her first story, or or or? When did this story truly begin? Not to get too philosophical about it or anything, but when does any person's story truly begin? We know now

THE ARCHETYPE OF THE JOURNEY

that even with our own biological conception, half of our genetic material—that egg we once were—was alive inside of our grandmother, and of course our story didn't begin with our grandmother, because her story began inside of her grandmother, and so on.

The memoirist as a creative writer gets to choose the moment when the story she is telling begins, its point of departure. Elizabeth Gilbert begins her journey by telling us about "the moment when this entire story began," when she was on her knees on the bathroom floor of the house she had recently purchased with her husband, after she had three insights—she didn't want to be married anymore, to live in that house, or to have a baby she knew she was supposed to want to have. Feeling herself in "a state of hopeless and life-threatening despair," she found herself unexpectedly praying, and that prayer began what she called "a religious conversation, ultimately leading to her departure from her marriage and her home and her life as she knew it.

Gilbert's aware she could have started her story with the beginning of her marriage and why fell apart, but she makes an argument for why she won't do so: it's too personal and sad; they both had their own issues and she doesn't feel like she can discuss his in public; and she's incapable of being unbiased. She'll skim right past all of it because the marriage itself, its beginning and its initiations and its end, is not the catalyst for the story. It's the prayer to God on the bathroom floor that she declares as her departure.

When my students struggle to define their departure, I typically ask them one question: What was the moment where you were called forth to start this journey, the moment so pivotal that the journey would not have happened without it? I'm after the catalytic moment, the one so critical that if you remove it from the equation, there might be no equation. If I hadn't had that first drink. If I hadn't lost the baby. If I hadn't won the lottery. If I hadn't taken that job. In Gilbert's case, it's if I hadn't gotten on my knees in prayer. It's the "if I hadn't" moment that defines the departure.

Of course, this can still be a house of mirrors. We could argue that if she hadn't married her husband, she would have never been in despair on the bathroom floor in the first place. But her argument is that if she hadn't prayed, she wouldn't have been compelled to go on a spiritual journey. She might have just continued therapy, fallen in love with her divorce lawyer, gone home to visit her parents, and written a book about the virtues of being childless.

And listen, if you're still struggling with how to define the departure, here's the good news. Backstory. Let's imagine someone writing a memoir about their alcohol addiction. Their addiction story obviously begins with their first drink—if they never had a drink at all, they wouldn't have become an addict. But maybe they come from a long line of alcoholics—it's in their DNA. Maybe they grew up in an alcoholic or abusive home, and that led them to the attitude that drinking was a valid choice for pain management or escapism. Though these may be valid factors in their propensity toward alcoholism, still, without that first drink, there would be no journey through addiction. However, through backstory and through flashbacks, they get to include it all.

Now let's look at the other place many memoirists get stuck—the return stage.

There are two common forms of the return. First, there's the literal, physical return. You leave your home, you go out and have a journey, you return home. A natural ending for Elizabeth Gilbert's memoir would be her return to the United States at the end of her year of travel. But she doesn't choose to end it there—she chooses a different kind of return altogether. She ends the book near the end of her year abroad, when she and her Brazilian lover Filipe travel to the tiny island of Gili Meno in the Indonesian archipelago, a place she had visited two years earlier, right in the middle of the four-year collapse of her marriage. She calls that previous visit to the island "the very worst of that entire dark journey." So she returns to it with Filipe, this time "under notably different circumstances," full of the pleasure that comes with eating, the enlightenment that comes with praying, and the ecstasy that comes with new love.

She uses this final chapter to summarize for us the journey she had taken in those two years:

I've circled the world, settled my divorce, survived my final separation from David, erased all mood-altering medications from my system, learned to speak a new language, sat upon God's palm for a few unforgettable moments in India, studied at the feet of an Indonesian medicine man and purchased a home for a family who sorely needed a place to live. I am happy and healthy and balanced. And, yes, I cannot help but notice that I am sailing to this pretty little tropical island with my Brazilian lover.

It's a fantastic choice for a place to conclude—to return to a place where you were incredibly miserable when you're in a state of perfect bliss, and I would imagine it's a much more climactic ending than what happened when she returned to the US.

The second common form of return is a state return, or a return to some prior status quo or state of being. Many memoirs follow this pattern: life was going along as normal, something happened that created chaos (the departure from normalcy), chaos ensued and it had to be navigated (the initiation), but then it ended and life normalized again (the return). A new normal, of course, because you're now carrying with you what you've learned from your time in the chaos. Illness memoirs often follow this journey structure, with diagnosis as departure, illness as initiation, and recovery as the return (death and dying memoirs promise the ultimate return to your afterlife belief of choice). As with addiction memoirs with their journey from sobriety to addiction back to sobriety again, the return is almost a given with the genre. It's almost unimaginable that an addiction memoir would end with the author still as addicted as they were throughout the book.

Relationship memoirs may follow this pattern—there's a catalyst that causes the relationship to falter, such as infidelity or some secret life revealed, or there's an external event that disturbs the status quo, such as an accident or illness or challenge with a child. After the relationship goes through its initiation, it may return restored to a new normal again. If the relationship ends, the author may return to a restored peace of mind they had before the catalytic event occurred, or their new normal may be another, better relationship (à la Elizabeth Gilbert's relationship with Filipe).

Whatever the nature of the return, what's important is that the author returns with some earned wisdom. In Joseph Campbell's language, this is the "boon," the gift the journeyer receives as a result of the journey that they in turn offer the community for its benefit. In memoir writing, the memoir itself can be the boon. The author has earned some wisdom on their journey and they're offering that wisdom to their community of readers.

Elizabeth Gilbert tells us in her last chapter what the gift of her journey has been: she returns with a "solid truth, a truth which has veritably built my bones over the last few years–I was not rescued by a prince; I was the administrator of my own rescue." She continues, "I think about the woman I have become lately, about the life that I am now living, and about how much I always wanted to be this person and live this life, liberated from the farce of pretending to be anyone other than myself." In a very real sense, Gilbert returns from her journey with more of herself than she left with.

For the millions of readers of her memoir, she gifted them the catalyst for their own journey toward liberation. In her preface to the 10th-anniversary edition, she marvels at the success of the book, and explains it to herself like this: "Millions of women seem to have used the book as a recovery manual for their own heartbreaks and spiritual explorations." The human instruction manual that is Eat, Pray, Love tells readers, in Gilbert's words, "If your life has become a trash compactor, then you are allowed to try to escape that trash compactor, whatever it takes. By escaping your own trash compactor of an existence, you can revive, reinvigorate and reinvent yourself, almost at a cellular level." That is the boon of the book, the wisdom she earns through her journey.

She acknowledges that this is not a message women are used to receiving. "On the contrary, society's message to women has always been the opposite: Embrace the trash compactor that is your life. Bow down beneath your burdens and shut your mouth about it. Be a good sport. Give up more. Work harder. Surrender more. Endure more. Sacrifice more. Become a good martyr. Remember that your life is not your own; your life belongs to everyone else. Your life belongs to your father, your husband, your children, your community. . . ." In contrast, her memoir asks, "'What if your life belongs to you?'"

The Question Itself as a Journey Structure

Not all journeys end with the big bang of a return. We don't all get Filipes or Gili Meno moments. We may start sick and journey toward health and still end up sick in the end. We may have a difficult relationship with our father that we journey toward resolving, and we simply can't. We may start single and journey toward finding a partner and find one—there's no return to being single in the end. Still, we need to share our earned wisdom from the journey if we want to make a contribution to the human instruction manual.

If our journey doesn't fit neatly into the three-part journey structure—if we haven't yet or perhaps cannot offer the boon through our return—we can ask a question and offer an answer as the boon.

The connection between a question and a journey is right there in the root of the word itself—*quest*. When we ask a question, we quest. Meaning we journey or travel in search of the answer. It is a journey with purpose and intentionality. And it, too, follows the three-part journey structure. The question arises and we depart on a journey to seek answers. We go through trials and errors and missteps and dead ends and frustrations and moments of grace during the initiation phase, and in the end, we return to our lives with the answer to our question. A failed quest is of course possible, but in memoir, it would usually mean that though we didn't find the answer we were looking for, we return with something else of value instead—maybe we discover we've been asking the wrong question, and we lay it to rest. For example, a woman who sets out to answer the question, "How do I learn to forgive my perpetrator?" may come back with the answer, "I can't. But I can learn to forgive myself."

"What if my life belonged to me?" Gilbert asks. "This is the question that I asked myself back when I was lost in a fog of sickness, shame and sadness." And that question obviously resonated with millions of readers. Gilbert writes:

> For me, the most gratifying thing is to see how people, mostly women, took that story and then applied its questions to their own life and made changes in their own lives based on what they had read. Because, as outrageously insane as this may seem in 2016, there are enormous numbers of women out there in the world who still have not gotten the memo that their lives belong to them. . . . All of a sudden they realized about a situation in their own life, *Maybe it doesn't need to look like this anymore. Maybe I can change everything. . . . Maybe I have agency.*

Gilbert believes the book owes its popularity to those women who "used this story as a permission slip to ask themselves their own questions—often for the first time in their lives."

Gilbert writes, "My journey began with a series of questions. That's how all journeys begin. The shape of my journey was a reflection of my own personal answers to those questions. The shape of your journey will be different from mine, but at bottom, our questions will be the same. These are not easy questions by the way. They are merely the biggest and oldest questions of any human life." She then lists what we can imagine are archetypal questions, those asked by seekers forever and a day, here there and everywhere:

> Who am I?
> Who does my life belong to?
> What is my relationship to divinity?
> What have I come here to do?
> Do I have the right to change my own path?
> With whom do I want to share my path—if anyone?
> Do I have the right to experience pleasure and peace?
> If so, what would bring me pleasure and peace?

If story is indeed the human instruction manual, then these are the kinds of essential questions we're seeking instruction on. And of course there are more, many more, including:

> Where do I belong?
> How did I come to this place in my life, and how else might I live?
> What makes life worth living?
> What are my values?
> How can I be in right relationship with others?
> How do I survive in the face of suffering or loss?
> How do I forgive those who have betrayed me?

In some ways, the answers you discover matter less than the questions you pose. "The wise man doesn't give the right answers, he poses the right questions," said Claude Lévi-Strauss. I teach a course on essential questions, and invariably someone will ask, "I know my question, but what if I don't know the answer yet?" One woman shared, "I know my question is how do I learn to feel at home in my body, but I'm not even sure what that means yet, let alone have any answers." I typically offer two responses.

First, keep writing. It's very possible that you will write your way into an answer, that writing itself will shake the answer off the tree. We'll discuss this more in Chapter VIII, how in writing memoir, we're not just reporting on what we already know about the past, but we're also in the process of discovering more about ourselves in the present as we write. As depth psychologists, we believe we are all only partially conscious human beings, and writing is definitely a method of consciousness-raising, sometimes just as good as therapy.

Second, readers don't need you to have all the answers yet, if ever. Answers are for self-help books, while questions are for memoir—the former is written by an author who's telling you the answers, while the latter is written by an author who's telling you the story of how she grappled with the questions, and what meaning she made in her journey toward answering them (we'll talk more about the importance of meaning-making in the next chapter). Self-help books typically are tidy while memoirs are messy, and we love them for the mess because we too are messy human beings bumbling forward and backward and in all manner of circles with two left feet at times.

Five More Granular Journey Structures

So far we've looked at a three-part journey structure, the most elegant construction, and the quest journey, the journey in search of answers. Now, I want to share with you five other structures you may find useful as well, five other maps of the human journey.

First, let me say I'm not a purist when it comes to these maps. While you may find one that is an exact fit to your journey, in my experience, that's not often the case (though it's really cool when it happens). Though they are laid out linearly, we don't always move through them in that exact order. We don't always get to the last stage, and often we'll skip a stage or two or pass through them unremarkably. Sometimes my students will find themselves wanting to mix and match a couple of journey structures to fit their particular story, and I see nothing wrong with that. I see nothing wrong with choosing to focus on only a couple of stages of the journey, rather than trying to write a narrative that moves through them from start to finish, though I see nothing wrong with doing that either! As you can see, I take a very utilitarian and pragmatic approach to these journey structures. I'm not married to any, but I don't mind dating them.

I offer these structures to my students, not so they'll write their memoir organized around them, although they often do. I offer them instead as tools for consciousness-raising and memory recall. Sometimes a writer will think a stage doesn't apply to them, but on further reflection, they'll realize it does. More than once, while reading Maureen Murdock's 10 stages of the heroine's journey, I'll hear a woman say, "I thought I had skipped Stage 2, the identification with the masculine, but now that I think about it, I remember. . . ."

I also offer them as tools for contemplation, for considering the patterned nature of our lives and how we move through them, as well as the patterned nature of human experience writ large. It can be helpful to give names to stages, and it can be comforting to know you're not the only one who experienced something—helpful and comforting to you as a writer struggling to make sense of your story in your pages, and helpful and comforting to the readers of those pages, who can better make sense of their story through yours.

Because each of these structures is easily googleable or purchasable or check-outable from your library, I'll just summarize them here or highlight the salient points, but please, if one feels resonant or intriguing to you, do spend more time with it—the payoff can be powerful. When I teach these structures, I give my students a worksheet with two columns, the one on the left printed with each stage of the journey, and the one on the right left blank for them to map each stage with their own plot points. You may find that helpful as well.

Joseph Campbell's 17 Stages of *The Hero's Journey*

The American mythologist Joseph Campbell delineated 17 stages of the hero's journey in his 1949 book, *The Hero With a Thousand Faces*, based upon his study of cross-cultural mythology. Inside of the tripart structure of departure, initiation, and return, he added sub-stages. For instance, inside of departure there are five sub-stages: the call to adventure; the refusal of the call; receiving supernatural aid; crossing the first threshold; and entering the belly of the whale. This leads to initiation, with its six sub-stages, and return, with another six sub-stages.

Campbell's work has been criticized, and rightly so, for its gender essentialism—all the heroes are men, and women appear in two stages during the initiation phase: the meeting with the goddess, and the woman as temptress. It's the classic Madonna/whore split, which also assumes a cisgendered hero. There's a sub-stage in initiation called "Atonement With the Father" but there's no equivalent stage with the mother. Because others have found so much value in general in Campbell's model, they have revised it and sometimes simplified it to be more gender-neutral, more archetypally applicable to a broader swath of heroes alike. Still, some of my female students have been able to look past the essentialism and find the journey structure helpful.

Christopher Vogler's 12 Stages of *The Writer's Journey*

Christopher Vogler is an influential teacher and story consultant in the film community. He published the 1992 classic book, *The Writer's Journey,* where he simplified the hero's journey into 12 stages and applied them to the three-act story structure so popular in fairytale, myth, and film. Notably, Vogler removes the gender essentialism of the initiation phase by clumping "Meeting With the Goddess," "Woman as Temptress," and "Atonement With the Father" together into one sub-stage he calls "Ordeal."

I want to note that the book's title is a bit misleading. It's not about the journey of writers at all—it's about how writers can tap into the hero's journey to create more compelling stories. Vogler's subtitle is more accurate: "Mythic Structures for Writers."

Maureen Murdock's 10 Stages *The Heroine's Journey*

A direct counter to the hero's journey is Jungian analyst and memoir writer and teacher Maureen Murdock's book *The Heroine's Journey: Woman's Quest for Wholeness*, a book first published in 1990, then republished in 2020 as a 30th-anniversary edition. A conversation she had with Joseph Campbell in 1981 inspired the book. She came to believe that the focus of the heroine's journey was "to heal the internal split between woman and her feminine nature" and she wanted to know Campbell's thoughts. His response? Women don't need to make the journey at all. He told her, "'In the whole mythological tradition the woman is *there*. All she has to do is to realize that she's the place that people are trying to get to. When a woman realizes what her wonderful character is, she's not going to get messed up with the notion of being pseudomale.'"

Eww.

Eww is right, thought Maureen. Two years later, an image came to her of a circular path that moved clockwise through 10 stages, beginning with "Separation From the Feminine" and ending with "Integration of the Masculine and Feminine." The heroine's journey, in Murdock's formulation, is one where women "embrace their feminine nature, learning how to value themselves as women and to heal the deep wound of the feminine." The question at the heart of the journey is, "Who am I as a woman, as a Self unto myself, not merely in relationship to the patriarchy, to the masculine?" Though she explicitly states that the journey is not only for women, most of the book skews toward gender essentialism as well. Still, I have worked with men in my memoir courses who have found her schema quite helpful in healing their own broken relationship with the feminine.

Craig Chalquist's 10 Stages of *The Journey of Reenchantment*

Craig Chalquist is a depth psychologist, teacher, and author who in 2015 published a HuffPost essay titled "Why I Seldom Teach the Hero's Journey Any More—And What I Teach Instead." In his essay, he argues that "we Americans have a troubling history of overidentification with this [the hero] archetype." Not everyone is a hero or ascribes to be one, leading Chalquist to question, "What in the end does the Hero's Journey offer people who are not Heroes? A way to understand them, perhaps, but certainly not a path open to everyone." This left him wondering about "what model might surface from tales that deal with how non-Heroes journey, struggle, and with a bit of luck find fulfillment."

Enter his answer: the 10 stages of "The Journey of Reenchantment." Stage one begins with our childhoods, a time of magical enchantment with the world. Animals speak, Santa Claus and the Tooth Fairy visit, and all of nature is alive. But then, we grow up, becoming disenchanted as we learn to adapt to the outer world where suddenly this glorious thing called our imaginations is discounted as "it's *just* your imagination." In stages three and four, we become more alienated and may sink into an underworld experience.

But something turns, if we're lucky, and in stages five through seven, we begin seeking for new truths, new meanings, new experiences, and new ways to live our lives congruent with our values. In stage eight, we "find the magic door," something we can walk through, and/or someone we can walk with. In stage nine, we learn to live in both worlds, "the dayworld of consensus reality and the moonlit realm of intuition and dream." The journey ends at stage 10, "Opening the Door For Others," where we share how we navigated our journey and invite others to journey too, adding to the human instruction manual.

This structure is particularly useful for memoirs covering childhood through early adulthood. There's a limitation in the tripart journey from enchantment to disenchantment to reenchantment—those who grew up with very early childhood trauma may never have experienced enchantment to begin with.

Gloria E. Anzaldúa's Seven Stages of *The Path of Conocimiento*

Gloria E. Anzaldúa was a feminist, queer theorist, and a prolific author. She offers a seven-stage journey of transformation in her essay "now let us shift . . . the path of conocimiento . . . inner work, public acts," which is a chapter in the book *This Bridge We Call Home: Radical Visions for Transformation*, edited by Anzaldúa and AnaLouise Keating.

Conocimiento roughly translates from Spanish to English as transformative knowledge or consciousness. In her words:

> You too are driven by the desire to understand . . . . Beneath your desire for knowledge writhes the hunger to understand and love yourself. . . . You struggle each day to know the world you live in, to come to grips with the problems of life. Motivated by the need

to understand, you crave to be what and who you are. A spiritual hunger rumbles deep in your belly, the yearning to live up to your potential. You question the doctrines claiming to be the only right way to live. These ways no longer accommodate the person you are, or the life you're living. They no longer help you with your central task—to determine what your life means.

Anzaldúa calls the first stage of the journey "the earthquake," where something happens that suddenly rocks your world, tilts your axis, knocks you flat on your ass. In stages two and three, you enter the underworld until stage four happens, when something pulls you out of despair and you reconnect with spirit and "undergo a conversion." In the fifth and sixth stages, you bring your new awareness into the world, where it may get challenged by family, friends, or the status quo. In the seventh stage, which she calls "the turning point of transformation," you begin to work with allies on behalf of a more mature, wizened worldview which she calls "acting out the vision or spiritual activism."

This is an intensely psychological journey of transformation, from ignorance (*desconocimiento*) to awareness (*conocimiento*). It maps perfectly onto my feminist awakening when I entered the earthquake called the university and converted from an apolitical Republican to a politically active Democrat, a new awareness that was not welcomed by my family! Many of my students have applied this structure to their own consciousness-raising journeys around issues of religious oppression, homophobia, sexism, militarism, economic injustice and inequality, racism, ablism, etc.

Joseph Campbell's Simplified Two-Stage Version of *The Hero's Journey*

The above five journey structures are complex, containing anywhere from seven to 17 stages. But there's a simpler one. In the popular "The Power of Myth" television series, Joseph Campbell told Bill Moyers that the death and resurrection motif is the most simplified version of the hero's journey. He defines this motif as "leaving one condition, finding the source of life to bring you forth in a richer or more mature or other condition." It's the journey in the song "Amazing Grace," where we once were lost, but now, we're found, where we once were blind, but now we see. It echoes Gloria Anzaldúa's path of *conocimiento* where an earthquake happens in our lives and something inside us dies, only to be reborn through struggle.

I think this simplified journey structure has much to offer memoir writers who are writing about major transformations in life. We can ask ourselves, what died in me? How did it die? What was the cause of death? Who assisted in the murder of this part of me? Who stood by and watched it happen? How long did it take to die? The answer to the last question will vary, of course. For some people, the dying may be incremental, death by a thousand cuts, as often happens in memoirs of difficult childhoods, in stories of the dissolution of a relationship, or in addiction and some illness memoirs. For other people, the death may be instant, like Anzaldúa's earthquake, a sudden rupture that cleaves our lives into before and after—a terrible accident, a distressing diagnosis, a secret suddenly revealed—any bomb which drops bad news that bursts our lives open.

Whether a thousand cuts or an instant death, this journey structure would then turn the focus to resurrection, to rebirth. We can ask ourselves questions like: What brought me back to life? Who or what helped midwife me into a new life? What parts of myself did I leave behind, what parts of myself did I carry forward, and what new parts of myself were birthed into being? What did I discover about myself as a result of my experience of (symbolic) death? What wisdom do I now have to bring forward to my readers?

Jennifer's Seven Mythic Moments in The Underworld Journey, or *Katabasis*

Now, to all these archetypal journey structures, let me add my own. You may have noticed that all these journeys, except the quest to answer a question journey, contain a descent into the underworld, also known as *katabasis* in Greek. It's there in Campbell's death phase in his simplified version, and in his "Belly of the Whale" stage in his more complex 17-stage model; it's in Vogler's "Ordeal" stage; it's in Murdock's "Initiation and Descent Into the Goddess," stage; it's in Anzaldúa's "Coatlicue State of Despair" stage; it's in Chalquist's "Rupture and Underworld Descent" stage. This is a ubiquitous stage in the human journey cycle for obvious reasons—no one can escape underworld experiences that bring about depression, despair, grief, suffering, anguish, torment, loss, confusion, any number of dark nights and dark seasons of the soul. Anyone who lives a full life will end up in the underworld at some time in their lives, maybe many times, and those times may be shorter sojourns into the wilderness lasting a few days or a few weeks, or longer stays of months, years, even a decade or more.

It's also a very common stage to write about in memoir. So many memoirs catalog underworld journeys either as part of a simplified structure—"I entered the underworld (death), and I came out of the underworld (rebirth)"—or as part of a longer journey structure in which the underworld portion only spans a chapter or two. Underworld experiences include such archetypal experiences such as poverty, war, addiction, deformity or disfiguration, illness, divorce, verbal and/or sexual abuse or assault, adverse childhood experiences, accidents, mental disease and disorders, racism and prejudice, violence and victimization, death and dying, and grief.

I give grief its own category of underworld experiences, but in truth, we might imagine all underworld experiences are mourning tales marked by grief. In illness memoirs, there is grief over the loss of our health and vitality. In divorce memoirs, there is grief over the loss of a partner and sometimes a family. We experience literal losses in the underworld of the bodies of our beloveds and of the health of our bodies, but we also experience psychological losses, like the loss of our sense of being active agents and authors of our own lives, as we lament that we can't do anything about what's just happened to us. We can't go back and change the past, we can't bring back the dead, and we can't undo the violence that's been done to us.

In underworld experiences, what's often grieved is the loss of the sense of self. Some underworld journeys are descents into our own shadow, are blows to our egos who learn we are not who we think we are—we are far darker, far more dysfunctional than we thought we were. Many addiction memoirs follow this underworld pattern, where the addict must descend or hit rock bottom, and ask the questions, "What has become of me?" and "How did I get here?" and "How did I lose myself?" followed by the pivotal question, "Am I willing to let this self die, to be reborn into a new self?" Linda Lappin, in her essay "Your Journey From Hell and Back" published in *The Writer* magazine, describes the psychological aspects of the underworld journey: "It is a time of solitude and doubt, mourning and danger, anguish, fear, alienation, often estrangement from what we hold most dear: our sense of who we are."

And some of us may not make it out of the underworld. Some experiences may leave us with a depression so deep that our souls never see sunlight again, and we become a mere shadow of ourselves. Some experiences may not be survivable—the addict may overdose, the mourner may succumb to suicide, or the victim of violence may die a violent death. But if we don't die a psychological or literal death, we may return to the ordinary world, though forever changed. Lappin writes, "After katabasis, the return to our ordinary realm may not necessarily bring perfect happiness . . . but it does confer upon us a new identity and a new awareness of our strengths and limitations as human beings subjected to greater laws in which both faith and hope have a role to play."

Yet even though underworld experiences are so ubiquitous, when I looked around at journey structures, I couldn't find anything that broke the journey into stages or pointed to what I call "the stations of the cross" that mark the topography of the underworld experience. I could only find it in psychological broad-strokes in Elisabeth Kübler-Ross's five emotional stages of death and dying (which was later applied to grief in general)—denial, bargaining, anger, depression, and acceptance. Kübler-Ross acknowledged these stages were not linear nor a predictable progression, and her work has been critiqued for not being universally applicable to how people grieve across cultures. Still, it has been a helpful model for many, as it gives name to the varying emotional states we move through during our underworld experiences, sometimes all in the course of one day.

Still, despite coming up short in my research, I wanted to offer my memoir students some structure to use to examine their time in the underworld, some common language that we could share to understand our own stories, and a lens we could use to look at underworld journey memoirs. So I did what Joseph Campbell did. I turned to myths of the underworld journey, of which there are many across cultures, to see what they might have in common, and to glean any signposts that pointed to archetypal way stations along the journey.

Like theorists of other journey structures, I'll caveat these stages as nonlinear and non-progressive. In looking back at your underworld journey/s, you may find that you were stuck at one way station for a long time, or you might have frenetically moved through many of them during a single week or series of days. There may be way stations you never visited, or, when you see a way station named, you may realize you did visit it after all. I offer this journey structure in the same spirit with which I've offered the other structures—with the hope that it will help you understand your journey better, add flesh to its tell it in such a way that your readers will resonate with it, having gone through similar journeys themselves.

It's not my purpose here to create a scholarly tome such as *The Hero With a Thousand Faces*, with its generous dollop of myths for every one of the 17 stages. I'll just draw upon one myth per way station, highlighting the most salient archetypal moments in these myths. You may wish to read more about the myths that resonate with or mirror your own experience of the underworld.

Way Station # 1
Love's Failure Against Death – The Norse Myth of Baldur

Baldur is the son of Odin and Frigg, two of the main Norse gods. He is universally loved as a beautiful young god, so beautiful it's said he gave off light. Frigg wants to protect him from death, so she travels the world asking all creatures and beings to do him no harm. She thinks she's been successful and secured his safety, so all the gods amuse themselves by throwing objects and weapons at Baldur, laughing as these bounce off him, leaving him unharmed. Loki, the trickster god, asks Frigg if she's sure she secured promises from ALL beings, and she tells him she didn't ask the mistletoe because it's so small and harmless. Loki seizes upon this and crafts a spear with mistletoe at the end, which he gives to a blind god who uses it to accidentally kill Baldur. Of course Frigg wants him back, as do all the gods and creatures and beings. Hel, the goddess who rules the underworld, says she'll restore Baldur's life if everything and everyone in the world weeps for him. And everything and everyone does, except for the trickster Loki, so Baldur must stay in the underworld.

This myth applies to any parent whose love failed to keep their child safe and secure or alive, despite all intentions and efforts, despite how wonderful and full of light that child is or was. Of course, we can also deliteralize the myth and apply it to a child who tries to protect a parent, or a lover who tries to protect their beloved, or a father who tries to protect his family or his home. The pattern is the same—love is not enough in the end.

A memoir focused on this stage of the underworld journey is *Blinded by Hope: My Journey Through My Son's Bipolar Illness and Addiction* by Meg McGuire (a pseudonym). The back cover summary offers this question: "How does a mother cope when love is not enough?" McGuire is unable to save her son from either his bipolar disease or his addiction, nor keep him out of psychiatric institutions and prisons, despite all of her efforts and her training as a psychotherapist. As the book nears its close, she has to face her own addiction to rescuing him and admit her powerlessness, though it is not easy. She writes, "I still struggle to find compassion for my powerlessness in the face of his challenges." She finds solace when visiting a replica of the Pietà in San Francisco's Saints Peter and Paul Church. She's struck by the way Mary cradles the body of Jesus on her lap, "holding him with her right hand, her left hand open to the heavens in a gesture of surrender. She had witnessed her son's life journey, but she could not prevent his suffering and death. She was powerless over his destiny; she had done all she could do." McGuire, like Frigg and Mary, has to admit love's failure against symbolic or literal death.

Way Station #2
The Backward Glance – The Greek Myth of Orpheus and Eurydice

The marriage of Orpheus and Eurydice is a blissful one, until Eurydice is killed by a poisonous snake as she tries to flee a potential rapist. Orpheus' grief is so deep that he follows her to the underworld. There he plays music that so charms the King of the Underworld, Hades, that he gives Eurydice back, on one condition—Orpheus must lead her out of the underworld without looking back at her. He agrees and begins leading her out, but succumbs to temptation and turns to look at her, whereupon she is whisked back to the land of the dead. Orpheus, wild with grief, wanders the world in mourning, vowing to never love again, until a hoard of angry, jealous women rip him to shreds.

This myth illustrates how we may not survive our own underworld experience because we can't stop looking backward, and thus we can't move forward. Stuck in the past, we can't be in the present or imagine a future for our selves or our relationships or our status in life, so we remain in the underworld. We cannot accept that what's done is done; we are stuck in a cycle of nostalgia and grief for what is lost. We may be tortured by intrusive memories, we may batter ourselves with "what ifs," we may be unable to forgive and forget.

There can be many emotions that accompany this stage—anger, grief, regret, resentment, bitterness, depression, and deep sorrow—depending on the nature and circumstances of the loss. For example, a woman whose spouse died at a ripe old age after decades of a wonderful marriage may feel very differently when she glances backward in contrast to a woman whose spouse died relatively young and she finds out he had a secret life made up of multiple affairs and a plethora of lies.

If you think I'm being oddly specific here, I am! Contrast Joan Didion's memoir *The Year of Magical Thinking*, which chronicles a year-long backward glance after Didion's beloved husband of nearly 40 years dies, with Julie Metz' *Perfection: A Memoir of Betrayal and Renewal*, where Metz' husband of 12 years dies and leaves her a widow at 44, only to discover that he had a string of affairs, including one with a close friend. Didion is in abject grief for the year, unable to move forward, focused on the past, while Metz is angry, resentful, and bitter, spending her time after his death unable to move forward until she tracks down every lover of his, confronts every woman he slept with, to try to understand how she missed all the signs of his betrayals.

Same story—the sudden death of a spouse that drop-kicks the other into the underworld. Same mythic way station—the backward glance. But very different emotions.

Way Station #3
Stripping of the Self – The Sumerian Myth of Inanna

The mythic story of Inanna, the Sumerian goddess and Queen of Heaven, is rich in detail, but the most well-known part of the myth is her descent into the underworld where her sister Ereshkigal rules as Queen, in an attempt to usurp her power. Like many cultures' stories of the underworld, it is known as a place where once you visit, you can't return, with very few exceptions, so Inanna lines up some gods to rescue her if she isn't able to come back. She dresses in all her finest clothing and jewelry, as befits her station as the goddess of wisdom, war, power, and love. But when she gets to the underworld, she discovers she has to go through seven gates, and at each gate, a guard demands she take off one piece of clothing or jewelry. By the time she enters the underworld, she is naked and stripped of all her earthly powers. Once inside the underworld, her sister is enraged and turns her into a corpse, hanging her on a meat hook like all the other corpses, until she is rescued three days later by the god Enki's two minions, who revive her with the food and water of life, giving her strength to leave the underworld.

In this way station, we learn about the sacrifices that must be made in the underworld, and those losses are blows to the ego and its need to hold on to power and control. Inanna has nothing in the underworld—she has been stripped bare, and is at the mercy of forces greater than her. In our underworld journeys, we may lose signs of our earthly powers—our money, our careers, our homes and other valuable possessions, our reputations, our dreams for the future, parts of our body or our health or our mental acuity, our family members or friends. All can be stripped away from us by disasters natural and human-made.

We may also suffer psychological losses like the loss of innocence, the loss of identity, the loss of the fantasy of control, the loss of self-esteem, the loss of our pride and dignity. Our loss may be singular and perhaps more bearable, or our losses may compound like Inanna's, seven gates with seven losses, a "and then I lost, and then I lost, and then I lost" compilation that brings us to our knees. We may be rescued or we may be left to rot or leave ourselves to rot, though the odds are very good that if we have the wherewithal to write and publish a memoir, we've found our way back out again!

One memoir that exemplifies every way station of the underworld journey, but particularly illustrates this "and then I lost and then I lost" stripping down before the seven gates of hell, is Chanel Miller's *Know My Name*. Miller was sexually assaulted on Stanford University's campus, where one drunken evening she went from Chanel Miller, a rather ordinary young woman, to Emily Doe, a rape victim. During the 15 months between agreeing to press charges and her assailant's guilty verdict on three felonies, Miller describes in unrelenting detail all that was stripped away from her. Besides her very identity, Miller loses her job, loses her savings, loses sleep, loses her sense of safety in the world. She becomes terrified of being alone, afraid of the dark, and unable to enjoy sex with her loving boyfriend as she feels "unhomed" from her own body.

At the end of the testimony in the trial, she writes, "My basic functions began to falter: I stopped sleeping, forgot to eat, couldn't even shit properly. By the end of the two weeks, my mind had withdrawn, my body withered." In her victim impact statement, which she read aloud before sentencing, she tells her assailant about what he has stripped from her. "You have dragged me through hell with you, dipped me back into that night again and again. . . . You took away my worth, my privacy, my energy, my time, my safety, my intimacy, my confidence, my own voice." Sometimes she thinks she shouldn't have pressed charges at all and instead suffered her rape alone, rather than "face the dismembering that comes with seeking support" through the criminal justice system, which left her "retraumatized, publicly shamed, psychologically tormented, and verbally mauled." The assault harmed her physically, but she writes, "there were bigger things that got broken. Broken trust in institutions. Broken faith in the place I thought would protect me." The physical and psychological losses are devastating, a compounding of losses, a cascade of losses, until in the end she emerges from the underworld and reclaims her identity by writing *Know My Name* and using her real name, Chanel Miller.

Way Station # 4
Lost and Wandering – The Greek Myth of Demeter and Persephone

There is a sense of timelessness when we're deep in the underworld. Time often stands still while all we can do is wander around, dazed and lost. We see this in the myth of Demeter and Persephone. After Hades, the King of the Underworld, abducts her beloved Persephone, taking her into his domain to be his queen, Demeter wanders around for nine long days trying to find her. Demeter is in her version of hell—even though she's in the upperworld, she's psychologically in the underworld. She's lost too—she wanders, she grieves, she withdraws, and she expresses her terrible anger and acts out by scorching the earth to force the gods to help her.

While lost and wandering in the underworld, we may wonder if we'll ever recover, or if recovery is even possible. We may want to die, like Orpheus did during his time of wandering after losing Eurydice for the second time. We may not care if we live. We may act out in anger; we may harm ourselves or others. Or we may withdraw from the world, curling up into our mourning so deeply that we almost entirely disappear into the shell of ourselves.

We see this way station clearly in Gregory Orr's memoir, *The Blessing*, about his accidental killing of his younger brother when Orr was 12 years old. After the death, Orr becomes numb, withdrawn, and disconnected from his family. No one speaks to him about his brother's death. No one helps him to deal with his grief, amplified by such terrible guilt. Orr writes, "Whenever I thought of Peter, my feelings were so tangled up in guilt that I, too, wanted to be dead." The only way he can sleep for years afterward is to lie flat on his back with his arms crossed on his chest and his legs crossed at the ankles, "in the pose of a mummy in an Egyptian sarcophagus"–literally, the sleep of death. Orr notes that after violent trauma, the only way back "is to reconnect the self to the world," but he was unable to do this for years. He suddenly identifies with the Old Testament Cain. "Cain lived in a vacuum. He was a desert wanderer and fugitive." Orr turned to wandering in solitude in the natural world.

After three years of being that lost and wandering fugitive, and after the death of his mother, Orr moves from wandering in nature to what he calls "the Netherworld" of a dark establishment called Lawlor's. Its owner, Ray Lawlor, is "no less than Hades himself," and Lawlor's wife is "Persephone the Maiden," a woman who hadn't changed at all from the day of her abduction. Orr tells us, "I entered their lair, their underworld," this store that was alternately a soda fountain, a pinball and jukebox joint, and a bookstore store selling men's adventure and girlie magazines, comic books, and cheap paperbacks. Orr wanders there for a while until he finds his thread out of the underworld/netherworld. But I'll save that story for Way Station #6.

Way Station #5
The Re-Membering – The Egyptian Myth of Isis and Osiris

Osiris is murdered by his brother, and in one version of the myth, his body is cut into 14 parts and scattered all over the land. His wife Isis sets about to find all his parts, and slowly, piece by piece, she puts him back together. She re-members him—and here I'm using the etymology of the word "member," which is Old French from the Latin *membrum* meaning "limb." Limb by limb, part by part, Isis restores the body of Osiris, except for one very important member she can't find—his penis, which has been thrown into a body of water and eaten by fish. In one version of the myth, the gods are touched by her efforts, so they send Osiris to the underworld to reign there as king.

This mythic moment applies well when we've suffered a literal death of a beloved, and in our grief, we try to remember our beloved, to gather the pieces of them back together again. We may create a scrapbook or film, we may donate a bench to their favorite park as a memorial, we may tell endless stories about them to anyone who will listen, and if we're a writer, we may memorialize them in our memoir.

We can imagine Gregory Orr's memoir as a way of re-membering his brother, but it goes beyond that. Much of the poetry he's written that defines his adult career is also about his brother, whom he refers to as one of his "beloveds." He calls his book of poetry, *Concerning the Body That Is the Beloved*, a book that is "the resurrection of the body of the beloved," his dear Peter and his mother.

Re-membering in memoir also happens for writers who know they are dying, like Paul Kalanithi in *When Breath Becomes Air* and Nina

Riggs' in *The Bright Hour: A Memoir of Living and Dying*. Already in the underworld of disease (lung cancer for Kalanithi, breast cancer for Riggs), they write in part to re-member themselves, to bind together the parts of their lives into a story they can leave behind for their loved ones, including Kalanithi's infant daughter and Riggs' two young boys. They are without a symbolic penis, impotent to rise from the underworld, but by using their pens instead, they become an Isis to their own Osiris, searching like Isis to piece together the story of their lives before they become Osiris and enter the land of the dead.

But this stage is not limited to literal death. We can memorialize a broken relationship, a city changed by a natural disaster, a bygone era, the loss of our innocence, a life cleaved in two by a before and an after. Roxane Gay does this at the beginning of her memoir *Hunger: A Memoir of (My) Body*. She writes there of the gang rape she suffered at age 12 which dropped her immediately into the underworld and cleaved her life into two: before, when she was a relatively normal child, and after, when she put on pound after pound to protect her body from men, to build a fortress and a cage in which to hide inside until she became, in her words, super morbidly obese. In an early chapter, she goes back and describes photographs of her as a child, grateful she has them because there's so much she doesn't remember about her childhood. The photos help her re-member herself. She calls them "artifacts of a time when I was happy and whole. They are evidence that, once, I was pretty and sometimes sweet."

This way station is marked by grief, but we may also feel other emotions like melancholy, remorse, sadness, wistfulness, and certainly nostalgia. There also may be moments of joy remembered and a certain bittersweet satisfaction that comes with memorializing what has been lost. For the memoir writer, we recreate our lost self or the self of others with our word memorials, our book monuments.

Way Station #6
Following the Thread – The Greek Myth of Theseus and Ariadne

King Minos' wife slept with a bull sent to her by Zeus and gave birth to the Minotaur, a creature half man and half bull. Minos hides the bull in an elaborate labyrinth so complicated that no one, not the enemies he sends there, nor the seven young men and women he sacrifices there each year, can find their way out. The demi-god and war hero Theseus decides he will kill the Minotaur himself to stop the brutal sacrifices.

King Minos knows there's no way Theseus will find his way out of the labyrinth and thus will die. Enter his daughter, Princess Ariadne, who falls madly in love with Theseus and determines to save his life by offering him a thread he can unravel as he enters the labyrinth and follow on his way back out. Success! He slays the Minotaur and safely exits the underworld. It is Ariadne's love that saved him from death in the underworld—it is Ariadne's thread. There's often a thread that leads us out the labyrinth of our suffering; there's often a rope we find or we're thrown to help us climb out of the underworld and back into daylight.

Gregory Orr finds his thread after three years in the underworld of grief and his sojourn into the netherworld of Lawlor's. He finds not one but "three slender threads" in Lawlor's. The first connects him to comic books, returning him with nostalgia to his lost childhood, helping him to re-member. The second is cheap paperback mysteries and classics that "were like little buoys that kept me afloat on the night sea as long as I read them." The third is the girlie magazines, the women with smiles and bare breasts that "seemed to speak of the body's possible joys" that made him feel "almost alive" with "a yearning for intimacy and the meaning that might come from it." He calls these three threads "spider threads, while the substantial thread, a rope really, was "the precious thread of poetry." He writes, "Once I had hold of it, I knew I might find my way out of the labyrinth of my own consciousness." He admits he is not Theseus, with his heroic actions, and he had no Ariadne, who placed the thread of poetry in his hands. "I'd simply woken in the dark with the thread of poetry gripped in my fist and—perhaps—the nightmare combat already behind me." It took him years to get out of the labyrinth, and he wonders if he could have died there in the dark of the underworld. He writes, "But I did know this: if I once let go of that thread, I would certainly die."

The thread may be finding our creativity or our vocation or both, as in Orr's case. Threads may be trips or adventures we take (Cheryl Strayed's Pacific Crest Trail adventure in *Wild* or Elizabeth Gilbert's year-long sojourn in *Eat, Pray, Love*). Quite commonly, the thread may be a person—a mentor or an ally who shows us the way out of the darkness, such as a sponsor in a 12-step program, or a therapist or friend or beloved. The thread may even be an animal. In *Pack of Two: The Intricate Bond Between People and Dogs*, a journalistic memoir, Carolyn Knapp shares her dual underworld experience of addiction and then grief after losing both her parents. She finds her way out of the underworld and stabilizes her newfound sobriety with the help of a dog. She writes, "I was wandering around in a haze of uncertainty"–and that's a great description of being lost in the underworld–until she adopts Lucille. "In her," Knapp writes, "I have found solace, joy, a bridge to the world."

Both Orr and Knapp write of emotions like relief, release, and reprieve, of comfort and a sense of consolation that comes with reconnection, even a feeling of being born again. Solace and joy may accompany the experience of being above ground again, which may be experienced as a triumph or a victory, or a gift of grace or, as in the title of Orr's memoir, a blessing. This isn't to say that the darker emotions like anger, sadness, frustration, disappointment, and grief will not still visit us once out of the underworld, but we aren't entombed inside of them any longer. We have survived, and can see, and mostly live, in the light.

Way Station #7
Gifts of the Underworld – Multiple Myths

Finally, there are many myths which name the gifts of the underworld journey. In the myth of Inanna, she is released from the underworld with help from Enki, the god of wisdom, which symbolizes how, when we rise from the underworld, our old self may have been stripped, but a wiser self is born. We also mature through our underworld experiences, like Persephone did. She was a young maiden when Hades abducted her into the underworld, but through her experiences there, she becomes a mature queen with newfound powers. In the Greek myth of Psyche and Eros, when Psyche comes back from the underworld after being saved by Eros, by love, she gives birth to their child named Joy or Pleasure, and we too may experience a newfound feeling of joy and pleasure after our descent. And, of course, in the traditional hero's journey, the hero always comes out from the descent into the underworld with a boon, a gift for the community, as in the classic case of Jesus' descent after his crucifixion, when he returns resurrected with the gift of salvation for all of humankind.

Of course, most of us would prefer to have the gifts of the underworld without having to spend any actual time there, but wisdom tells us there's no other way to become so seasoned. For this reason, you hear so many people say of their dark experiences, "I wouldn't trade my (illness, addiction, loss, accident . . . fill in the blank) for anything, because it made me who I am." Orr states that clearly in the title of his book and the first chapter, "Blessing." His opening line is, "Do I dare to say my brother's death was a blessing?" He knows a reader will recoil from this, and he recoils as well, but he stays with the idea by unpacking the word itself. In French, he tells us, the verb *blesser* means "to wound." In English, to bless is "to confer spiritual power on someone or something by words or gestures." And the Old English *bletsian* means "to sprinkle with blood," to literally be baptized by blood. All three meanings of the word blessing intersect with the violent tragedy of his life: "To wound, to confer spiritual power, to sprinkle with blood." So in our underworld journeys, we are wounded, we are baptized with blood, and if we survive, we are given spiritual power. We are all metaphorical Jesus', baptized in blood on our own particular crosses, entombed in the underworld for a time, until we roll back the stone, resurrected, with our memoir as "the good book" chronicling our holy journey.

A Stage By Any Other Name?

If we choose to scaffold our stories using any of these journey structures, the question arises, should we name names? Should we pull back the curtain on the structure we're using, and share that with our readers? Should we overtly name the stages we're in as we move through them?

Sue Monk Kidd's 1996 bestseller, *The Dance of the Dissident Daughter: A Woman's Journey from Christian Tradition to the Sacred Feminine*, follows the 10 stages of Maureen Murdock's heroine's journey quite exactly. But Kidd never mentions the heroine's journey explicitly. Let's assume she read the book when it came out in 1990—since Kidd was studying Jungian psychology and female spirituality and Murdock's book is a classic in both, there's every reason to assume she did. I offer this as an example to my students—you can use a known journey structure to inform and organize your memoir without pointing out the scaffolding (though if it's something that's been really useful to you, crediting the author and calling attention to the structure for your readers so they can learn more about it is a double act of acknowledgment and generosity).

And look, whether Kidd was consciously aware of this journey structure or whether she unconsciously tapped into the same vein of gold that Murdock tapped into, the end result is the same–the archetypal resonance that both books struck with their readers is evidenced by their best-selling status, the number of languages the books have been translated into (showing a universal appeal across cultures), and the perennial interest in them–Kidd's book with its 20th-anniversary edition, Murdock's with her 30th-anniversary edition.

In contrast, we have Lissa Rankin's self-help memoir, *The Anatomy of a Calling: A Doctor's Journey from the Head to the Heart and a Prescription for Finding Your Life's Purpose*. Rankin was very conscious about structuring her story using the stages of Campbell's hero's journey. In describing her writing process, she shares:

> So when I embarked upon the journey of writing a memoir, I figured I'd go back to my old notes and make sure that I crafted my true story along the story arc of the hero's journey.
>
> The strange thing I discovered was that my actual true life story was already perfectly organized along this story arc. As I started interviewing other people who were finding and fulfilling their calling, I realized their true life stories were following the same formula. We were not trying to live riveting story lives; it's simply what was happening as we journeyed into our own true essence and stepped into our sacred purpose. That's when I realized life itself is a hero's journey, especially when you say YES to that which calls you. And so my book began.

Rankin is speaking of the premise of this book–that our lives are often lived and experienced as following archetypal patterns, those deep grooves in the psyche. She didn't have to self-consciously go rooting around for evidence of this stage or that–they were all right there in her story. And Rankin does expose the scaffolding, drawing on Campbell's stages and language in every chapter.

Theo Pauline Nestor's combination craft guide and memoir, *Writing Is My Drink,* also names its structure, but only in the table of contents, where she uses the three-part structure of departure, initiation, and return to organize her writer's journey. The chapters in "Departure" show her desire to become a writer, and all the fears and stumbling blocks in her way. It ends with her breaking through her thesis block by discovering the power of writing for 15 minutes at a time. The chapters in "Initiation" chronicle her years teaching, with no real writing to show for it, her years in her MFA in creative writing program, and some encounters with writers Frank McCourt, Terry Tempest Williams, and Joyce Carol Oates who mentored and inspired her into her first major publication: a "Modern Love" column in *The New York Times.* In the chapters in "Return," she's now a published author of her first memoir, *How to Sleep Alone in a King-Size Bed*, and she offers the boon, the wisdom she earned in her journey from frightened student writer to successfully published author.

Somewhere in between Kidd's no mention of the journey structure, Rankin's complete reliance on it, and Nestor's naming of it only in the table of contents, is Viola Davis' celebrity memoir *Finding Me.* In her first chapter, she summarizes the hero's journey for her readers.

> For my speaking gigs, the title of my presentations is always the same: "The Journey of a Hero." I learned from writer Joseph Campbell that a hero is someone born into a world where they don't fit in. They are then summoned on a call to an adventure that they are reluctant to take. What is the adventure? A revolutionary transformation of self. The final goal is to find the elixir. The magic potion that is the answer to unlocking HER. Then she comes home to this ordinary life transformed and shares her story of survival with others.

Davis tells us, "That's exactly how I describe my story." She does use some of Campbell's language in the rest of the book. She describes her much older sister Dianne as her "supernatural ally" (stage 3 in Campbell's journey). It was Dianne who started Davis' "call to adventure" (stage 1) when she asked her, quite simply, "What do you want to be?" In a chapter called "The Calling," Davis sees Miss Cicely Tyson on television for the first time in *The Autobiography of Miss Jane Pittman*, and she knows the answer to Dianne's question—her calling is to be an actor. She calls her time training at Julliard "the belly of the beast" (stage 5). She ends her book by naming the "elixir" she found on her journey, the magic healing potion, typically the last stage in Campbell's truncated 12-stage format. But she doesn't make a point of naming other stages, though we can certainly find evidence of them in her memoir. By framing her memoir as a universal hero's journey, Davis takes her extraordinary story and makes it an archetypal one, elevating the celebrity memoir with its *me me me* focus in so doing.

These three examples offer a range of ways we write journey structures into our memoir—completely in the background, completely in the foreground, and somewhere in the middle. Whether they're a tool for organizing our story and for telling our story, they are definitely a tool for *understanding* our story, making conscious the universal way stations we've visited on our journey.

Conclusion

In *I Could Tell You Stories: Sojourns in the Land of Memory*, memoirist Patricia Hampl writes, "Our most ancient metaphor says life is a journey. Memoir is travel writing, then, notes taken along the way, telling how things looked and what thoughts occurred. The memoirist is not a tourist. This is the traveler who goes on foot, living the journey, taking on mountains, enduring deserts, marveling at the lush green places. Moving through it all faithfully, not so much a survivor with a harrowing tale to tell as a pilgrim, seeking, wondering."

I like this metaphor of memoir as travel writing. In memoir, we tell our stories of transition, of moving from one place to another, either physically or psychologically, and often both. We are pilgrims, seekers, often packing questions into our satchel and carrying it with us in search of answers. Along the way, we tell "what thoughts occurred," something we'll take up in Chapter V on the archetype of meaning.

There are two ways to imagine our readers within this metaphor. In the first, we return from our journey with a slide carousel of images. We imagine our readers as our audience, sitting them down on the couch as we click through the slides, narrating our journey to them in mostly a monologue. In this metaphor, we stand inside our own circle in the spotlight as the reader watches from the outside.

In the second, we imagine our readers instead as companions, as fellow wanderers and wonderers who've had their own journeys as well, or who may be in the beginning or middle of a similar one as ours. We still bring our slide carousel along—we still want to share image-stories of our journey, but not to a passive audience. We make room for our fellow seekers' experiences as well—we acknowledge the "we" of our story and the "you" to whom we tell our story. In this metaphor, we invite the reader into the center of the mandorla with us, where we read together from the human instruction manual.

But before we dive into the archetype of meaning, let's spend some time in the next chapter looking at the person who is taking the journey, who is discerning its meaning—you, the main character of your memoir.

THE ARCHETYPE OF CHARACTER
Connecting to the Heart of Your Readers Through
Five Universal Character Qualities

Despite the "me" in *memoir*, and despite the fact that our character is uniquely ours and bears our one-of-a-kind fingerprint, character itself is archetypal—we all have one (for better or for worse!)—and within our unique characters lie universal qualities. In this chapter, we'll look at five fingers on the hand of character: emotions and feelings, yearnings, values, tragic flaws, and the struggles and challenges of change.

There are more qualities of character we could talk about, of course, another hand's worth and maybe a foot too, but I want to attach these five qualities to your right hand and ask you to place that hand over your heart. Because that's what I want to explore in this chapter—how to make a heart-to-heart connection with our readers.

Donald Maass writes in his book *The Emotional Craft of Fiction*: "When readers feel strongly, their hearts are open. Your stories can not only reach them for a moment, but they can change them forever. I don't care about what you write, how you write it, your choices in publishing, or what you want out of your career. What I want is to feel deeply as I read your work. I want to feel connected to you and your characters." This applies to memoir and fiction both—the only difference is that you *are* a character in your memoir. You are our proxy, our point of view, our guide through the story, even if your story centralizes another character.

Whether we feel connected to your story depends on whether we feel connected to you, and that depends on whether you're willing to lead us into your heartland, the beating, pulsing heart of you, or whether you leave us at the hinterland, removed and remote. Maass writes, "We open our hearts to those whose hearts are first open to us." Will you open your heart to your readers? Will you be vulnerable, and show us your brilliant and broken humanity, and thus make room for ours? Will you reveal your character in all its complexity?

Let's look at five ways to do so. And in this chapter, I'm going to mix it up a little—instead of offering you examples from multiple memoirs, I'm going to focus on a single memoir—Ashley C. Ford's 2021 memoir *Somebody's Daughter*. Ford's memoir was highly acclaimed and an instant *New York Times* bestseller, and rightfully so—it's a gorgeous, compelling read, and if you haven't already read it, I'd suggest you put a bookmark in this chapter and read it first—some of my examples contain spoilers, and the book deserves to be read in its entirety first before it is parsed into the sum of its parts.

Ford's book is a case study of what a deep memoir is, a how-to guide for using an archetypal approach to deepen a story and broaden its appeal. Two endorsements get to the deep and the broad. "Ashley C. Ford went **deep** into the well of herself" (Saeed Jones) and, "This exquisite, honest memoir will **resound widely**" (Book Marks). Some endorsements speak of the universality of her memoir, such as, "Her story is **particular** to her, but it's also about **every single one of us**" (Abby Wambach). Others speak to her contribution to the human instruction manual—"Her understanding that **the ones we love are imperfect** crafts a shining star for the reader to follow" (*San Francisco Chronicle*) and, "Her coming-of-age story gets at **how to both acknowledge and break away from what we're born into**" (*Cosmopolitan*).

Several endorsements speak to the heart that's at the heart of this chapter—"It's Ford's willingness to share her thoughts and observations, warts and all, that sets her memoir apart. She's a woman unafraid to face herself and share what she sees, which she does with admirable realism, humor—and especially, **heart**" (Yahoo Life) and, "A memoir so clear, sharp, and smooth that the reader sees, in vivid focus, Ashley C. Ford's complicated childhood, brilliant mind, and golden **heart**" (Glennon

Doyle) and, "Ashley C. Ford's talent is on full display, as is her **heart**" (Isaac Fitzgerald).

Let me offer a quick summary of the book before we look at how Ford displays that golden heart of hers, and how we can do so as well. *Somebody's Daughter* is a coming-of-age memoir chronicling Ford's childhood growing up as a poor Black girl in Indiana. She has a fraught relationship with her often emotionally and physically abusive mother and her cantankerous but adoring grandmother, who share responsibility for raising her in the absence of her father, who went to prison when Ashley was only a few months old. The book opens with the news that he's being released from prison after nearly 30 years, and closes with his return, with a linear structure in between. Thematically, it's a story of family love and loyalty, of losing and regaining one's identity, of learning how to loathe oneself and then love oneself.

Finger One–Emotions and Feelings

The first way to connect with your readers, the first finger on the right hand over your heart, is through sharing your emotions and feelings.

Though we tend to use these words interchangeably, they are actually distinct, though related. An emotion is something that originates in our bodies, a body-based reaction that typically falls upon us outside of our control quite autonomously. A feeling comes after an emotion—it's what we tell ourselves about our emotions, how we interpret them. The simplest way to understand the distinction is that an emotion comes from the body and a feeling comes from the mind.

Let's look at an example. Imagine two people knocking on the door to enter a raucous party. Both of them feel their hearts racing and their agitation rising, evidenced by the tap tap tapping of one of their feet on the floor. One person labels the feeling as excitement—*Yay, I get to go to a party! So many people!* The other person labels the feeling as dread—*Really, do I have to go to this party? Too many people!* Both bodies had the same emotional response, but both minds attached different feelings to it.

It's possible to describe an emotion without connecting it to a feeling. To write, "My throat closed and I was unable to speak" is to describe an emotional response without naming the specific feeling attached to it. It's also possible to name a feeling without attaching it to an emotion. To write, "I felt sad about her reaction" is to name a feeling without showing us the body's emotional response. If we could draw such a distinction, we might say describing an emotion is showing, while naming a feeling is telling.

If you've been using emotions and feelings interchangeably, no worries—you're in good company. I do it too. Even Donald Maass, who wrote *The Emotional Craft of Fiction*, does so, making no distinction between the two. In talking about the complexities of character, he offers examples using both words. He writes, "Human beings are complex. We have emotions on the surface and emotions underneath. There are emotions that we minimize, hide, and deny. There are emotions that embarrass us, reveal too much, and make us vulnerable. Our emotions can be profoundly trivial or so elevated that they're silly." Later he writes, "Our feelings are . . . dynamic. They change. They can reverse in an instant. We can be torn, confused, and frustrated, which only means that our feelings are in conflict. We can be stuck, shut down, apathetic, or a mess. We can be dead inside or newly alive. We experience awakenings, self-awareness, hope, and joy." I can see no difference in how he's using the words.

And look, ultimately I don't care whether you use the words synonymously. I only name this distinction for one very important reason—because memoirists sometimes neglect writing their bodies into their text, neglect showing us the visceral nature of raw emotions before we digest them into feelings that can be told. In my mantra of "show *and* tell," it's great when we do both, because our readers can relate—they also have bodies that emote and feelings that interpret those emotions. And because in the main, we are empathetic human beings, the more we can share both our emotions and feelings with our readers, the more empathetic resonance we're likely to evoke.

Ashley C. Ford is adept at writing both her emotions and feelings, and in the order they arrive—first the emotion, then the feeling, if she's able to name the latter. She begins her book this way. On an ordinary night while having dinner with her boyfriend, she receives a call from her mother telling her that after nearly 30 years, her beloved father is being released from prison. Ford describes her body's emotional response: "My breath caught between my mouth and lungs, unsure in which direction it was most needed. My heart hit the gas, rushing blood to parts of my body calling out for it, and my hands trembled. . . . My heartbeat traveled to every end of me, pumping pumping pumping through my ears. . . . My head spun with words, images, bits of conversations, music, and colors making up a swirl of debris zipping past my face, and returning seconds later, moving too quickly for me to reach out and hold onto anything long enough to make sense of the patterns they made, or whatever they tried to tell me. . . . My emotions moved through me faster than I could name them."

Naming her emotions moves her into feeling territory, and of this she writes, "Feeling any of it felt like the beginning of losing control, and losing control felt like certain death in my body, if not my mind. If I didn't process the feeling, I wouldn't feel it, and if I didn't feel it, it wouldn't kill me."

When she hangs up and returns to the table to tell her boyfriend the news, he asks her how it makes her feel. "I don't know," she replies. She stops eating and begins sobbing, telling him, "I really don't know how I feel."

Ford has me on her side from Chapter 1. I resonate with hearing complicated news that overwhelms the body. I resonate with not being able to name my feelings, even as I know they are big ones. I am moved by her, so moved I imagine reaching across that dinner table and putting my hand on her hand, the way her boyfriend does. My curiosity is piqued—I want to know more about this relationship with her father that has her react so emotionally to his release. I want to know why it's so confusing to her that she can't discern her feelings, not yet. I have a glimpse into her broken heart and I want to know what broke it and if it can or will heal throughout the course of the book.

Sometimes, Ford describes the emotion and names the feelings in tandem. After learning that a female cousin has been sexually abused by her stepfather, and enduring her mother's rather hysterical rants and raves and warnings about the dangers boys and men pose to pre-teen Ashley, even her male relatives, she learns to feel fear. "Ever since I learned my cousin's secret, a secret she kept but hadn't chosen, I lost something that made me feel generally okay. It was replaced by the steady drum of fear that made my heart race and my stomach drop." She continues, "The fear that bloomed in my center was foreign to me, unlike any I'd ever felt before. It was the kind of fear that made you cry before anything even happened." The feeling–fear. The body's emotional response–heart racing, stomach dropping, and preemptive tears.

One feeling that women tend to "minimize, hide, and deny," to use Maass' words, is anger. Sure, we have the emotional response–our blood boils, our hearts pound in our chests, our eyes narrow–but most of us have been socialized to clench our jaws and remain silent. Ford shows us her very angry mother, someone who is quick to kick or hit, someone who lashes out verbally and volatilely. She describes how her mother wears her anger: "My mother's tongue was coated in venom, her familiar anger rising in the back of her throat." Young Ashley learns to silence herself against that familiar anger–not because she was socialized to do so because of her gender, but because she is terrorized by her mother if she does not–expressing her anger only leads to more abuse. Even as a young adult who no longer lives with her mother, she stifles her anger in order to keep the uneasy peace.

But she doesn't minimize, hide, or deny her anger from us. Her anger is twofold, beginning in Chapter 1 with anger at herself for her response to her mother. When her mother tells her she can always come home, Ford wants to tell her she'd "fistfight every stranger I run across on the street before we live under the same roof again." She recognizes this is a "hyperbolic expression of a feeling" that she doesn't allow herself to verbalize, and then she writes, "I got angry with myself for even thinking the thought because I knew it would hurt her to know it had ever been in my mind. I got mad at myself too, for not saying it out loud anyway. For not caring if it hurt her, if it meant telling the truth." Ford immediately introduces us to the complexity of her feelings. She doesn't want to hurt her mother, and she wants to tell the truth which would hurt her mother. This tension is one we're sure to relate to, the "damned if I do, damned if I don't" dilemma that comes when we wish or want or need to get a feeling off our plate that will be unpalatable to its recipient.

Ford also tells us about the anger she feels toward her mother. There's a scene later in the book when her mother's appendix bursts, and she fails to go to the hospital until she almost dies from septicemia. Ford writes that she might have had more empathy for her mother had she been afraid of doctors, or didn't have the money to pay for hospital bills or the time to take off from work, but none of those apply to her mother. Instead, she says it was her mother's fear of dying that kept her from, ironically, almost dying. The fear is less about her own death, but about leaving her four children as orphans. While some of us might read that and think that's misguided, for sure, but appreciate her concern for her children and feel a little heartstring pull, not Ford–she's just angry, at least at first, when she hears the news. She admits, "When it comes to my mother, I have always needed less than a nudge to find myself full and hot with self-righteous anger. And when I catch myself being angry that way, I've usually found a way to blame her for that too."

But as Maass notes, our feelings are subject to change, to quick reversals, and this happens to Ford when she visits her mother. When she sees her in her hospital bed, so near death, not the formidable woman who raised her, Ford writes, "I wanted to be angry. Instead, I was deeply, startlingly sad." Ford leans into the complexity and contradictory nature of her feelings, something we all share as human beings.

She does it again later in the memoir when her grandmother is dying. Ford offers to give up a major career move to stay and shepherd her through her death, but her grandmother refuses the offer. Ford writes, "I was both relieved and disgusted at myself for the heft of my relief." Maass tells us, "We're clear. We're vague. We hate. We love. . . . We are walking contradictions. We are encyclopedias of the heart." Indeed, as author and writing teacher Janet Burroway encourages us, characters "need to exhibit enough conflict and contradiction that we can recognize them as belonging to the contradictory human race." Ford's exploration of her feelings about her mother gives permission to all daughters and sons to name and claim their complex feelings about their parents, as we nod our heads and sigh, "Me too. I know that encyclopedia by heart."

I think there are three takeaways from Ford on writing about emotions and feelings. The first two are explored above–first, describe emotions and name feelings both, even the ones we've been socialized away from expressing, and second, don't shy away from naming the complex and contradictory nature of our feelings. The third takeaway is the careful way she crafts those emotions and feelings on the page. Too much emotion and feeling can render a memoir maudlin, mawkish, shmaltzy, sappy, or overly sentimental. Too little emotion and feeling can render a memoir too matter-of-fact, cold, dry, impassive, or flat. Too much emotion and feeling can overwhelm and suffocate a reader; too little emotion and feeling can underwhelm and distance a reader. There's a Goldilockian sweet mean in there—not too hot, not too cold, but just right.

The question for memoir writers then becomes, how to get it just right? The playwright Anton Chekhov offers a suggestion in a letter he wrote in 1892 critiquing a writer's story. It's very simple—the more "miserable and unfortunate" a situation is, the colder the writer should describe it, in order for the reader to have room for their own emotional response. Donald Maass states it similarly: "When character emotions are highly painful, pull back." Comedians know this—they don't have to yuck it up to get a laugh out of their audience. They tell the joke, and we laugh. Humor memoirists know this as well—they write the funny anecdote, and we laugh—if they have to tell us how funny it is, we don't get the pleasure of finding the funny ourselves. So Chekhov's advice—show the pathos, and let us feel.

I think Ashley C. Ford gets it just right—there's enough description and enough telling, but also enough breathing room for us to feel our feels. One strategy she uses—and I see this used all the time in well-crafted memoirs—is to end a paragraph with a strong emotional moment, and then have a section break, or similarly, end a chapter on a strong emotional moment before starting the next. Both kinds of breaks allow us to recover from the sucker punch of emotion and the naming of feelings, to stare off into the blank space for a time as we process our own emotional responses and feelings.

In one such effective scene break, Ford receives her report card that says she passed kindergarten. The next day, in a rare occurrence, her always adoring though almost entirely absent father calls from prison. When her mother hands her the phone, Ford yells into the receiver, "'I passed kindergarten, Daddy! I passed!" Her father replies, "'I'm so proud of you, baby girl,'" and Ford writes, "I could hear his smile, his pride, and I soaked it up." She ends the section with his next words: "'I've got me a smart child.'" She doesn't need to tell us how she feels about this—the scene stands alone. Maass writes, "Details have the power of suggestion. Suggestion evokes feelings in readers, drawing them out rather than pounding them with emotional hammer blows." The tone of her father's voice, smiling and full of pride, and the words he speaks are all the details we need to know to know how to read this scene, and the section break gives us space to feel young Ashley's pride and pleasure.

Ford is masterful at knowing how to end chapters on emotional notes, both high and low. Open to the end of any chapter, and you'll see what I mean. Just one more example. At the end of one chapter, Ford's long-term, completely supportive, almost-perfect boyfriend lobbies a question to her that delivers such an emotional hammer blow. When Ford questions why he feels distant from her, he replies, "'Why do you need something to be wrong?'" Ford gives us room to draw our own conclusions—instead of answering him or telling us, she simply ends the chapter with, "And I wondered why I did." Her wondering gives us room to wonder ourselves. Maass writes, "When characters struggle with their feelings, readers must referee. They seek to resolve characters' inner conflicts. They render judgments." The blank space between the end of this chapter and the beginning of the next allows us the space to feel the heft of her boyfriend's question, and to referee, resolve, and render our own interpretation of Ford's psychology.

Dara Marks writes of the "sacred trust that is bestowed upon storytellers—to lead humanity to a higher place by holding up a candle so that the path ahead is illuminated and made a little less treacherous. If we simply acknowledge in our stories that the events in our life do impact us, we connect on the most fundamental level to everyone else. We confirm that the wide range of human emotions—including pain, loneliness, sorrow, disappointment, as well as passion, joy, love, and hope—are not only felt by us, but by all of humanity." Ford earns our sacred trust. She vulnerably shares the impactful events of her life with us, and we feel connected to her as a result, invested in her emotionally, in love with her humanity and affirmed in ours.

Finger Two—Yearnings

Memoirist and teacher Heather Sellers writes about the importance of leaning into yearnings to create a connection between the reader and the memoir's characters. She writes, "If the creative nonfiction piece . . . has as its focus on a person, or people, storytelling skill demands attention to yearning. In order to get the reader to hook into the characters or narrator, she has to feel some kind of a strong pull forward, towards something, or the story flatlines, tension drops, game over." She credits the author Robert Olen Butler for teaching her about the importance of yearning in creative non-fiction, fiction, memoir, you name it—if it's story-based, then yearning is what propels the story forward. I teach her memoir *You Don't Look Like Anyone I Know: A True Story of Family, Face-blindness, and Forgiveness* as an example of placing yearning on the page.

Butler writes, "I use the word 'yearning' with my students because it suggests the deepest level of desire." He's come to believe that there's "a unified field of yearning": "I think that if you dig deeply enough, the yearning at the center of great literature is *I yearn for the self. I yearn for an identity. I yearn for a place in the universe.* That's the great thing, the great 'Who the hell am I?' which we ask ourselves every day." This unified field of yearning is another way of saying yearning is archetypal, yearning is universal.

Butler's suggestion that the über-yearning is for the self, for the answer to the question, "Who am I?" is very consistent with depth psychology. This goes all the way back to ancient Greece, to an inscription at the Temple of Apollo that read "Know Thyself," which Socrates and later Freud himself was quite taken with. If we take seriously the depth psychological idea that we are all partially unconscious human beings, this means we don't inherently know ourselves, or at least, there are parts of us that are unknown to ourselves, so the great yearning that the ancient Greeks and Socrates and Freud and depth psychology and Butler all point toward is the yearning to know the answer to the question, "Who am I?"

Dara Marks calls "the quest to know ourselves . . . the grand journey of our lives. When writers touch even a small part of this level of self-reflection, they reach into the soul of everyone." In asking the question "Who am I?" and searching for an answer, we model a similar inquiry for our readers, who may (rightfully) be less interested in who we are than in who *they* are, and they're looking toward the human instruction manual of our memoir for clues and insights about how to know their own souls more deeply.

Ashley C. Ford never overtly raises the question "Who am I?" in *Somebody's Daughter,* but it's there in her character arc. The first two-thirds of the memoir tells the story of how she lost herself and her voice, making herself invisible in order to survive, and the last third tells how she found herself and her voice, claiming her visibility in the world. But I want to save this example for another finger in this chapter, and look at different yearnings in this section.

An ancillary yearning to "Who am I?" is the question, "Who are we?" This is the archetypal yearning to know ourselves in relation to our partnerships, our families, our ethnicity, race, gender, religion, region, culture, country, political party—from our smallest tribe of two increasing in numbers up to our largest tribe as global citizens. "Who are we?" is commonly explored in memoir—who are we as friends (Hua Hsu's *Stay True*); who are we as a married couple (Elizabeth Alexander's *The Light of the World*); who are we as an ethnicity and a culture (Jemela S. Macer's *Between Two Worlds: An Armenian-American Woman's Journey home*); who are we as a gender (Juliet Jacques' *Trans: A Memoir*); who are we as a region (Octavio Solis' *Retablos: Stories From a Life Lived Along the Border*), etc.

While Ford's memoir could have addressed the question, "Who are we as black people?" or "Who are we as black women?" that's not her memoir's emphasis. Instead, the book concentrates more on the question, "Who are we as a family?" But I want to save this example for later in this chapter as well. I save them in part because I want to concentrate here on what I think are her two biggest yearnings in the memoir—the archetypal yearning for love, especially her father's love, and the yearning to be seen and understood.

Though her father appears on very few pages of the memoir, and in the first 30 years of Ford's life, she only remembers seeing him twice, he plays an outsized role in her heart. He writes her many letters throughout the book, and talks to her on the phone, always saying how proud he is of her, how lucky he is to be her father, how much he loves her. She writes, "All my life, my father represented love to me. Deep, enduring, irrevocable love. So many times I thought all the problems of my life could be solved if I'd just had him there to hold me and tell me who I am, and how much he loved that person." When she finally decides to visit him on her own at age 25, after not seeing him for 13 years, she writes, "I was . . . busy dreaming about our inevitable reunion, and his inevitable adoration of the woman his daughter had become." She tells us, "Despite everything my father had done, I was still so eager to be claimed by him. To be protected by him. To the world he was a bad man. To me, he was my dad who did a bad thing. I was still trying to figure out what it meant to love someone who had done such a bad thing, but I did love him."

And he loves her. When they reunite in the prison visiting room, he embraces her and tells her over and over again how much he loves her. She writes, "My father loved me as much in person as he did in his letters. Maybe more."

Her yearning for her father's love is also attached to the yearning to be seen and understood. Yes, he loves her unconditionally, but he doesn't really know her—before this moment, he had seen her once 13 years earlier and before then only in the first few months of her life. She barely writes to him, and her mother doesn't stay in touch with him much either, so there's little he knows of her. He seems to love the idea of her, and she wants more. In the memoir's opening, she shares, "He wrote that I was his favorite girl, I was brilliant, and I was the best daughter anyone could ever hope for. For a long time, that was all I needed. Until, of course, I needed more."

The more she needed was for her father to know all of her, to love her for who she really is and not the dream or the fantasy of her. She yearns for him to love her unconditionally while knowing her, seeing her, and understanding her. She writes, "I felt like my father would understand me, if I could just tell him what was happening inside me. I wanted to tell him everything, to confess the bad parts of myself and have someone say, 'I still love you. That will never change.'" What child, what young adult, what adult of any age would not resonate with a yearning to hear such words from a parent?

Another archetypal yearning is the yearning to belong, and Ford feels that as well with her father. It's right there in the title, the yearning to belong to a parent, to be "somebody's daughter." It's there when she says she longs to be "claimed" by her father. In the prison visiting room, as her father holds her and tells her he loves her, she writes, "In that moment, I felt like someone's little girl. And I'd been waiting a long time to feel like somebody's daughter."

Ford's memoir also explores the archetypal yearning for freedom. Her childhood is full of restrictions under her at-times overbearing grandmother and almost-always overcontrolling mother. When she's finally able to break free and go away to college, she experiences an overwhelming sense of freedom. Her mother allows her to choose her own major and Ford writes, "I didn't really know what I wanted to do, but I was intoxicated with the freedom to decide for myself, when so many of my more fortunate classmates didn't have that option. My freedom to choose, unwatched, became precious to me, and I felt like I might float right out of my shoes." In soccer star and leader Abby Wambach's review of the memoir, she writes that it's "a master class on how to love your family and still live with individuality and freedom," but that's the payoff at the end of the memoir—it takes a long time for Ford to get there, and we feel her yearning for freedom so strongly that it's a huge sigh of relief for us when she finds it.

There are a few other archetypal yearnings I'll mention here. Ford touches on them all, but I want to offer them to you to amplify in your own writing. To the yearnings to know oneself, to know one's family and tribe, to be loved, to be seen and understood, to belong (which is also the yearning for home), and to be free, I would add the yearnings to know our life's purpose and meaning, the yearning to express ourselves (which is also the yearning to create), the yearning for safety, the yearning to be free from suffering, and the yearning for power, achievement, and efficacy.

Author Leslie Jamieson writes, "Yearning is our most powerful narrative engine." This is what Heather Sellers means, that "in order to get the reader to hook into the characters or narrator, she has to feel some kind of a strong pull forward, towards something." Yearning is the engine that pulls a reader forward, that propels a narrative. And so we ask ourselves, in each of our chapters and even each of our scenes, what am I yearning for here? How am I expressing that yearning?

And the same goes for the other important characters in our memoir. We ask ourselves, in this scene I have written with my grandmother, what is she yearning for? In this scene with my mother, what is she yearning for? Can I make those yearnings clearer, amplify them more, turn up the heat?

Yearning is not only a powerful narrative engine, but it's also a powerful explanation for conflict or tension between people. When Ford goes to live with her grandmother for a time, she never wants to go back to live with her mother. Ford is yearning for freedom from suffering, but her grandmother makes her return because her yearning is for family, for a sense of belonging (we'll explore this below). The constant tension between Ashley C. Ford and her mother can be explained by conflicting yearnings—in so many scenes, Ford yearns for her mother to understand and see her, but her mother seems to yearn for little other than power. It's not until the end of the memoir that Ford's mother relinquishes some of that need for power over her daughter, and is able to see her for the adult that she's becoming.

Finger Three—Values

Another universal quality human beings share is the important role of values in our lives, values such as love, belonging, self-expression, family, home, power, etc. If this list sounds familiar, it's because we've just explored these as archetypal yearnings as well. And this makes sense, doesn't it?—we yearn for what we value. If we don't value loyalty, we won't yearn for it. If we don't value creativity, we might not understand someone else's yearning for it. But we're hardwired to understand *it*, the value itself. Patriotism might not be high on my list of values, but I inherently understand what patriotism is when I see it and read about it. Selflessness may not be something you value personally, but you can recognize it in others, even if you don't resonate with it.

Because values are closely connected to our hearts—*we love what we value*—expressing our values in our memoir is a great way to share our hearts and connect to the hearts of our readers. Even if we don't share the same values as a memoirist, if and when we understand why that value is important to them and how much they yearn for the full expression of it, we have a window into their hearts and an opportunity to root for their fulfillment. It's also a great way to add to the human instruction manual—as readers, we may be unconscious of the importance of certain values until a memoirist brings them to our attention and demonstrates for us how to live into those values. Of course, we don't want to get preachy about our values nor shove them down the throats of our readers either, but leaning into what we value, making it clear on our pages and in our scenes, is another good way for our readers to feel us.

Donald Maass notes, "Generally characters who are the most universally appealing are models for what we might call heart values" which he lists as "compassion, insight, a commitment to justice, family, love, steadfastness, sacrifice, [and] selflessness." I suppose these "heart values" are in contrast to values such as money, control, power, achievement, and discipline, though we can put those values in service to a heart value—we might value money as a means to care for our family, or value power as a means to effect social justice, or value discipline as a means to sacrifice. In other words, any value can be a heart value if we explain and express it as such.

Without thinking too much about it, we are bound to write our values into our memoir—how could we not? We're writing about something important to us or we wouldn't bother writing, and what's important to us is deeply connected to what we value. But as with everything in this book, I'm suggesting we bring more consciousness to writing into archetypes—in this case, the archetypal values we are expressing in our memoir—I'm suggesting we amplify them for maximum resonance and connection with our readers.

I've already discussed some values in Ashley C. Ford's memoir, including love, belonging, and freedom, but what I want to explore here is the value she places on family because that value changes over the course of her memoir. Let's set her father aside here—we've already looked at how much she values his love and values belonging to him, but in so many ways, he's tangential to the main family to which Ford belongs—the family led by her grandmother and her mother, with her three siblings and her extended family of aunts and uncles and cousins galore, almost all of whom live near each other in the same town and sometimes on the same street and even in the same house.

When the book opens, we know her relationship with her family is fraught—she tells us she'd rather fistfight strangers than go back home to her mother's, and we know she hasn't spent time with her nuclear family since her father entered prison before she even cut a tooth. She's wondering if she and her boyfriend Kelly can become a family together: she calls them "lovers who lived together, trying to find out if we had whatever turned two people in love into the kind of family either of us wanted."

In the next chapter, she goes back in time to when she was four years old or so, living with her mother and her beloved little brother R.C. With her mother, it's far more complicated. She tells us there's "Mama," "the loving mother we knew before whatever sparked her ire," and there's "the Mother," the ire-filled, hot-tempered, verbally and physically abusive one who leaves young Ashley constantly feeling like she's bad and wrong—not just that she does bad or wrong things, but that she's fundamentally bad and wrong. Her mother sends Ford some crazy-making mixed messages—for example, in front of the extended family, she says, "'I would die first. . . . I would die before I let anybody hurt my kids,'" but she is the one who is constantly hurting her kids. Her love is tied up in her abuse—she'll kick or hit Ashley and then pull her close to her chest and laugh. She is incapable of apology, and until one important moment near the end of the book, incapable of owning her form of crazy.

Ford enjoys her extended family in many scenes and particularly enjoys spending time with her maternal grandmother, who is prickly and difficult, but who treats Ford well. It is from her grandmother that she learns the most important lesson about the value of family. Her grandmother has taken a young Ashley away for a year to live with her father, Ford's great-grandfather, after her mother suffers from a stillborn birth and enters the underworld of depression. Ford loves living on her great-grandfather's farmland, feeling peaceful and free to be a child there without vigilance. When Ford and her grandmother return home for Christmas, her mother turns into the Mother again, kicking her from behind and face-planting her on the living room carpet for a minor indiscretion. When Ford and her grandmother return to the farmland, and Ford implores her grandmother to never make her go back home again, that's when her grandmother steps in to teach her about the importance of family.

Her grandmother grabs a shovel and a burlap bag, and they walk out to the wild part of the land. Her grandmother digs a hole in the dirt, and points out a bunch of garden snakes in the hole, "in some sort of a knot though not stuck together. They moved quickly and deliberately over and around one another. They were not fighting, and they did not seem to be trying to get away from us or anything." When Ford asks her grandmother what they're doing, she says, "'They're loving each other, baby.'" Then she takes lighter fluid out of the burlap sack, pours it into the hole, and throws in a match. Ford watches in horror as the snakes hold each other tighter while burning. "Even as the scales melted from their bodies, their inclination was to squeeze closer to the other snakes wrapped around them." Her grandmother uses this as an object lesson, telling Ford that both of them will have to go home. Looking at the burning snakes, she tells her granddaughter, "These things catch fire without letting each other go. We don't give up on our people. We don't stop loving them. . . . Not even when we're burning alive." Her grandmother tells her, "When it comes to family, all we have is each other."

It's a lesson Ford hears, but she doesn't internalize yet. She and her grandmother return home within a year, and nothing has changed—the Mother continues to rampage, and home is still not a safe place. As she grows older, she spends more and more time away from home, until she finally escapes to college. Her relationship with her beloved siblings becomes strained due to lack of proximity, but she writes, "My love for my family was in direct conflict with my need to be gone, out, and away." She does what many of us do when we go to college—we make a family out of our friends, our classmates, our co-workers, our boyfriends and girlfriends. Similar to the taste of freedom she had on her great-grandfather's farmland one year in her childhood, once she gets a taste of the freedom of college, she never wants to move back home.

Still, she struggles, writing, "My mother was adamant that all we had, and all we'd ever need, was family. If she was right, I had everything I needed. . . . Even then, I felt guilty about wanting more." She feels like she's failing them by being physically distant. "If family was everything, the source of all that was needed to complete the picture, I was a willfully missing piece of the puzzle. And though I loved these people, I knew this was not my home anymore." She simply cannot be herself there, and be seen for who she truly is. But with time, and three major family events—her mother's near death from her burst appendix, her final visit to her father in prison, and her grandmother's death from cancer—she begins to reconsider the value of family.

In the next to last chapter concerning the death of her grandmother, she writes, "Up until my grandmother died, I'd just accepted the way things were, resigned to my role as the member of my family no one quite understood. It had been enough, maybe even part of the fuel that kept me going in the warped way these things do sometimes, but now, I wanted more. I wanted their closeness. I wanted to start over, and let them see me as I am. I wanted to trust them. I wanted us to be as we are, people who love each other." She sees how she has abandoned her home in Indiana for her home in New York with Kelly, but she realizes, "It didn't have to be that way. However complicated, I could exist in both, as me, fully me. I could be strong enough, because I had to be—if I didn't want to lose this. And I knew I didn't." In the end, "I knew now that moving forward required going back." She has now internalized her grandmother's message about the value of family—families don't stop loving each other, and they never give up on each other.

This message is brought home in the final chapter, the last three pages of the book. She returns to Indiana to welcome her father home from prison. He has committed terrible crimes against two women, but Ford realizes, "It wasn't, and isn't, my place to forgive him for what's done. But my father is part of me, and I couldn't turn away from that. I couldn't turn away from him. I didn't want to." Even knowing what he's done, she doesn't stop loving him and she doesn't give up on him. We are left in the end with a strong testimony about the value of family.

As you write into your values, don't shy away from showing conflicts, complexities, and nuances. Things are seldom black and white when it comes to values, and our values may shift or solidify over time. Readers will resonate with your struggles to clarify your values, to distinguish them from the values of others, and to live a value-laden life.

The Fourth Finger—Tragic Flaws

Another great character quality to write into our memoirs is what's known as "the tragic flaw." The concept comes primarily from ancient Greek tragedy, as described in Aristotle's book *Poetics*, using the term *hamartia*. Hamartia translates into "to miss the mark" or "to err," to "fail in one's purpose" and in Christianity, "to sin." It's whatever our fault is, if we think of fault as in a fault line in the psyche, a crack in our soul's surface that leaves us vulnerable to psychological earthquakes. You can call it a defect, a shortcoming, a failure of judgment, a moral defect, a blind spot, a weakness, and we all have them, darn it, because we're all flawed human beings. It doesn't get more archetypal than that!

In ancient Greek tragedies, the most typical tragic flaw was hubris, or pride, which often meant a hero who thought he was invincible, who could fool the gods. Take Oedipus, for example. He is told by the Oracle at Delphi that he is destined to kill his father and murder his mother. His pride (of course coupled with fear) leads him to attempt to escape his destiny, to outrun the gods, and, well, we all know how that turned out. Another common tragic flaw is too much ambition coupled with arrogance which we see in any number of Shakespearean dramas, like *Macbeth* or *King Lear*. Jealousy is the tragic flaw of Othello, although jealousy is often connected with pride—suspecting someone of infidelity, as Othello suspected his wife, Desdemona, can be a wound to one's pride. Romeo and Juliet shared a tragic flaw in their impulsiveness, which led to their mutual deaths, making their tragic flaw literally a fatal flaw—another term that's often used synonymously.

In Greek mythology, all the heroes have tragic flaws. A classic example is Achilles, who had that dang heel that didn't get dipped in immortality, making him vulnerable there. That's a literal tragic flaw on the body, but he also suffered from the psychological tragic flaw of hubris, and when his pride was wounded, he was angry and vengeful and wreaked all sorts of havoc. Even the gods in Greek mythology are flawed—Hera and Aphrodite have their jealousy, Zeus and most of the gods have their lust and subsequent infidelity, Artemis and Apollo have their pride, Poseidon has his egoic rage. The message for us—if even heroes and gods are flawed, then so too are we as mere mortals.

Whether our flaw is tragic or not, meaning it leads to tragedy, to our downfall, or whether our flaw is fatal or not, meaning it leads to the demise of something (the end of our marriages or our jobs or our relationships with others)—well, I'd argue, this is simply a matter of degree. One person can get drunk a bunch of times in college and not turn into an addict. Another person can experience jealousy and not seek revenge. Another person can steal a few office supplies now and then and not turn into a white-collar criminal. We're all made up of and capable of minor flaws, but I'd suggest here that it's our major flaws, our major fault lines, that are worth exploring in our memoirs.

Now I don't want to wade too much into the nature/nurture debate here. This debate would have us ask, are we born flawed, or made flawed? Are there people who are just born bad seeds, or is their seed spoiled by the soil they were planted in? I don't know if the answer is both nature and nurture, but what I do know is that nurture plays a big part, maybe the main part, in the development of our tragic flaws. A child who experiences early betrayal may turn into an adult whose tragic flaw is distrust, causing them to sabotage all relationships. A child who experiences sexual abuse may turn into an adult flawed by sexual dys-function, or may become abusive themselves. A child who is teased mercilessly for some perceived default may turn into an adult whose tragic flaw is a lack of self-esteem, causing them to stay in an abusive relationship. This moves us away from original sin (nature) into psycho-logical dis-ease (nurture) as the main cause of our tragic flaws.

In *Inside Story: The Power of the Transformational Arc*, Dara Marks uses the term "the fatal flaw" and defines it this way: "The FATAL FLAW is a struggle within a character to maintain a survival system long after it has outlived its usefulness." Let's unpack that definition, starting with "a survival system." Something wounds us, usually when we are young, and that wound creates a fault line in the psyche, a crack or a fissure. In order to not fall into it and give in to the darkness, we create survival systems, and those survival systems are very useful, necessary even, for our psychological and sometimes physical survival. A girl is sexually abused, and told by her abuser that he'll kill her family if she tells any-one, and that girl learns how to keep her secrets buried deep inside. She must, in order to survive. A boy grows up with a violent father, and in order to survive his home life, he learns to escape into his room and be invisible. Another girl grows up in a chaotic home, and the only way she knows how to survive it is through obsessive counting and magic rituals where she can create order.

These are all useful survival systems, but the key part of Marks' defi-nition is that these survival systems can become fatal or tragic to the adult who is unable to shake them off, even when they are no longer useful. The girl who was abused may become the mother who ignores her own daughter's abuse, keeping the secret of abuse still. The boy with the violent father may still hide as an adult, so conflict adverse that he can't stand up to a bullying boss at work. The girl who grew up in the chaotic home may become the woman who can't let go of her obses-sive-compulsive behaviors, even when she's in a safe home as an adult. The terrible irony here is that what saved us as a child can destroy us as adults; what we developed to stay safe as a child may make us a danger to ourselves and to others. As Nietzsche wrote, what doesn't kill us makes us stronger, but the truth is also this—what doesn't kill us (as children) makes us weaker (as adults).

The examples I've offered of early wounding in life—sexual abuse, physical abuse, a chaotic home—are some of the deepest wounds a child can suffer, and Ashley C. Ford suffered them all. Perhaps your childhood was relatively normal (whatever that means!). Perhaps you're wondering, do I have a tragic flaw? Perhaps your childhood wasn't something you needed to survive. And here again, I'll go back to a matter of degree. Maybe your tragic flaw is more minor. Maybe you grew up with four siblings and you had to fight for your parents' attention (your survival system), so your "tragic" flaw as an adult is constantly needing attention. That's not likely to destroy you or make you a danger to others—maybe just a minor irritant! But it could wreak havoc on friendships or a marriage, or cause troubles in the workplace. Maybe you were always in the shadow of a high-achieving sibling whom you couldn't keep up with, so your survival system was to act like you didn't care— your "tragic" flaw as an adult may be self-sabotage by purposefully underachieving. Or maybe you grew up in a "too nice" home where conflict was to be avoided at all costs for the sake of getting along, and your "tragic" flaw as an adult is never speaking up in uncomfortable situations or expressing any less-than-positive feelings.

Point being, whether you have a TRAGIC FLAW or a tragic flaw is simply a matter of degree.

Coming-of-age memoirs are a great place to explore tragic flaws, because they deal with the time in our lives when we're most likely to develop them—childhood and adolescence. If a coming-of-age memoir takes us through the author's early adulthood, we may not only see the survival mechanism that developed, but the second part of Marks' definition—how that survival system has outlived its usefulness, and may cause unnecessary suffering or strife in the author's life.

We see that in Ford's coming-of-age memoir. Ford's tragic flaw is her propensity toward invisibility, toward hiding and silencing herself. It's completely understandable, given her childhood growing up with a volatile and violent mother. She writes that by the age of four, "self-preservation had already been imprinted upon me as a requirement [for survival]." As we explored above, she comes to believe, through her mother's punishments, that she's a bad girl, and she does everything to hide that badness from others. She writes, "I'd found this secret place inside to shield my bad self, the part that chose not to tell the truth, but it had never occurred to me everyone might have a secret bad self. A self that didn't tell the truth because it had learned the same lessons I'd learned and knew the quiet and the dark could be good places to hide from screams and slaps." She writes, "I knew how to disappear. Sometimes my mother needed me to disappear."

Ford calls invisibility her "superpower," and this language makes sense—our survival systems *are* our superpowers, the thing that keeps us physically and psychologically safe during childhood. *But not without its cost.* Ford was sexually assaulted twice during her childhood and early adolescence, once by a "family friend" who forced his tongue down her throat on New Year's Eve, and once by a "boyfriend" who raped her as she was trying to break up with him. Neither time does she tell her mother—she simply doesn't feel safe to do so, fearing her wrath, fearing confirmation that she really is bad, that her choices are wrong. Not telling her mother about the rape is particularly costly, since the boy stays in Ford's life, stalking her, and she fears he'll do it again. We imagine that even if she told her mother and she initially flew into a rage, she would have also stepped up and offered protection for Ford, and sought punishment for her rapist.

The cost of Ford's silence and invisibility in these examples is stark, but no less costly was the daily wear and tear on her soul from hiding her true self from her family, and later in college, from her friends. All those years of feeling like she's bad and wrong, all those years of making herself invisible, take a terrible toll on her self-esteem. There's a touching scene in the book when Ford returns home from college for a visit that illustrates this toll. She has to spend 10 minutes looking at herself in the mirror, "reciting the same phrase like my therapist had taught me: I like myself the way I am. I like myself the way I am. I like myself the way I am. I like myself the way I am." But it's hard for her to remember this when she's around her family, and the price she has to pay for a modicum of self-esteem is her estrangement from them.

Part of being vulnerable with our readers is to place our tragic flaws on the page, to expose our woundedness, to name our survival systems,

THE ARCHETYPE OF CHARACTER

and to explore how they have outgrown their usefulness and have negatively impacted our adult lives. Even if we're not writing a coming-of-age memoir and instead are focusing on our adult lives, our readers will understand what drives our decisions and motivates our behaviors in those lives if they understand the patterns that got put in place during our childhood. Even if we're writing about events that take place in our 50s, we can flash back to childhood and our survival systems then and the repercussions now. In doing so, we create an opportunity for an empathetic, heart-felt connection with our readers who have their own tragic flaws as well. They'll be rooting for us to overcome ours, and if their flaw is similar, we may inspire them to make changes in their lives.

The Fifth Finger—The Struggles and Challenges of Change

The fifth finger on the hand of the archetype of character is the change. Donald Maass writes, "Change is a universal experience. We've all gone through it. We cannot avoid it. The passages of life guarantee it. Change is necessary, difficult, wrenching, and individual." As such, he writes, "It's the most powerful way to stir feelings in our reader."

The archetype of change lies at the core of the majority of memoirs—remember my argument in Chapter I that the main archetype in memoir is transition, or change. Readers are constantly facing changes in their lives, and they often come to the human instruction manual of memoir to see how memoirists struggle with their own changes, both external and internal. We know the struggle is real, so if a memoirist wants to keep it real with their readers, they'll put their struggles with changes and changing on the page. They'll lean into what Dara Marks calls the most powerful part of story, "the transformational arc," showing us who they were and who they became, without skipping all the messy middle that transformation requires.

Often, what needs to change or transform is our tragic flaw itself. Even if there's no direct causal relationship between our tragic flaw and the change-situation before us—for instance, our tragic flaw didn't cause "x" to happen—how we survive "x" may be greatly influenced by our tragic flaw, and usually not for the better.

To transform our tragic flaws, we don't succumb to those survival systems that are no longer useful, but we become conscious of them and let them go. Oh, were it so easy as those three words—*let them go*—suggest. That's why I use the word "struggle" here, which is another word for the literary term "conflict," and conflict, as we know, is essential to story. All children learn this in school—the six central elements of a story are character, plot, setting, point of view, theme, and conflict (sometimes you only see five elements of story, with resolution replacing point of view and theme, but point being, conflict is always there). These are the archetypal elements of story.

We're taught by our literature teachers that there are two kinds of conflict, internal and external, the conflict within ourselves and the conflicts with others (nature is also considered an other). I don't think there's ever anything that's purely external conflict, because of course we bring our internal conflicted selves to our external conflicts, as in the example above of the man who accepts bullying from his boss because of his internal struggle with his outdated survival system from childhood.

What depth psychology adds to this discussion on struggle is that sometimes our internal conflicts are struggles of consciousness; that is, we must struggle to make conscious our own unconscious survival systems. This is the first struggle—to become conscious of the tragic flaw in our psychological design. Then the second struggle becomes to let it go, to transform it, to replace it with more age and situation-appropriate responses. The abused child no longer needs to disassociate when she's a woman having sex with a safe partner. The girl who grew up in the chaotic home no longer needs as a woman to count the kitchen tiles 10 times before she's safe to make dinner. First, the struggle for consciousness. Then, the challenge of transformation. First, "Oh, shit, I do that?" Then, "Let's see if I can change."

If we want to write a memoir that harnesses the power of the transformational arc (ala Marks), and that powerfully stirs feelings in our readers (ala Maass), then we have to write down and write into our own tragic flaws. We have to tell on ourselves. We have to lift the lid of the toilet and expose our shit before we flush it away (how's that for a metaphor?). If we're going to show how we got from point B to point C, we might want to take our readers back to point A and show how we got to point B to begin with. Because they're probably going to wonder, anyway. When we read addiction memoirs, for instance, yes we want to know how the addict (point B) got sober (point C), but if we're psychologically minded at all (and I think we can safely assume memoir readers are, and that's why they're drawn to the genre), we'll also want to know what caused the addiction in the first place (point A). If we don't write about point A, we risk our readers thinking we haven't done our psychological work, that we haven't struggled with consciousness, that we're either not reflective enough, or we're withholding our reflections from the reader (slice-of-life and humorous memoirs are often exceptions to this rule).

And what if we never get to point C, the end of the transformational arc? Or what if we get there, and then relapse? Well, that's life too, right? Sometimes life doesn't provide a happy ending. Sometimes our flaws remain tragic, and they kill us or kill something in our life in the end. Sometimes we start out miserable and we end up still pretty miserable. Sometimes we don't survive our own survival systems. But a complete defeat is rare in memoir. Sometimes, in the struggle to change, we only manage to move the gears a little, to flush away a little bit of the shit, to dismantle only a wall or a window frame in our houses of pain. It's okay to be honest and show that too.

Ford's memoir offers a good example of this. Toward the end of the book, we see her relationship with her mother start to change, to soften. We see it when Ford moves from anger at her mother over almost letting herself die of a burst appendix, to feeling sad instead. At the end of that chapter, she writes, "My mother wasn't perfect. Our relationship was complicated, and difficult. She was my imperfect mother. We were two different people, and found that hard to accept in one another. But I was hers and she was mine. That's how it had always been. Who would I be, if not hers? I didn't want to be without her."

This was a major epiphany for Ford, who had spent much of her time before this trying to escape from her mother. And we saw above that part of her survival system was to withhold the truth to her mother, a way of escaping psychologically from her judgment. But there's a moment when that changes too. She makes the decision to finally tell her mother about the rape, and in this scene, we see how her mother has changed as well, as she offers Ford some much-needed absolution. "'I understand why you didn't tell me,'" she says. "'I was crazy back then.'" It's a quiet moment, but the reader feels its import—my emotional reaction to reading that scene was to lay the book on my lap and exhale the deepest sigh of relief.

These changes in her relationship with her mother, alongside her life-changing visit with her father in prison and the insights into the importance of family after her grandmother's death, leave Ford determined to break down her survival system of invisibility and allow herself to be seen and known by her family, to allow herself to tell the truth. The biggest turning point in this arc comes during her visit with her father, when she asks for his permission to write about him and their relationship, and he gracefully grants it. Not only that, but he says, "'Do me a favor, Ashley? When you write about you and me? Just tell the truth. Your truth. Don't worry about nobody's feelings, especially not mine. You gotta be tough to tell your truth, but it's the only thing worth doing next to loving somebody.'" After she leaves the prison, she tells us, "For half a minute, I was flying. For half a minute, I knew I had it in me to tell the truth, and be loved anyway."

For half a minute. Because change is challenging. Because insights and epiphanies can sometimes only live in the world for half a minute. Because that's life. Because that's what it's like to be human.

Ford tries to hold onto the transformational arc through the end of the book. "I didn't want to run from my family. I wanted to be who I was, and I didn't know if that person fit among them anymore. My lessons hadn't always come the way I wanted or hoped, but I was not ashamed of how I had changed, and I was determined to remember that." Right before she enters her grandmother's hospital room for what will be the last time, she notes, "If this was the last time I saw her alive, and she saw me, what would I want her to see? I would want her to see me. All of me. Even the parts she would hate, just to give her the chance to see the full breadth of who I really was, and maybe, just for a moment, a real idea of who I might become." The scene pays off beautifully when the only words her grandmother speaks to her are, "'Your hair. . . . is so beautiful.'" Her grandmother had always disliked Ford's decision to let her hair go natural, and here she is telling Ford that she's beautiful, just the way she is. Another quiet moment, but rich with symbolic import.

In the last moment on the transformational arc of this memoir, when Ford's father comes home from prison, she writes, "We looked at each other, wondering who the other might be, excited to find out. There was a new road to pave together, and I wanted to do the work beside him just as I am. Just as I've always been." It's a beautiful ending, a promising ending, a fulfilling ending of the book, but the transformational arc is not complete. Her relationship with her family and father is not restored, but is instead re-storying. There is more work to be done. We're reminded that at the beginning of the book, in the scene where Ford's mother calls her to say her father is coming home, that her relationship with her mother is not fraught-less, but it is less fraught. She tells us then:

> She called every few weeks—I answered every other call—and we usually had a good time talking for ten to fifteen minutes. I'd taught myself to keep our phone conversations light, or as I liked to think of it, complication-free, without lying. I didn't want to lie to her. I wanted to be able to talk to my mother the way I could with most other people, as myself. But she wasn't just anybody. She was my mother, so that was impossible. There were limits. We only dove into subjects that wouldn't end in arguments, which was mostly whatever would make us both laugh.

Complication-free, but without lying. Not a healed relationship, no, but one that is healing. The survival system of deception is gone, but the survival system of not poking the bear is still intact. We appreciate Ford's honesty, the way she shows her work, the way she acknowledges that the work is not done, but the arc is bent toward transformation. After all, she's 34 years old when the book is published, and we who have lived a good deal longer than Ford would be doubtful if she claimed to have completely banished her tragic flaw and faced no more struggles. We don't need the arc from flawed to flawless in our memoirists. Sometimes flawed to less flawed is enough.

Conclusion

In *Unreliable Truth: On Memoir and Memory*, Maureen Murdock writes, "The memoir presupposes that there is a certain unity to human experience, that we all share similar hopes, dreams and desires." That certain unity is our character, as unique as our fingerprints, as universal as our fingers. In this chapter, we put our fingers on the archetypal pulse of character, its beating heart, what we as characters all share in common—our body's emotions and our mind's feelings, our yearnings that drive us, our commitment to our values, our wrestling with our tragic flaws, and our struggles and challenges with change. To create a memoir with the deepest possible story and the broadest possible appeal, we write into those character qualities honestly and vulnerably, reaching across the human divide in the spirit of generosity, one open heart to another.

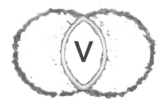

THE ARCHETYPE OF MEANING
Putting the Deep in Memoir Through Theme, Reflection, and Takeaways

If we return to the idea that story is the human instruction manual for living our lives, then we can imagine one of the central questions that manual must answer is, "What's the meaning of it all?" and a myriad of similarly worded questions: "What is the meaning of life? What does it mean that these things happened to me? What meaning can I take away from what happened? What makes life meaningful? How do I make meaning from the seemingly meaningless experiences that have befallen me? How do I live my life in the most meaningful way possible?" Meaning is the boon we offer our readers from our journey through life's vicissitudes. Meaning is a gift we bring out of the underworld to offer to the readers of our memoirs. I quoted the psychiatrist C. G. Jung in Chapter I, who wrote, "Meaning makes a great many things endurable—perhaps everything." Our memoirs are humble offerings to our readers—we say, "I endured this, and here's the meaning I found or here's the meaning I made of it all. Perhaps it will be meaningful to you as well."

Meaning is closely tied in my mind with reflection. The etymology of "reflect" means to turn or look back. When we turn and look back on our lives or on a period in our lives, we typically do so to find meaning there. It's not just a "so that happened," but rather, a "that happened—so what?" Meaning is what we make of what happened to us upon reflection. Cheryl Strayed tells us, "I'm not interested in confession. I'm interested in revelation. When I'm reading, I don't want to know every terrible thing that happened to the author just for the sake of knowing. I want to know what meaning he or she made of what happened." In *Writing is My Drink*, memoirist Theo Pauline Nestor says the same thing: "I'm not so much interested in the events the narrator has endured as I am in the narrator's insight into the experience. There are all sorts of crazy life stories out there, but to me what's interesting is what the story *means* to the writer."

Me too.

I'm going to admit something really sacrilegious here. Don't tell Mary Karr, but I'm not a huge fan of her classic and widely praised memoir, *The Liar's Club*. I enjoyed it, I should say, and felt it was a riveting story, well-written and full of unique and quirky details, a crazy life story. But I was disappointed in it as a memoir because I felt it stayed pretty close to recounting the events of her childhood. There were so many times I wanted to put down the book and ask Karr, "What did you think about when that happened? What did you feel about her then? What was that experience like for you?" I felt like she was telling her story from a bit of a remove, and thus, it didn't touch my heart and soul like other memoirs do. And, even more, what I missed in the book was reflection. I wanted Mary Karr to reflect upon the meaning of her crazy and off-beat experiences of childhood. I got a lot of the "so that happened" and very little of the "that happened—so what?"

There is an important genre distinction here. If *The Liar's Club* had been fiction, I would've gone along for the wild ride just fine, because I wouldn't expect a piece of fiction to reflect upon the meaning of itself, of its own narrative. Or I would have written my own meaning into it, done what a good student of literature does and reflect upon the work and name its themes. But I expect something different from memoir. I expect a reflective author. I expect some form of "this is who I've become as a result of having these experiences" or "this is what I now know about life as a result of going through this experience." When I read memoir, I invest in a person, not just a plot, and in my favorite memoirs, the author is both storyteller and meaning-maker. As Patricia Hampl writes in *I Could Tell You Stories*, "Memoir is the intersection of narration and reflection." *The Liar's Club*, to me, was all narration, little to no reflection—not an intersection, but a one-way street. Not a mandorla, but a circle. I liked it, but I couldn't find the *there there,* and I couldn't find the *me* there.[*]

In *Handling the Truth,* Beth Kephart is very hard on memoirists who just narrate their story, calling them "pseudo-memoirists." She writes, "The pseudos haven't climbed out of their own small circles yet. The pseudos haven't connected with the larger world, or with their readers. The pseudos are confusing anecdote with memoir." She continues, "It's not that we don't want their details. It's that we need to know what it all means, and how it relates to us. Simple truths. It's just not memoir without them." While I wouldn't go that far, wouldn't dismiss someone as a pseudo-memoirist if they're not a meaning-maker or decline to call a book a memoir if it doesn't contain reflection that relates to us, I would call it a missed opportunity to, in the words in this book's subtitle, deepen your story and broaden its appeal, and add something to the human instruction manual.

It's also a missed opportunity to make your memoir stand out to a publisher. Publishers make money when a memoir appeals to the widest possible audience. Every now and then, a one-way street of a memoir will become a phenomenon, like J.D. Vance's *Hillbilly Elegy* and Tara Westover's *Educated,* neither of which contain much reflection at all. But publishers are also interested in the intersection between narration and reflection because the intersection is where the reader and the audience meet.

Let's look again at Gregory Orr's memoir *The Blessing.* On the surface, the events he's recounting in the memoir are not something the vast majority of us can relate to—we have most likely never accidentally killed a family member in our youth, or even know someone who did. Orr could have stayed on the surface in his memoir, did what Cheryl Strayed calls "confession," telling us "every terrible thing that happened to [him] just for the sake of knowing." But Orr doesn't do that: he offers us the "revelation" that so appeals to Strayed. On the book jacket cover, we are promised that revelation: "Eventually, his experiences would lead him to an unexpected epiphany and a clear answer to one of life's basic questions: How do we find meaning in the face of death?"

---

[*] To be fair, Karr published *The Liar's Club* at the beginning of the memoir revolution that came in the late '80s and '90s. Many early memoirs focused primarily on storytelling and were light on meaning and reflection, including Frank McCourt's *Angela's Ashes* and Tobias Wolf's *This Boy's Life.*

That's what Orr is searching to do in the aftermath of the accident, to find the meaning of it. He writes, "It's not possible to live in a world without meaning. . . . But all the meanings, all the childish understanding of life that had sustained me up until that day were suddenly and completely eradicated by Peter's death." His memoir is about finding meaning again when we suffer tragedies that eradicate all meaning, and his clear answer is his contribution to the human instruction manual, because again, while the vast majority of us will never accidentally kill anyone, all of us will grapple with finding meaning in the face of suffering, tragedy, and death.

And all of us is a big audience.

Essential Questions

In Chapter III, we explored the way a question can be used to structure a memoir—we pose a question, or life poses a question to us, and our memoir chronicles the journey toward the answer. Orr does this in several places. On the jacket cover is the question, "How do we find meaning in the face of death?" In the first chapter, the question is raised, "Why was I spared?" The final chapter offers answers to both those questions, while the middle chapters show the journey from question to answer, and from meaninglessness to meaningfulness. I don't think Karr has a question in *The Liar's Club*. Her memoir is more along the lines of "this shit happened and it was tragic and kinda funny."

I am a huge fan of including essential questions in every memoir—those big, broad, universal questions like Elizabeth Gilbert's "What if my life belonged to me?" and the other ones she and I list in Chapter III. If your memoir addresses essential questions, you've already made the case for why your particular story is universal, and you're already connected to a curious reader, standing at the intersection together, questing toward answers. I ask all my memoir students, what is the universal question or questions your story is an attempt to answer? Then, I step in to assure them, don't worry if your question seems generic—the big questions *will* be generic. And don't worry if your question has already been explored by two dozen or two hundred other memoirists—the point is that the questions are so big and broad and deep and there is no definitive answer, there is only *my answer* and *your answer* and *his*

THE ARCHETYPE OF MEANING

answer and *her answer* and we need *a chorus of answers* to provide us with as many models as possible for how to live our lives with meaning and purpose in the face of x, y, and z.

Sometimes it takes some drilling down into our stories to find our bedrock questions, the ones that will connect us with the greatest possible audience. I use the example of Carol E. Anderson and her memoir *You Can't Buy Love Like That: Growing Up Gay in the Sixties.* Her book asks and answers the question, "What was it like to grow up gay in the sixties to evangelical parents?" To relate to that question on the surface, you need to be 1) gay and/or 2) growing up in the 60s and/or 3) a child of evangelical parents. It's specific, not universal. And Anderson is aware that her question is not relevant to all readers. In an interview in *The Magic of Memoir*, she shares, "My hope in telling my truth is to help people see why what happened to me would have meaning in their life—how the struggle to be authentic while keeping a secret would be relevant to them, even though they might not be gay." There's the larger question many people can relate to. "How can I be authentic while keeping a secret?" There's the intersection that's going to appeal to a publisher—this very specific story, this very general question.

It's quite common for these essential questions to be used as marketing text on the book's back cover, like Orr's publisher did with the question, "How do we find meaning in the face of death?" Beth Kephart explains, "The questions, themes, and concerns that fuel a memoir are often best enunciated at the start," and the cover is certainly the place where we typically start. The question is a hook (the mark itself even looks like a hook!), a way of reeling a reader in and indicating that this story will be one drop in a much larger ocean that they may be swimming as well.

For Dani Shapiro's memoir *Hourglass: Time, Memory, Marriage,* the publisher chose not one, not two, but three "hook marks" to place on the back cover, large questions with questions within the questions.

> What are the forces that shape our most elemental bonds? How do we make lifelong commitments in the face of identities that are continuously shifting, and commit ourselves for all time when the self is so often in flux? What happens to love in the face of the unexpected, in the face of disappointment and compromise—

how do we wrest beauty from imperfection, find grace in the ordinary, desire what we have rather than what we lack?

Those questions cast a wide net, gathering in so many fish in the sea who may be struggling with the changes that come with their long-term relationships.

If the questions are not in the back cover summary, publishers will often choose endorsements that lay the questions bare. This is the case with Carol E. Anderson's book. The summary stays close to the specifics of Anderson's story—gay, 60s, fundamentalist Christian home. It broadens out into revelation—"*You Can't Buy Love Like That* reveals the complex, invisible dynamics that arise for gay people who are forced to hide their true selves in order to survive." Even if you aren't gay, of course, you may find this revelation intriguing and want to read the book to learn more about those dynamics. But the first endorsement offers an essential question that casts the widest net—author Judy Goldman writes, "At the heart of this book is a question: 'What is love?'" Suddenly every one of us is swooped up. And Goldman promises us, "After reading these pages, you will be much wiser about the ways of the heart," clearly naming this book as a contribution to the human instruction manual.

Brooke Warner's She Writes Press is the publisher of Anderson's book. In her previous position as acquisitions editor for Seal Press, she knew that when she presented possible titles, the marketing team would want to know what the story was beyond the story, the answer to the question, "What will the reader get out of your book?" She shares, "If it wasn't apparent, the book wasn't acquirable." So it doesn't surprise me that the first endorsement points to what the reader will get out of the book—we'll be much wiser about the ways of the heart. The second endorsement assures us that despite the specificity of Anderson's story, there's something in it for us. Madeleine Blais writes, "Written with candor, compassion, and humor, *You Can't Buy Love Like That* is, like all great memoirs, both specific and universal in its appeal." And the third endorsement points to the memoir's universal themes. Stacy Blake-Beard writes, "Truthful and beautifully written, Anderson's insightful journey is a reminder of the privilege of choice, the importance of voice, and the power of love." The back cover text is brilliantly inclusive, promising the *me* (Anderson's story), the *we* (gay people's story), and the *us* (our story) in the center of the mandorla.

A Useful Distinction Between a Memoir's Topic and its Theme

Let's turn now to explore theme as a site of meaning-making for memoirists. In *Inside Story*, Dara Marks is emphatic about the importance of theme: "It is the *theme* that makes our writing meaningful. It opens up the story's inner value system, so that writers can make *conscious* connection with what the story *really* wants to communicate to them and through them."

Given the importance of theme as a vessel for meaning-making in memoir, I've been surprised that a lot of writing craft books, teachers, and critics use the term "topic" and "theme" interchangeably. For example, take this blurb from *Garden and Gun* magazine about Ashley C. Ford's *Somebody's Daughter*. "Ashley C. Ford writes with lyrical vulnerability. . . . Her most powerful personal essays have delved into her girlhood, race, incarceration, poverty, and family ties—themes she expands on in this recollection of her childhood and her father's imprisonment."

I want to draw a distinction that will be useful in this chapter. I don't think "girlhood, race, incarceration, poverty, and family ties" are themes. They are topics, the subject matter of the book. In Elizabeth Gilbert's *Eat, Pray, Love*, eating, praying, and loving are not themes, but topics. In Dani Shapiro's *Hourglass: Time, Memory, Marriage*, time, memory, and marriage are not themes, they are topics. In Linda Joy Myers' *Song of the Plains: A Memoir of Family, Secrets, and Silence*, the subtitle names her topics too, a typical placement for topics.

Even some dictionaries don't make such a distinction. In Wikipedia's definition, "a theme is a central topic, subject." Another online dictionary definition of theme is "the subject of a talk, a piece of writing, a person's thoughts: a topic." But that definition just confuses me. The subject or topic of a piece of writing is not synonymous with a person's thoughts. You can write a bunch of facts about a topic and never include your thoughts about it. To me, a theme is a person's thoughts on a topic. As Stacy Blake-Beard states in her endorsements, Anderson's thoughts on growing up gay in the 60s are that it's a privilege to have a choice, important to have a voice, and powerful to have love. Those are her themes, while growing up gay in the 60s is her topic.

That same online dictionary gets to my distinction in its second definition of theme, calling it "an idea that recurs in or pervades a work of art or literature." Wikipedia also gets to the distinction when it calls theme the "message within a narrative." These definitions are more helpful–theme is our *ideas* about the topic. Theme is our *message* about the topic. Lisa Cron defines theme in *Wired For Story* as "the underlying point the narrative makes."

Why is this distinction between topic and theme so important? I'm not just parsing words here. I believe, along with Lisa Cron, that "since theme is the underlying point the narrative makes about the human experience, it's also where the universal lies." Theme is where we write the human instruction manual and is our opportunity to add our perspective, our point of view, our earned wisdom, to topics of concern to us all.

Gail Caldwell's memoir *Let's Take the Long Way Home: A Memoir of Friendship* names her topic in the subtitle, but her theme is named in the book's description: "*Let's Take the Long Way Home* is a celebration of the profound transformations that come from intimate connection." Tell me it's a memoir about friendship and I'm like, meh, okay. But tell me it's a memoir about how friendship is an intimate connection that can bring about profound transformations, and my credit card is already out.

Putting the theme in the book's description (or as we've seen, in the endorsements) is a common tactic to garner interest in the book–just naming the topic is rarely enough. The description for Shapiro's memoir on the topics of time, memory, and marriage reads: "*Hourglass* is an inquiry into how marriage is transformed by time–abraded, strengthened, shaped in miraculous and sometimes terrifying ways by accident and experience." We don't know her underlying point about memory in this sentence, but we know her perspective on marriage and time, and if we're interested in that perspective, we'll pick up the book to see how she develops the theme–the evidence she lays out to argue or illustrate that underlying point.

A helpful metaphor here in thinking about topics and themes is a string of pearls. The topic is a necklace, the pearls are the individual stories you'll share on that topic, and the string is the theme that holds the stories together, the memoir's throughline. Most memoirists come to writing with clearly identified topics. For example, they might think, "I want to write about my relationship with my autistic son" or "I want to write about the stroke I had when I was a child." They know their necklace. But they may not yet know their theme, the throughline of their story. As a teacher, it's always an exciting moment when my memoirists identify their themes, when they say, "So that's what this really is about. That's what I've been trying to say all along." And once they know their themes, they can begin to carry them through their larger story, selecting scenes or anecdotes to illustrate them, while removing material that digresses too far from them as off-point. To return to the necklace analogy, if you know you're writing the story of a pearl necklace, you'll realize that the blue bead of a story over there, while pretty, doesn't belong on this particular necklace, and that earring you just wrote, that's a whole different topic entirely.

A Useful Distinction Between Reflection and Takeaways

Once we settle on our themes, then we can begin to write our reflections on them, our ideas or takes or positions or beliefs on those themes—what they mean to us, why they matter to us—based on the experiences we are recounting in our memoir, based on the story we are telling. If our theme is the profound transformations that come from intimate connection, for example, we can offer reflections on our own intimate connections, what we learned from them, how those intimate connections felt, why we value them, and how they've transformed us.

In Gregory Orr's memoir, he offers us the following reflection. "Whenever I thought of Peter, my feelings were so tangled up in guilt that I, too, wanted to be dead. And I thought of him constantly in those days and weeks and months after his death." Here Orr is reflecting on two of his themes—the destructive nature of guilt, and the intrusive nature of grief.

But in the paragraph right above this one, Orr offers something else—a takeaway. Brooke Warner writes that takeaways are "a form of reflection—specific kinds of reflections that turn outward and serve as little arrows that pierce readers' hearts." Orr's reflection above is turned inward—he's talking about his heart. But in the paragraph preceding it, he turns outward, writing, "When someone you love dies suddenly, the process of surviving them is complex. Part of the difficulty is separating out your entangled identities. Grieving, you celebrate the love bond between you and the dead one, but also, as you grieve, you are distinguishing yourself from the dead one." See the difference? Reflections are *about* the author, how the author makes meaning of their experience, but "takeaways are *for* the reader," as Warner and Linda Joy Myers note in their book, *Breaking Ground On Your Memoir*.

Warner tells us, "Often when I read takeaway in memoirs, I'm compelled to stop and take a moment. These are deep, connective moments between writer and reader, when the writer moves beyond writing just her own story and acknowledges and reaches for universal human truths." That's how I experience them too. I know the author has offered me a takeaway when I am arrested while reading, where I stop and look out the window, or stare into space. I stop thinking about the writer's life and I begin to think of my own—how does this resonate with me? What questions does it pose to my life? It's a form of recognition—I know this feeling. I've thought this same thought. It may be a moment where I nod in agreement, or find myself wanting to write "Yes!" in the margins. I call these "highlighter moments"—those moments when I stop reading and reach for my highlighter because something pierced my heart and I want to remember it.

One brilliant memoir that I burned through an entire highlighter while reading is Kathryn Schulz's *Lost & Found*. Pierced my heart? On nearly every page. You might expect as much in a memoir exploring losing your beloved father and finding your soulmate, but really, the memoir is over-the-top piercing. Two examples. On grieving her father: "But grief makes reckless cosmologists of us all, and I thought it possible, in an impossible kind of way, that if I went out looking, I might find myself, however briefly or inexplicably, in my father's company again." On waking up in the morning and seeing her lover's eyes: "*All I ever want is this,* I think in those moments and countless others, *over and over and over again for a hundred thousand years.* That is the essence of requited love and, surely, the luckiest of all conditions: to wish only for what we already have."

Yes, and yes. I've thought both thoughts, felt both feelings. Sometimes I'll highlight a particularly poetic passage that I want to remember for its beauty or power or craft. But more commonly, what I highlight in a memoir is a takeaway that moves *me* or resonates with *me* or *I* want to remember *for me*. Notice the italicized first-person pronouns here—I don't highlight something that the writer learned for *herself*, but rather, I highlight something that matters to *myself*. Reflections are circles about the "me" of the author, while takeaways are mandorlas, always about something larger, something more universal, something that connects the "me" of the author with the "you" of the reader.

This is more than just pronoun play. I think it's a really useful craft distinction and one that I teach my students—the surest way to know you're writing a takeaway is to step away from the first-person singular pronoun of "I" and into the first-person plural pronoun of "we" or the second-person plural pronoun of "you" or the third person-plural pronoun of "they."

Orr does that in his takeaway, shifting into the second-person plural, the collective "you."

> When someone you love dies suddenly, the process of surviving them is complex. Part of the difficulty is separating out your entangled identities. Grieving, you celebrate the love bond between you and the dead one, but also, as you grieve, you are distinguishing yourself from the dead one.

He could have also chosen to use the first-person plural "we."

> When someone we love dies suddenly, the process of surviving them is complex. Part of the difficulty is separating out our entangled identities. Grieving, we celebrate the love bond between us and the dead one, but also, as we grieve, we are distinguishing ourselves from the dead one.

A bit more removed, but still in plural pronouns, is the third-person plural "they." Orr could have written his takeaway:

> When people experience someone in their lives dying suddenly, the process of surviving them is complex. Part of the difficulty is separating out their entangled identities. Grieving, they celebrate

the love bond between them and the dead one, but also, as they grieve, they are distinguishing themselves from the dead one.

If "I" is the pronoun of choice for reflection, is there a pronoun of choice for takeaways? I think this is a matter of your personal preference and style. Third person creates more objectivity, but also more distance. Second person, speaking directly to the reader as a "you," creates more direct intimacy with the reader, but it comes with a particular risk. If a reader doesn't recognize themselves in your *you*-niversalizing, it could alienate them. You risk speaking on behalf of your reader, and instead of highlighting your takeaway, they may wish to cross it out or write in the margins, "No! Not me." The same thing can happen with first-person plural, with gathering the reader into a "we." They may not appreciate you speaking on their behalf if their experience is very different.

Some authors move liberally through all levels of pronouns. Let's take Gina Frangello's memoir *Blow Your House Down: A Story of Family, Feminism, and Treason* as an example. Frangello's book is a master class in theme, reflection, and takeaways, worth studying for the meaning she wrings out of her very personal story of her adulterous relationship and how it implodes her family and her life. Her takeaways cross the gamut of pronoun choices.

First-person plural

- "We are always permeable, shifting. We are all only one strange leap away from becoming inconceivable to our former selves."
- "The greatest lesson we teach our children is how to survive us."

Second person

- "When you hate yourself enough, there is a sharp tinge of satisfaction in unhappiness."
- "This, I came to understand, was what freedom tasted like. It wasn't a heady illusion in the safety of a time-shared bed, seeking the approval of the person whose heart you are breaking. It is being willing to have your own heart broken and not blaming the outcome on anyone. It is being an

orphan, and love not being an obligation or prescription, but always a risky, transformative choice."

Third-person singular

- "But what happens to the young girl who isn't beautiful? What happens to a girl who grows up under a male gaze that renders her inconsequential, with nothing much of importance to lose?"

Third-person plural

- "Only people who also live with pain want to know anything about that narrative—most others are spending far too much energy pretending to themselves that it will never happen to them, and assigning value judgments to those who are sick to determine what that person may have done to 'invite' the problem (if not outright deserve it)."

She also writes takeaways without pronouns at all, writing about "men" and "women" and "people" in general, such as in this sentence: "The ways in which women both love and support one another, and mistrust and betray and undermine one another, may be the most complex thing in the universe." She writes takeaways as philosophical statements such as "Sometimes love just isn't enough to make something possible" and "There is only one way to tell the truth, but there are myriad ways to live a lie."

Frangello frequently begins with a reflection, then attaches a takeaway to it. In this sentence, she begins by reflecting on her own grief, but then she opens it up to a takeaway about our grief: "I miss her more with every passing day because, just as words once written can never be unwritten, grief is not a thing that ends. Sometimes, though, it cracks us open and exposes the places we've hidden, and that can be a kind of gift." In another example, she opens with a reflection on having to make the decision to stay in her marriage or leave, then offers a takeaway: "Staying would not have rendered me weak—an inconsequential June Cleaver—just as cheating didn't make me a coldhearted monster. The clean reduction of a woman to any prime number is always a lie, even if some lies are prettier than others."

In my copy of *Blow Your House Down*, I've highlighted something on almost every page, and often, several times on the same page—it's that well-crafted. Though she probably never came across Linda K. Thomas' blog post, "Your Memoir's All-important Takeaways," Frangello clearly lives by its wisdom. Thomas admonishes us:

> Dedicate quality time to crafting your takeaways. *Specify* what was the *most important message or lesson* you took away from that experience (the one you're reflecting on). *Boil it down*, write a *concise message for your readers*. . . . At first your takeaways will resemble diamonds-in-the-rough. Your job is to *cut* and *polish* and *make those gems sparkle*. Doing so *adds to their value* for both *you* and *your readers*.

I agree. Though of course we want every aspect of our writing to be strong and polished, we especially want this for our takeaways. Takeaways are gifts for your readers, and you want to craft the best gift possible to say thank you. Thank you for your time. Thank you for your money. I want this to be worth it for you. Here's a little something you can take away with you. A hostess gift, of sorts" If a reader is going to highlight or underline this important gift in your writing, you want it to be the absolute best, truest, most heart-felt and generous and as close to perfectly written sentence/s you can craft. Takeaways are frequently used as back cover quotes or highlighted in your book's description, and they often make their way onto your book's Goodreads quotations page, so it's worth every effort to make them shine.

Strategies for the Reluctant Takeawayer

In my experience teaching memoir, I find that most writers err on the side of caution when it comes to offering takeaways, especially women, who all too often don't claim their voices and their knowledge and their hard-earned wisdom. Brooke Warner has experienced this too. She shares:

I've found with my own students that mastering takeaway is about trusting themselves as writers. You have to believe that it's okay to have an opinion, to make an assertion. There is no takeaway without stating what you believe to be true. People fear that takeaway is preachy, or "telling," but done well it never should be. Done well it's an opportunity to take the reader to realms beyond your story, inviting them to consider their experiences and how they see the world—and in this way, takeaway alone has the power to impact readers in ways that no other aspect of memoir writing can.

I have a mantra I offer my students. "Own it all and give it all away." Own the wisdom you've gleaned from living your life—after all, you must think there's something important in your story, or you wouldn't make the kind of sacrifices it takes to write it down. Own what you know, own what you've earned, own what you've learned, and then, give it all away, a generous gift to your readers. Don't be stingy, stockpiling your life's lessons in a hope chest, as in, "I hope this book will make a difference in someone's life." Warner's last line is worth highlighting here: "Takeaway alone has the power to impact readers in ways that no other aspect of memoir writing can." That's a takeaway about takeaways for sure!

Sometimes my students shy away from takeaways, saying things like, "I don't want to speak on behalf of anyone else," or "I don't want to make assumptions about other people's experiences." They'd rather hide behind their story, and let the reader get what they get. Warner has seen that too. She writes, "Lots of writers fail to truly express what their takeaways are because they think they're inherent." She suggests that if you've already written a lot or completed your memoir and "you've never considered takeaways, find ways to go into the work and draw them out. Most likely they're already there, laying tangled or hidden in the story. As the writer of a memoir, your job is to show them to the reader. You can do this subtly or overtly, depending on your voice, your style, and your skill."

For the still-reluctant takeawayer, let me offer you eight simple strategies for doing your job—eight more subtle placements for takeaways in your writing.

1. Put them in your epigraphs.

Many writers include an epigraph, a short quotation that opens a book, and the epigraphs often signal the takeaway. *When Breath Becomes Air*, the story of Paul Kalanithi's battle with lung cancer in his mid-thirties, uses this strategy. His epigraph reads:

> You that seek what life is in death,
> Now find air that once was breath.
> New names unknown, old names gone:
> Till time end bodies, but souls none.
> Reader! then make time, while you be
> But steps to your eternity.
> ~Baron Brooke Fulke Greville, "Caelica 83"

The epigraph serves dual purposes. It explains the title and offers the takeaway—make time while you are alive and seek life, even as you move toward death.

In *Fat Girl*, Judith Moore places an epigraph before every chapter that suggests its theme and sometimes the takeaway. At the beginning of Chapter 6, when she is diving into her childhood wounds, she quotes a line from Franz Kafka: "It's good when your conscience receives big wounds, because that makes it more sensitive to every twinge." If you're going to use this strategy, you'll need to make sure there's a tight fit between the epigraph and the chapter's contents. It's okay if it's cryptic when the reader begins the chapter, but by the end, it should make total sense.

2. Use someone else's quote in your chapter.

If you're shy about offering your own wisdom, let someone else do it for you—find a quote that offers the takeaway, and work it into your chapter. Portia de Rossi does this in her eating disorder memoir, *Unbearable Lightness: A Story of Loss and Gain*. The last chapter ends with her marriage ceremony to Ellen DeGeneres. De Rossi is practicing her vows in front of her mother. "You treat me better than I've ever treated myself," she reads, and her mom, concerned about the possibility of Portia's relapse, interrupts her and says, "But you're all better now, aren't you?" The chapter ends with this:

> I look at my reflection in the mirror and I like what I see. I'm not looking at a childhood fantasy of what I should look like on my wedding day or a bride in a wedding dress. I am looking at me. I contemplate the idea of being better and it brings to mind my favorite quote from Wayne Dyer, our friend and the man who is about to marry me to the woman of my dreams. "True nobility isn't about being better than anyone else; it's about being better than you used to be."
> "Yes, Ma. I am better."
> I am better than I used to be.

This is such a fabulous takeaway for an eating disorder memoir, since eating disorders are often fueled by the search for perfection. You don't need to be perfect, de Rossi offers her reader through the Dyer quote. Just go for better.

3. Put the takeaway in dialogue.

If you're worried about sounding didactic, you can place your takeaway in dialogue, like de Rossi does in the above example. Julie Metz does this in her memoir *Perfection: A Memoir of Betrayal and Renewal*. After her husband's sudden death, she finds out he was having multiple affairs. By the end of the book, she's in a relationship with a new man, Will. She uses a line of dialogue as a jumping off place for a takeaway.

> During one of my long talks with Will, early in our relationship, he said something that I knew was difficult but correct: "You have to forgive him for us to move on together."
> Forgiveness is a wonderful thing, the only truth that saves us from eating ourselves alive and causing damage to everyone we love. I continue to work on forgiveness.

Be sure your takeaway sounds like people talk, and not like a sermon squeezed into quotation marks. Unless, of course, you're quoting dialogue from a sermon!

4. State your takeaway as your beliefs or thoughts rather than as a statement of fact or truth.

If you want to offer a takeaway, but don't want to speak on behalf of a collective, you can couch it as your belief using an "I" statement. Judith Moore does this in *Fat Girl*. "I believed that inside every fat person was a hole the size of the world: I believed that every fat person wanted to fill that hole by eating the world."

Now whether this is a takeaway that applies to every fat person doesn't matter. She clearly states it as her belief, giving us room to choose to believe it ourselves, or not. She could have dropped the "I believed that" and just told us, "Inside every fat person. . . ." This is fine rhetorically, but you risk alienating a reader who disagrees with you, or who resents you for speaking on their behalf. You'll need to decide how emphatic you want to be.

Similarly, you can state your takeaway as *your* thought, *your* truth, using an "I" statement. Glennon Doyle does that when she writes in *Untamed*, "I think we are only bitter about other people's joy in direct proportion to our commitment to keep joy from ourselves." Notice two things here. She could have dropped the "I think" and just stated the takeaway more overtly. And, she could have stayed in reflection by staying in the first-person singular: "I think *I* am only bitter about other people's joy in direct proportion to *my* commitment to keep joy from *myself*." She gets the best of both worlds here. She qualifies her takeaway by placing it inside a thought.

5. Put the takeaway at the top of the chapter before you go into a scene and story to anchor it.

Opening a chapter with a takeaway is a great way to grab the reader's attention right away, and make them wonder where you're going with this. Lidia Yuknavitch does this in *The Chronology of Water*. She begins her chapter "Nemesis" with a takeaway: "Anger is funny. It sits snarling in you your whole life just waiting for perfect ironic moments to emerge." Then she launches into a story of how her anger emerged when a professor who was a well-known author called her work "trite," which pissed her off so much that she decided to get a Ph.D. in literature. In the middle of the chapter, she adds another takeaway: "Sometimes the choices we make come from jealous lame petty places. But they are as real as it gets."

Terry Tempest Williams' *When Women Were Birds: Fifty-Four Variations on Voice* is full of takeaways. The story begins with Williams' opening her mother's journals after she died, and finding them all blank, a mystery she tries to understand throughout the book. In Chapter XIII, she opens with a takeaway. "What needs to be counted on to have a voice? Courage. Anger. Love. Something to say, someone to speak to; someone to listen." The rest of the chapter explores journal-keeping, how Williams has carried on a conversation with herself "religiously" in her journals, while her mother's voice was silent in the pages of all those blank journals.

6. Put the takeaway at the end of a chapter to "stick the dismount."

Placing the takeaway at the end of a chapter is a powerful way to stick the dismount, a metaphor I take from gymnastics. Dismounts are thrilling when they're landed perfectly. It's also thrilling when an author sticks the dismount at a chapter's end, offering the perfect takeaway that the whole chapter has been working up to. In one chapter in Gail Caldwell's *Let's Take the Long Way Home: A Memoir of Friendship*, she shares what it was like to live through the first year after her best friend's death. The last line of that chapter? "Like a starfish, the heart endures its amputation." Those eight words deliver a sucker punch straight to the gut.

In *One Hundred Daffodils: Finding Beauty, Grace, and Meaning When Things Fall Apart*, Rebecca Winn tells the story of her divorce after 25 years of marriage. In one chapter, she reflects on how terribly she's treated herself over the years, how she never felt like she was enough or deserving of love. She concludes the chapter with a takeaway, followed by a personal reflection. "We teach people how to treat us. I'm ready for a new lesson plan."

7. Put the takeaway at the very end of your memoir to stick the dismount of the entire story.

Maybe you want your memoir to be more pure storytelling. Yes, some reflections here and there, but you really want to stay with the story, stay with the voice of the narrator and her experience, not rise above the landscape of the experience to pull out takeaways for the reader.

Fine. All good.

But you can put your takeaways at the very end of the book, tucked away outside the mainframe in the conclusion, the epilogue, the afterword, whatever convention you want to use. It is most welcome there as well, and can create a very satisfying conclusion for the reader.

Darin Strauss does this, on the next to the last page of *Half a Life*. He's finally able to let go of his guilt over his role in the accidental death of his classmate, and he offers this takeaway.

> The accident taught me this.
>
> Things don't go away. They become you. There is no end, as T.S. Eliot somewhere says, but addition: the trailing consequence of further days and hours. No freedom from the past, or from the future.
>
> But we keep making our way, as we have to. We're all pretty much able to deal even with the worst that life can fire at us, if we simply admit that it is very difficult. I think that's the whole of the answer. We make our way, and effort and time give us cushion and dignity. And as we age, we're riding higher in the saddle, seeing more terrain.

"I think that's the whole of the answer," he tells us, to the implied question, how do we survive our tragedies?

Jesmyn Ward's memoir *Men We Reaped* tells the story of how she lost five young men in her small Mississippi town to accidents, murder, and suicide over the course of four years. She offers her own answer to the same question: How do we survive our tragedies?

> We who still live do what we must. Life is a hurricane, and we board up to save what we can and bow low to the earth to crouch

in that small space above the dirt where the wind will not reach. We honor anniversaries of deaths by cleaning graves and sitting next to them before fires, sharing food with those who will not eat again. We raise children and tell them other things about who they can be and what they are worth: to us, everything. We love each other fiercely, while we live and after we die. We survive; we are savages.

8. Offer your takeaways in the form of questions.

Questions are a great way for the shy memoirist to place a takeaway—you can always say you're just asking for a friend! Though Glennon Doyle is not a shy memoirist—her self-help memoirs are loaded with overt and emphatic takeaways—she does make use of this strategy. In a chapter in *Untamed*, she is debating divorcing her husband after she's fallen in love with someone else. She's decided that "good mothers don't break their children's hearts in order to follow their own." But then she has a "reckoning." She asks, "What if a mother's responsibility is teaching her children that love does not lock the lover away but *frees* her? What if a responsible mother is not one who shows her children how to slowly die but how to stay wildly alive until the day she dies? What if the call of motherhood is not to be a martyr but to be a *model*?"

Of course she could have stated these as the answers she came to rather than the questions she was asking herself. She could have written, "The call of motherhood is not to be a martyr but to be a *model*."

She makes use of stacking questions again in the book, writing, "But now I wonder, is love not a feeling but a place between two present people? A sacred place created when two people decide it's safe enough to let their real selves surface and touch each other? Is that why it's called in love? Because you have to visit there?"

If there's something you'd like to say, but you're a reluctant takeawayer, try asking it or wondering about it instead.

Conclusion

I wanted to end with Doyle because she's the queen of takeaways and she's an immensely popular best-selling author. And I don't think those two things are unrelated. Her primarily female audience eats up her books. They learn from them. They are inspired by them. They mark them up. They follow her on social media. They listen to her podcast. She's on Oprah's *Super Soul Sunday*, she's besties with Elizabeth Gilbert, and Reese Witherspoon has her on her book club. She is an f-ing phenomenon, and it's in large part because even though she wrote all three of her books in her late 30s and early 40s, she was not afraid to be vulnerable and reflective and to unabashedly opine and philosophize and psychologize and universalize and lay claim to what she knows from her experience. And to share it generously. She's a model worth studying.

Yet many of my students, primarily women a decade or two or three older than Doyle, have a hard time writing takeaways. They hide in humility. They blush at the suggestion that they have something to share, even though it's their deepest hope that they do. They want their lives and their stories to matter, but it's hard for them to name and claim their own wisdom.

So I give them this exercise. We read four lines from Mary Oliver's poem "Sometimes."

Instructions for living a life:
Pay attention.
Be astonished.
Tell about it.

Then, I offer them examples for how to summarize different sub-genres of memoir.

For a trauma memoir:

Instructions for living a life:
Life's not fair.
"Why me?" isn't useful.
Spin straw into gold instead.

For an addiction memoir:

> Instructions for living a life:
> Just say no.
> I said yes.
> It's not too late to change your answer.

For a grief memoir:

> Instructions for living a life:
> Loved ones die.
> Over too soon.
> But never really over.

For a spiritual memoir:

> Instructions for living a life:
> God here.
> God there.
> God everywhere.

Then, I ask them to write their own "Instructions for Living a Life" as if it was a summary of their memoir. Oliver writes, "Tell about it," so I ask my students, what is the "it" that you're here to tell us? What is the "it" that you want to add to the human instruction manual? What meaning have you made of "it"?

Something about this assignment loosens them up (probably the requirement of brevity!), and what they write is often profound.

So I offer this to you as well. Tell us about it. Tell us about your life. Tell us what it means. Tell us what it means to you.

But also, tell us what it means to us.

THE ARCHETYPE OF TRUTH
Its Uneasy (and Sometimes Queasy) Dance With Memory and Imagination

Hannah Engler, a writer and book publishing professional, makes a bold statement when she writes, "Fabrication is inherent in memoir writing." For readers of memoir who haven't really given the genre much thought, that statement must come as quite a shock. *Fabrication is inherent in memoir writing? What? Fiction fabricates, not nonfiction. I'm supposed to be reading the true story of someone's life. She must be referring to guys like James Frey who made stuff up and majorly exaggerated and got caught.*

No. She's not. She's referring to *all* memoir writers. All memoir writers fabricate. All memoir writers, to take it a step further, *must* fabricate. *What?*

Let's look at her whole quote.

Fabrication is inherent in memoir writing. Number one, it's impossible to have an unbiased view of your own life, period; number two, it's impossible to write about something in the past tense and not see it through the lens of the present. These factors, combined with the fact that real life hardly ever binds together in a coherent, readable narration, is what makes memoir such an interesting genre. It's composed of people telling the stories of themselves. These stories are all true, in a way; they're just not factual.

Oh boy, is there a lot to unpack here. I tried to split truth and memory into two separate chapters, but the truth is, they really can't be separated for a memoir writer. Both truth and memory are married to imagination, so this chapter is by necessity a ménage à trois. I wish I could say it's an elegant dance we're going to do here, but that's not the right metaphor. We're going to be hacking our way through some dense, deep, dark, and thorny thickets. It's gonna get swampy. There may be some head spinning followed by tail chasing. You may get queasy. A sledgehammer is going to appear in these pages—you may want to use it on this chapter. This chapter is either going to set you free from worrying about truth in memoir writing, or it's going to make you turn to fiction. But I promise, if you make it to the end, there's light there. As complicated as it's going to get, as many questions as it's going to raise, there are, in fact, some simple solutions, a couple of easy answers.

But you gotta wait for it.

Down the Rabbit Hole

A number of years ago, I had a conversation with my mother that tilted the axis of my world. When I was growing up, I remember my alcoholic stepfather getting drunk a couple of nights a week, and definitely every weekend. When I shared this memory with my mother, she said it was completely untrue, that he was drunk maybe a couple of times a month. I was shocked. She was shocked. I wondered if I had overestimated his drinking because it was so traumatic to me. I wondered if she had underestimated his drinking because she felt guilty about staying with him.

I'm sure you've had this experience before. You're telling a story from your past, let's say around the family dinner table, and one of your siblings or your parents tells you it didn't happen that way, that you're not remembering it right, and then they tell you what *really* happened. You may have had one of two reactions. First, you might become insistent that no, in fact, you are remembering it correctly, and *they're* the ones misremembering. Or, you might re-remember, your memory shaken and stirred by their memory, and realize they're right, that you have been remembering it wrong all along. The second scenario is hardest on a memoirist because once one memory is called into question, *memory itself* can be called into question. If you're mis-remembering *this*, you could be mis-remembering *that*. A whole lotta thats. Perhaps your memory cannot be trusted.

That's what happened to me in that head spinning, axis tilting conversation with my mother. I wondered, if I couldn't trust my memory of this defining trauma in my early life, could I trust any of my memories?

In *The Memoir and the Memoirist*, Thomas Larsen writes, "Families manifest typically the most primal and potentially the most duplicitous relationships we have." It's no wonder then that they are the site for so many differing or conflicting memories. And this raises ethical questions for me as a memoirist. If I write a memoir about my stepfather's drinking, is he drunk three times a week, or three times a month? Do I take the average of my memory and my mother's memory and call it a compromise? Split the difference? Do I put a footnote at the end of the story, or do I make an author's note at the beginning, adding a disclaimer where I share the conversation with my mom, and then state that for the purposes of this memoir, I'm just telling what I remember, making no claim for it as truth? Do I find another way to tell the story so I don't implicate the frequency element? Is that even possible? Or maybe I write my childhood as fiction, where I can write him drunk the way I remember it. Maybe my memory *is* fiction.

You can see how quickly I have fallen, along with many a memoirist, down the rabbit hole where memory and truth have an uneasy, entwined relationship.

In her book *Imaginal Remembering: Our Soul's Journey Through Memory and Imagination*, Daphne Dodson writes, "Despite extensive research, memory remains enigmatic, often discussed but never unequivocally unraveled." Memory is like Winston Churchill's saying: "a riddle wrapped in a mystery inside an enigma." Ben Yagoda, in *Memoir: A History*, writes, "Conventional wisdom casts memory as a retrieval system, like a videotape that plays back information that has been recorded onto it, or a computer that accesses the files of what really happened." Psychologists would agree, he writes, that this "is utter nonsense." Memory researcher Daniel L. Schacter agrees as well. Memories are not literal recordings of what happened, he tells us. There are not memory traces in the brain; our brains are not like computers, where files are stored and can be accessed. Instead, "the brain facilitates remembering rather than stores memory." In other words, remembering is a *process* our brains go through—memories are not a *product* stored in our brain.

And remembering as a process is fraught with problems. Before we can look at what we mean by "truth" in memoir, we have to deal with the pesky troublemaker—memory.

Memory Problems, or the Problem with Memory

Daniel L. Schacter has devoted much of his life to researching memory, and in particular, the enigmatic and problematic nature of memory, perhaps nowhere more clearly exposed than in his 2021 book, *The Seven Sins of Memory: How the Mind Forgets and Remembers (Updated Edition)*. The book focuses on seven of memory's imperfections, errors, and transgressions—the more precise words for what he calls "sins," no doubt a clever title foisted on him to recall the seven deadly sins. Two of the seven problematic qualities of memory that are not of specific concern to the project of memoir writing, though they may be irritating, are absent-mindedness and blocking (when you can't recall something on the tip of your tongue). It's the five remaining problems of *transience, misattribution, suggestibility, bias,* and *persistence* that make "truth" and "memory" distant relatives many times removed, or an incompatible couple who should probably file for divorce.

Allow me, supported by Schacter, to make my case about the problematic nature of memory.

Problem #1 – Transience

Transience, which Schacter calls perhaps the most pervasive of all memory's imperfections—and one that increases with age, damn it—is simply defined as forgetting an event over time. Schacter offers lots of research to illustrate this phenomenon, but of course, we all know this happens. I just don't think we know how *often* it happens, and just how *quickly* it happens.

He offers a case study that drives this point home and parks the car. Several days after the highly emotionally charged verdict in the O.J. Simpson double homicide case, college students were asked to describe in detail how they learned about the jury's acquittal. Fifteen months later, they were asked again, and only half the students remembered the moment accurately. Three years after the verdict, "less than 30 percent of students' recollections were accurate; nearly half were dotted with major errors." If three years is long enough for a young mind to produce such inaccuracies of memory around such a major event, imagine the implications for an older memoir writer recalling events from decades ago, even major events, let alone more minor ones.

Clearly, *remembering what happened is not the same thing as what happened.*

This is not to say we lose all our memory of what happened, though that could be the case. More often with transience, Schacter writes, we have "incomplete rather than total forgetting that leaves in its wake scattered shards of experience. Vague impressions of familiarity, general knowledge of what happened, or fragmentary details of experiences are the most common legacies of transience." Vague, general, and fragmentary are not adjectives that promise a compelling narrative. What we need then, to fill in the blanks, is our imagination, our best guess as to what might have happened. Research can sometimes help, and Schacter writes, "Countless studies have also shown that seemingly lost information can be recovered by cues or hints that remind us of how we initially encoded an experience." Returning to our childhood home can shake loose some memories, for example, that might otherwise stay lost. In my memoir retreats, I show my students images of television shows and vintage toys from various eras and lay out candy I buy at the old-timey candy store, and memories long forgotten come flooding in.

Schacter notes that "transience is perhaps the most terrifying of the seven sins: it undermines memory's role in connecting us to past thoughts and deeds that define who we are." By extension, transience should be the most terrifying sin for a memoir writer, because isn't this the point—that we're connecting to past thoughts and deeds that define us? And if we've lost those past thoughts or deeds, or only remember a small percentage of them accurately, then what? Do we throw out the baby of the book we're writing with the bathtub of the genre of memoir itself because they're both too unreliable? Or do we instead throw out the fantasy of telling the truth at all, and turn to other ways of imagining just what truth means to a memoir writer?

Hold on to those questions. We're only one problem in.

Problem #2 – Misattribution

Misattribution in memory is a form of wire crossing. We may remember a person, but misattribute the context in which we met or knew them—remembering, let's say, an older woman who babysat us who was in reality our Sunday school teacher. We may remember an object clearly, but misattribute who gave us that object. We may think it was our father, for example, who gave us our first baseball glove when it was really our grandfather. We may recall something that happened in high school, but that scene was actually in a movie we watched—it wasn't our teacher who told us to "seize the day," but it was Robin William's character in *Dead Poet's Society*. We may misattribute sardine breath to a boyfriend named Jack when in fact it was a later girlfriend named Jill.

In the process of misattribution, we've got the memory right, but we've linked it up to the wrong source. This is referred to as "memory binding." Binding failures account for our inability to remember if we actually did something versus we just imagined doing something. For example, in studies where someone is told to imagine holding an object, they sometimes claim they actually did hold that object years later when asked again. In memoir, this kind of misattribution between imagination and reality may occur if we spent a great deal of time in our high school, let's say, imagining kissing the girl next door—decades later, we may write that kiss into our memoir and be shocked when that girl next door tells us it never actually happened.

Another kind of binding failure is called "memory conjunction error." This is when our mind binds two or more things together into one. Schacter gives the example of meeting two people at work, Mr. Wilson and Mr. Albert. When asked to remember one of the men the next day, you confidently reply, Mr. Wilbert. In memoir writing, this may occur if you blend three ex-boyfriends together, remembering the one you're writing about as having blue eyes, hairy toes, and a crooked smile, when those traits instead each belonged to a different guy. It seems the brain is naturally good at creating composite characters.

Let me give you an example closer to home. I'm a lifelong Democrat, the bloodiest bleeding heart liberal. However, I've often told the story though of how I voted for Ronald Reagan in my first election. I've used that story in the classroom to talk about how we often swallow the political beliefs of our family without chewing. My whole close family is dyed-in-the-wool Republican, I would tell my students, and it wasn't until I went to college that I was able to differentiate from my family and form my own beliefs, and I never voted for another Republican again.

It's a good teaching story, but you know what? It's entirely untrue, something I didn't realize until recently. And do you know how I found out it was untrue? Math. In November 1980, I was only 16 years old, two years away from being able to vote at all, let alone for Ronald Reagan.

In querying this memory that's both estranged from history and so clear in my mind, I suspect what must have happened is some sort of a mock vote in one of my sophomore high school classes. So it's kind of true that I voted for Reagan—I do remember correctly—it's just that I didn't vote for him in the national election. I've conjoined a high school tick of a box with a real experience in the ballot box. Now this anecdote has become a different kind of teaching story, one about memory conjunction error.

Another form of false attribution is called "cryptomnesia," the experience of thinking something is new, when we've just forgotten we experienced it before. In memoir writing, cryptomnesia may occur, for example, if you write about the first time you took ballroom dancing lessons in preparation for your first dance at your wedding. Flipping through your yearbook later, you may discover that you took ballroom dancing lessons as part of your high school gym class. In this case, the misattribution is to an earlier event that you don't remember, most likely in conjunction with the problem of transience.

Problem #3 – The Problem of Suggestibility

Schacter writes, "Suggestibility in memory refers to an individual's tendency to incorporate misleading information from external sources—other people, written materials or pictures, even the media—into personal recollections." He offers the example of Edward Daly, a Korean War veteran "who made up elaborate–but imaginary–stories about his battle exploits, including his involvement in a terrible massacre in which he had not actually participated. While weaving his delusional tale, Daly talked to veterans who had participated in the massacre and 'reminded' them of his heroic deeds. His suggestions infiltrated their memories" until they reported with certainty that they knew he was there.

With this memory problem, there's an agent who does the suggesting, like a person or persons, written materials, or the media, but we might forget the agent entirely even as the memory persists. Imagine a mother who lashes out in anger at her young son, taking her hot curling iron and pressing it against his skin until it burns so badly that it leaves a scar. "Mommy didn't burn you," she tells her son. "It's your fault–you weren't supposed to be playing with the curling iron and you fell on top of it." The mother repeats this story to her son all day long, and when her husband comes home at night, she repeats it to him as the son listens and nods, too scared of his mother to tell the truth. In the sin of suggestibility, that same boy as a young man might actually remember having fallen on the curling iron when his lover asks how he got that scar. He might remember that story all the way up until his 60s when he enters a memoir course and begins to describe the scene, and it just doesn't make sense. Something starts niggling around in his memory until the truth breaks through–*my mom burned me with her curling iron*–followed by the next inevitable question–*what else about my childhood am I misremembering?*

The curling iron example illustrates how suggestibility can cause us to store a false memory of the past in our banks, but suggestibility can also apply to the present way we view a memory. The classic example is when we confront someone from our past with memories of how they abused us, and they vehemently deny it, which may cause us to question whether it happened that way at all. They may accuse us of "false memory syndrome," or they may gaslight us into thinking that our therapist or our memoir writing teacher planted those ideas in our head. If we believe them, or even entertain the belief, we may find ourselves with the same question as above–*what else about my childhood am I misremembering?* The clinical term for this, coined by Gísli Guðjónsson and James MacKeith in 1982, is "memory distrust syndrome," which we all have to some extent. It only reaches the level of a syndrome if it's extreme, and if we distrust our own memories so much that we have to rely on outside sources we deem more trustworthy than ourselves.

Because of the problem of suggestibility, many memoir teachers suggest not checking your memories against those of others until you've written down your own account, and not to withdraw your memory even if they say it didn't happen that way. Mary Karr recommends that we might want to write that conflicting account into our memoir. She does this several times in *The Liar's Club*. In one instance, she writes in a parenthetical, "If I gave my big sister a paragraph here, she would correct my memory." She then offers what her sister would have written, but sticks to her memory instead, allowing us to deal with that discrepancy however we see fit.

Problem #4 – The Problem of Bias

Schacter defines the memory error of bias as one where we experience "distorting influences of our present knowledge, beliefs, and feelings" on our memories. He describes five major kinds of biases, all of which I find applicable to memoir writers, and fascinating too.

The first two kinds of biases, *consistency and change biases*, "show how our theories about ourselves can lead us to reconstruct the past as overly similar to, or different from, the present." In short, "The way we were depends on the way we are." We might write about our 30 years of blissful marriage and recall a "love at first sight" meet-cute, until we find a journal from that time period and read about how irritated we were at our first meeting and how we resisted the relationship for several months. That's consistency bias—because we are in love now, we remember being in love then. In change bias, if we're in a 30-year marriage that we think has changed so much for the better over the years, we may remember the first decade of our marriage as more difficult than it actually was. In both biases, our theories about our marriages—whether it's stayed consistent or changed—shape how we remember the past.

The third bias is a *hindsight bias*, where "recollections of past events are filtered by current knowledge"—or as Albert Einstein wrote, "Memory is deceptive because it is colored by today's events." Schacter illustrates hindsight bias by another O.J. Simpson trial study, where college students were asked two hours before the verdict if they thought Simpson would be convicted, and then asked again two days later. They rated the likelihood of conviction lower than they had just 50 hours earlier, before they knew he would be convicted. If our hindsight bias can already distort our memory of an event in 50 hours, think about what it can do over years, even decades.

Imagine a woman who is writing about her pancreatic cancer experience 20 years after the fact. It's a positive story—after nearly a year of difficult treatment that often left her debilitated, she beat cancer and never had a recurrence. In her memoir, she writes about her fighting spirit, how she just knew she would triumph over cancer, and she's convinced this positive attitude kept her alive. In going back into her journals of the time to verify some dates, she finds weeks and weeks of entries where she was sure she was going to die, and had even left directions for her funeral in her journal. That's hindsight bias—because she knew it ended positively, she mis-remembered that it began negatively. Schacter writes, "Hindsight bias, then, is ubiquitous: people seem almost driven to reconstruct the past to fit what they know in the present. In light of the known outcome, people can more easily retrieve incidents and examples that confirm it."

A fourth kind of memory bias is *egocentric bias*, which Schacter tells us illustrates "the powerful role of the self in orchestrating perceptions and memories of reality." If we remember something different from someone else in our lives, even if that other person is certain they are right about what happened, our egocentricity makes us far more likely to think we are right and the other person is just remembering it wrong. Schacter notes studies of married and dating couples where each member of the couple remembers themselves as more responsible for various incidents than the other. A married couple is asked to remember a past vacation, and what percentage of the responsibility they took for planning it. One person might claim 80%, and the other 40%. Even if they agree that one of them did more than the other, they still overestimate their own contribution—and no surprise, we are motivated to think more highly of ourselves, to have what researcher Shelley Taylor referred to as "positive illusions."

THE ARCHETYPE OF TRUTH

Of course, this bias should be of concern to all memoir writers, but especially those writing about significant relationships. The tendency to remember ourselves more positively in relationships may lead us to draw conflict more sharply, and attribute less of the cause to ourselves, and more to the other. It's easy to see how villainization can occur and aspersions can be cast that distort both ourselves and others. One of my memoir students, about four years into his writing, noted with astonishment how much nicer his now-deceased grandmother had become in writing about her, and how much more he was, in his words, "a little shit." His egocentricity bias got the better of him in the beginning of the writing project, but through the encouragement and acceptance of his writing group, he was able to look at both his grandmother and himself with more clarity and acknowledge both as much more complex characters in his memoir.

Many memory researchers and memoir teachers alike note that what we remember may have everything to do with our sense of self. Maureen Murdock writes, "If the image of the event we have participated in does not match the image of the self we have carefully constructed, then we rarely remember the facts of the event at all." My student remembered himself as a victim of his neglectful grandmother, so he started off writing victim stories. When he began to reimagine himself as a difficult grandson whose grandmother did her best to raise him, different memories began to emerge that cast both of them in a different light.

The research shows that in egocentric bias, we tend to remember ourselves more favorably, but sometimes it can go the other way. Though less common, egocentricity bias can lead us to cast ourselves in a more unfavorable light. However, as researcher Michael Ross notes about this phenomenon, when we do speak less highly of ourselves in the past, it's often in order to draw our current self in a more favorable light. Memoirists who want to show a transformational arc in their life stories may exaggerate the sinner in order to elevate the saint, or exaggerate the rags in order to elevate the riches. Selective memory may be at play here, consciously or unconsciously, but regardless, it's still an egocentric bias that can lead us to such distortions of memory.

One of my favorite quotes on such distortions of memory comes from the philosopher Friedrich Nietzsche: "'I have done that,' says my memory. 'I cannot have done that,' says my pride, and remains inexorable. Eventually—memory yields." The kinds of memories that pride erases are *egodystonic*, meaning they are incongruent with our ego's sense of self. In the case of my student, he didn't want to remember himself as a little shit. Instead he initially drew on memories that were *egosyntonic* for him, ones more congruent with who he thinks he is and was. This line of thinking may explain the hysteria of Brett Kavanaugh's testimony in front the Senate Judiciary Committee in 2018, when Christine Blasey Ford accused him of sexual assault during high school. If he did assault her, it's possible he blocked that entire memory from his conscious mind because it was so egodystonic, but his emotional outburst may have betrayed him.

Finally, the fifth problem of memory bias is *stereotypical bias* whereby our generic stereotypes "shape interpretation of the world, even when we are unaware of their existence or influence," according to Schacter. In this sort of memory bias, if we are a white person recalling an experience with a teacher of color, we might unconsciously attribute to that teacher whatever stereotype we (and white culture) hold of them, distorting our memory of this particular teacher.

Imagine a memoir written by a man who was sexually abused in his teens by a Catholic priest. He carries a stereotype that all Catholic priests are either pedophiles or wanna-be pedophiles who have to work hard to keep their sexual lust for young boys under control. This stereotype is often reinforced in our culture after the Catholic Church sex scandals became so notarized in the mid-1980s. His abuse happened decades before then, but he's swallowed the stereotype whole, and as a result, in his memoir every Catholic priest he met prior to his victimization is recalled as being somewhere on the pervert scale. Any positive encounters with priests are either forgotten unconsciously or willfully not included because they don't reinforce the stereotype.

Problem #5 – Persistence

Schacter calls the sin of persistence—remembering things you wish you could forget—"perhaps [the] most debilitating." He admits it can be a mild irritant, using the example of song lyrics you can't get out of your head. But it's the intrusive memories of experiences we "desperately want to banish" that can be debilitating. By their nature, these would either be bad memories, or memories that were good at the time, but have become bad based on later outcomes. For example, your wedding day might be an extremely happy memory, but after your spouse dies, if that memory becomes intrusive and persistent, it might bring on further feelings of loss. Schacter names "the primary territory of persistence: disappointment, regret, failure, sadness, and trauma."

I used to believe we remember negative experiences more than positive ones, but Schacter says research doesn't bear that out. What the research does say is that we tend to remember negative experiences in more detail than positive ones—it's those very details that can be intrusive as we remember, review, and relive every moment leading up to, during, and after a traumatic memory (think post-traumatic stress disorder). A case in point is Joan Didion's continual review of the details of her husband's sudden death throughout the entirety of *The Year of Magical Thinking*—what came before his death (a mysterious comment he made days before, a visit to the hospital to see their daughter the day of, the book he was reading while Didion made dinner, the last words he spoke about his Scotch before he slumped over the table); what happened during his death (she tries to give him the Heimlich, he falls to the floor, she calls an ambulance); and what happened after his death (the ambulance crew clears his airways, uses a defibrillator on his heart, the paramedics take away his body, she rides in a second ambulance), etc. It's the details that haunt her, that she replays again and again, trying to make sense of them. It's the persistent details that intrude upon her everyday life, carrying with them Schacter's primary emotional territory—disappointment, regret, failure, sadness, and trauma.

Schacter does offer a bit of good news about negative memories: "Some data suggest that negative emotions may actually fade faster than positive ones, [that] raw hurt eventually dissipates." However, in bad news for memoir writers, "Reminders of difficult experiences can slow the normal fading of painful emotions over time. . . . Continual reminding can strengthen recall of the disturbing specifics of what happened to the point that persistence becomes unbearable." Memoirists who write about traumatic experiences are bound to stir up painful emotions as they purposefully trigger themselves by remembering as many details as possible. Perhaps Mary Karr had this in mind in a quote I shared earlier, that "writing a memoir is knocking yourself out with your own fist, if it's done right."

Schacter writes, "Reminders of unpleasant experiences can also induce us to engage in what psychologists call 'counterfactual thinking'– generating alternative scenarios of what might have been or should have been." We ruminate on endless "what ifs," we chide ourselves for what we did or didn't do, we curse God for his callousness or we rail against the Universe for being so cruel. Since persistence and counterfactual thinking are so common regarding difficult memories, I actually encourage my students to write their own list of "what ifs" and then, spinning the moment forward in time, imagining "what then"–what the future might have looked like had things gone better. Since persistence and counterfactual thinking seem to be hardwired into our brains, like it or not, it's a way to connect with your reader who may be interested in your what ifs and what thens because they have their own as well.

Closing Arguments

When I first saw the seven "sins" of memory in Schacter's title, I thought it was nothing other than a clever marketing ploy, a riff on the seven deadly sins in Christianity. But after I read the book, I realized memory does commit a sin–the sin of betrayal. We are betrayed by our memory all the time–our memory is prone to imperfections, distortions of truth, and outright errors; it's faulty and flawed and unstable and unreliable; it's inexact and inaccurate and prone to trickery. Putting the word "imperfect" before "memory" is redundant. Schacter and other memory researchers' work shows us that the very definition of memory is an imperfect recall of the past done by a person in the present.

For creative writers inside the genre of memoir, we would be well served to consider Ben Yagoda's assertion that memory itself is "a creative writer, cobbling together 'actual' memories, beliefs about the world, cues from a variety of sources, and memories of previous memories to plausibly imagine what might have been, and then, in a master stroke, packaging this scenario to the mind as the real one."

If memory is a creative writer and not a reporter who sticks to the facts, Ma'am, just to the facts, then what we are writing in our memoir is never the truth—the factual truth, that is. So if it's not the factual truth, what is it? What do we call the kind of truth we're struggling to set down on the page?

The Archetype of Truth

Let me return for a moment to that conversation with my mother about my stepfather's drinking. At first, it seemed really important for me to know the truth—*just how often was he drunk?*—but in fact, there was no way to find out the truth. Over three decades ago, my stepfather suffered a traumatic car accident that wiped out much of his long-term memory and replaced it with untruths. He still believes he once played basketball for the all-Black team, the Harlem Globetrotters, though he's hard-pressed to tell us how they let one white guy on the team. And even if he hadn't lost his memory, who's to say he'd remember more accurately how often he was drunk 45 years ago, what psychological dynamics might be at play in his own representation of the facts, what sins of memory he might commit?

According to Schacter, we need to move away from "a binary litmus test of true and false" when talking about memory. My mom's memory is no truer than mine, nor falser—these terms simply don't and can't apply to memory. Memory is not true or false, *memory just is*. No one can argue with you if you say, "But that's the way I remember it." The memory *is* your truth, and yes, you may get some knowledge down the road that changes your memory, but that doesn't mean your other memory was false—it was simply true for you at the time.

So I'm not wrong about my memory, though I may be wrong about the facts. I can't trust that my father was drunk every weekend, but I can trust that it's my memory's truth. This is why memoir as a genre carries a different ontological status than autobiography as a genre. One explores memories of a life; the other states knowledge and facts about a life. One says, "Here's how I *remember* my life," and the other says, "Here's how I *lived* my life."

Schacter makes a distinction here that I think is useful—he tells us there's a difference between "historical truth" and "narrative truth." Historical truth refers to the way things actually happened (the purview of autobiography), but narrative truth refers to what we think is true because of how we remember it (the purview of memoir). The writer Tim O'Brien in his memoir-adjacent novel *The Things They Carried* refers to the distinction as "happening truth" versus "story truth." Other memoir teachers refer to it as "factual truth" versus "emotional truth."

I can't recall the factual, historical truth about how often my stepfather was drunk, I can only relay what I remember. But when my mother's memory was so different from mine, it did give me pause. Even if we agree to split the difference on how often he was drunk, I wondered why my memory would ratchet up the number, and then I realized, it's my emotional truth. Despite the number of times per month he was drunk, it's emotionally true that I feared and loathed his drinking, and I felt like our home was not a safe place. It's emotionally true if I write that my father was drunk every weekend and sometimes during the week— the constancy of his drinking is critical to conveying the feeling of a lack of safety.

One writer who takes a passionate position on emotional truth in memoir is Richard Blanco, author of the memoir *The Prince of Los Cocuyos*. He ends his author's note by writing, "I've bent time and space in the way that the art of memory demands. My poet's soul believes that the emotional truth of these pages trumps everything. Read as you would read my poems, trusting that what is here is real, beyond what is real—that truer truth which we come to call a life."

So when my memoir students raise the inevitable questions, "Can my memory be trusted?" and "Are my memories true?" the answer I offer them is yes and yes. You can trust that your memory is your memory and you can trust that your memory is true. Truth is archetypal—that is, a form that we fill with content. For memoir writers, we can fill it with emotional truth, story truth, narrative truth, or simply marry it with memory and call it memory-truth.

Trust Issues

In *Memoir: A History*, Ben Yagoda tells the story of Judy Blunt who wrote a memoir called *Breaking Clean* about her unhappy domestic life on a ranch in Montana. She "recounts how her father-in-law picked up her typewriter, brought it outside, and 'killed it with a sledgehammer.'" Her father-in-law refuted the story and somehow *The New York Times* got wind of it and called her out. Her reply? "The machine's death by sledge-hammer was 'symbolic.' In reality, she said, 'the old man pulled the plug on the typewriter and shouted and screamed, but the typewriter survived.'"

Yagoda notes that when "'small' deceptions or fabrications" like these are reported, there's much handwringing in the literary world, with one of two positions typically arising. The first position is one of shock, "that a book labeled as 'memoir' and sold in the nonfiction section of the store should include untruths. Not only is that false advertising, but even one deception—whether deliberate or unwitting—undermines every other statement in the book."

The second position is, "Get a life, people. Human memory is flawed, and everybody knows it. And memoir, as a genre, is universally understood to offer subjective, impressionistic testimony. It doesn't pretend to offer *the* truth, just the *author's* truth."

Yagoda points out the flaws in both positions. The first, he writes, "presupposes an unrealistic and naïve moral absolutism." Some things in a memoir can be fact-checked, but the rest of memoir relies on "a matter of impression," and for a writer to craft a decent book, they "must express these impressions in the form of a narrative." Following this logic, we can perhaps vindicate Blunt. Her father-in-law's assault on her typewriter impressed her deeply, and to get across that impression, she turned to what it emotionally felt like—he had destroyed it with a sledge-hammer.

The second position has holes as well, Yagoda says. "Nonfactual assertions in a 'nonfiction' book matter. People respond to such books precisely because they are supposed to be true; it may be the biggest part of their appeal. . . . To the extent a memoir is shown to be false, it loses its identity, its authority, and its power." From this position, knowing Blunt isn't telling the truth about the typewriter calls into question her authority about anything she's authored in that memoir.

Sven Birkerts writes, "Memoir, unlike reportage, serves the spirit of the past, not the letter. Indeed, no one who reads memoir believes—how could they?—that exchanges happened exactly as set down, or that key events have not been inflected to achieve the necessary effect. The question is only *how much* departure is tolerable, and at what point does the modified recollection turn into fiction?" Was Blunt serving the spirit of the past by bringing in a sledgehammer? Was the sledgehammer a necessary inflection to convey just how unsupportive her family was of her writing? If only a plug was pulled, is it too much of a departure to bring in a sledgehammer? Did that modified recollection turn into fiction?

Yagoda acknowledges that yes, "there are truths and untruths. The key to a more nuanced view on this question is putting them into a hierarchy." Robert Root calls for "some sort of sliding scale of reliability" in *The Nonfictionist's Guide*. Neither men offer one, but Andrew Hudgins, in an essay titled "An Autobiographer's Lies," does just that, creating a list of the eight lies of autobiographers (including memoirists) and presenting them in hierarchical order.

"Loving Lies"

As a child himself, Hudgins tells us he read dozens of memoirs of childhood, and he came to believe the authors were all lying in their sentimental and too simplistic portrayals. He made a righteous vow to himself at age 15 that when he wrote his memoir, he'd be "scorchingly honest." But, he writes:

> As soon as I began writing in earnest, I realized that some lies—though now we literary sorts call them "fictions"—are inevitable. Others are merely convenient. Autobiography is in some ways a translation of actuality onto the page and in other ways a selective and imaginative re-creation of it, a work of art—and the two roles can go to bed together and enjoy their uneasy congress only by lying to each other. But the lies are loving lies, told with hope and good intentions.

Hudgins arranges the lies in ascending order of transgression, and admits he's committed them all.

1. **The lie of narrative cogency**, which he calls "the whitest lie, the lie that hardly troubles my conscience at all." This pertains to leaving details out, or condensing scenes or characters for clarity, or intensifying aspects of the story for aesthetic reasons. He

acknowledges this lie "falsifies experience: intensification and clarity are misrepresentations," but he'd rather that than "torture by exactitude."

2. **The lie of texture.** If the first lie tightens the story, the second expands it. Memory tends to forget details while retaining the emotion of the experience, while storytelling thrives on details and needs them to actually explain the emotional residue we're left with. He notes an "odd paradox," that we are "sometimes forced to invent details to make it more believable." I can't remember exactly what my stepfather drank, but I know there was a lot of beer. What brand, I don't remember either, but I'd feel comfortable picking a brand like Coors, which signals a certain economic class, and writing a scene where I came across a hidden stash of empty, crushed yellow cans, in order to add texture to my story.

3. **The lie of fictional convention,** where we make our life take on literary conventions. When we write memoir, we turn our lives into material, "and, once it is material, it, for some purposes, stops being life and becomes primarily material," and we begin to shape our story using "recognizable literary conventions"—or, in the language of this book, archetypal conventions. If we're writing our life as a hero's journey, we might exaggerate the belly of the whale part, paint our dark night of the soul a little darker and longer than it actually was, for dramatic effect. We might not remember the color of a dress we wore on a first date, but we name it red because we want to evoke the symbolism of love.

4. **The lie of emotional evasion**, which he calls "the sin of omission" where we become "evasive and shifty" and want to sidestep the truth. Hudgins admits we may do this unconsciously— we may evade the truth about ourselves without knowing it. But often we do it consciously, hiding facts from the reader that make us uncomfortable. He offers the example of remaining a virgin until he married. He writes, "It took many attempts before

I was able to mention, quickly and in passing, that my first sexual experience took place on my wedding night, and I only put it in the book because I felt I had to."

5. **The lie of the re-created self**, which notches up emotional evasion into flat out re-creation and thus becomes a "considerably more egregious lie." We make ourselves look good by what we emphasize, and we may concomitantly make others look worse to dramatize the gap. He writes, "For about six months after this discovery, I was enthralled by how I could be so much wittier, shrewder, kinder, more sensitive, and more knowledgeable on the page than I am in life. . . . But it was sleazy, this self-ennobling, and I knew it was sleazy." He then revolted by "putting unnecessarily ugly constructions on my own motives" because "presenting myself on the page as such packs an emotional kick for both writer and reader." This is also the lie of narrative cogency—Hudgins purposefully intensified an aspect of his character for artistic effect.

6. **The lie of extended consciousness**, which Hudgins splits into two separate offences. The first, and more egregious, is appropriating other people's experiences or stories as our own. We may have our justifications for this, such as "they won't mind" or "it could just as easily have happened to me" or "they probably don't even remember." The second offence in this category, the one he calls "less clearly transgressive," is applying adult consciousness to our child self's experiences which makes us sound wiser or more reflective than we were at the time. In a memoir poem he wrote, Hudgens says of himself, "The adult interprets that boy's life in ways the boy would not comprehend and would probably reject out of hand as making a big deal out of nothing." He applies this in the direction from the adult to the child, but I would add that a memoirist can do it to their younger self at any age. For example, the 60-year-old memoirist can ascribe more wisdom and consciousness to their 30-year-old self just as easily.

7. **The lie of interpretation**, where we attribute meaning and significance to what we've experienced that may "suppress ambivalence, ambiguity, and chance." Real life is messy, full of doubt,
uncertainty, confusion, second-guesses, and while that may be
true, he doesn't find that *life as lived* always makes for good and
satisfying *life as art*. So for aesthetic reasons, we clean up our
experience, giving it clear significance or an unambiguous
shape by offering an interpretation or meaning that cleanly colors between some messy lines.

8. **The lie of impressionism.** While the lie of interpretation says
"this means that," the lie of impressionism says "this felt like
that." In this lie, we may exaggerate our feelings to create a
certain impression on our reader, or even assign an experience a feeling that may not have been there. He writes, "I am
always astonished at how falsely I remember things, astonished at how plastic memory is. And even when I know a
memory is incorrect, part of my brain cleaves to the wrong,
imagined memory, and now I hold two images in my head,
two memories—and the false one is more vivid and more emotionally significant to me than the actual one. Which, then, is
the truest memory? It's convenient when the actual events adequately convey the emotional experience, but sometimes
they don't and the writer has to choose." Think unplugging a
typewriter versus sledgehammering it. He calls this "the biggest lie, the least defensible logically, ethically, or morally" and
yet argues that "it's inescapable for a writer attempting to create an artistically coherent work."

Hudgins is ultimately uneasy with the "illogical, unethical, and immoral position" that writing about our past leads us to, if we want to
create art out of experience. But then he admits, "The trust I bring to
reading an autobiography [or memoir] is a reader's trust in a convinc-
ingly told tale, not the trust I bring to reading *The New York Times* or a
history of Assyria, in which aesthetics are secondary to factual accuracy."
Autobiographical writing "dances on the shifting middle ground between

fact and fiction, reportage and imagination, actuality and art; and different writers will draw their lines on that ground in different places."

Though I would have arranged the lies in a different order, I find Hudgins' list useful, if only for trying to tease out the gradations of a memoirist's fabrications. In the first months of writing, I give my memoir students the assignment to go through the list and draw their own lines. Though I've never done it before, it occurs to me now that if I were to remind them of those lines four or five years later after they've crafted their stories into art, I bet they've crossed their own lines, and for perfectly logical reasons. Hudgins ends his essay by writing, "We read memoirs precisely to find out what one writer thinks his life means and how that life felt to the one who lived it." In looking back at his own memoir, filled with every lie in his list, he concludes, "Yes, that *is* what my childhood means, and yes that *is* how it felt. And, to make those two affirmations, I accept, however uneasily, the lies I had to tell."

A Dip in the Etymological Pool

By this time in the chapter, I imagine some head-scratching or spinning by you who hold this book in your hands. "Wait," I can imagine you saying. "If there are 'truer truths' and 'emotional truths' and 'narrative truths' and you can tell a truer truth by lying, what the heck is truth anyway?" Maybe a dip in the etymological pool will clear our heads.

Etymologically, truth comes from the Old English *triewð* meaning "faith, faithfulness, fidelity, loyalty; veracity." As memoirists, what are we being faithful and loyal to? *To memory itself.* Not facts. Facts are the purview of journalism. No, when we write memoir, we are loyal to our memories, we are faithful to the facts *as we remember them*, we vouch for the veracity of the memory. It is perfectly fine for me to say that I *remember* my stepfather being drunk several days a week, and really, I don't even need to qualify that this is a memory if the word "memoir" is stamped on the front cover of my book, right?

Another etymological root of the word truth is from the Germanic abstract noun *treuwitho*, meaning "having or characterized by good faith." When we read a memoir, we ascribe good faith to the author. We expect she is telling the truth, not the factual truth, but memory-truth. Still, whenever it is possible to fact-check a memory, like finding an exact date or name or location, or something available in the historical record, perhaps we should do so, and if the fact contradicts the memory, I think we should say so. Andy Rooney opens his memoir *My War* with this humorous statement: "This is a memoir, not a history book, but in an effort to make it accurate, I've tried to check my memory against the facts. It is distressing for me to note how infrequently the facts concur with my memory of what happened. I assume, in cases like this, that the facts are wrong."

In his essay about writing his coming-of-age memoir *Firebird* ("Return to Sender: Memory, Betrayal, and Memoir"), Mark Doty ponders his decision not to research his childhood. "I could have found the sites of childhood scenes, and interviewed relatives, seeking corrections or corroboration, but that wasn't my book's project." Instead, he writes, "What interested me was memory itself, the architectures memory constructs, the interpretive act of remembering." Doty's decision exemplifies the Old English definition of truth as faithfulness and fidelity, as he stayed true to memory. As readers, we assume his good faith, in the Germanic definition, especially because he writes his questions about the truthiness of his memoir into the text, a strategy I'll explore later in this chapter.

The Bipolar Players in the Truth-Telling Game

In all my reading on truth in memoir, I find that authors tend to fall into three teams: on one extreme we have Team Loosey Goosey, on the other extreme Team Tighty Whitey, while most memoirists sit on the bench somewhere in between.

Dani Shapiro is on Team Loosey Goosey. She writes, "The idea of truth in memoir is absurd. Memory is utterly mutable, changeable, and constantly in motion. You can't fact-check memory." Her definition of truth cleaves closest to the Old English, that of being faithful to memory. She writes, "There are truths of a sort—the truth of adhering to what one remembers." Her position aligns with Mark Doty's above.

Mary Karr plays for Team Tighty Whitey, which she explores in *The Art of Memoir* in the chapter, "The Truth Contract Twixt Writer and Reader." She's black and white about it—no making anything up, except dialogue, and even then, she doesn't write her dialogue in quotation marks so the reader knows it's just an approximation. She writes, "My own humble practices wholly oppose making stuff up." She admits, "Truth may have become a foggy, fuzzy nether area. But untruth is simple: making up events with the intention to deceive." Her definition of truth seems to cleave to the second definition—she wants the memoir writer to write in good faith, fulfilling a truth contract with the reader. For Karr, good faith means you don't deceive the reader with any fabrications if you want your reader to trust you. She writes, "It niggles the hell out of me never to know exactly what parts the fabricators have fudged."

Mary Karr does not trust serial memoirist Vivian Gornick, who writes:

> This word "truth" is one I never employ. I never think about it and I never use it. My idea of what a memoirist owes a reader is honesty, however that is constructed. The reader must feel that the narrator, the memoirist, is trying to get to the bottom of the experience that one is writing about, whatever that experience is. The truth seeker—that's how I think of the duty of the memoirist. The truth of one's self. The truth of what one is trying to understand and puzzle out. It doesn't have to do with factual memories.

Gornick doesn't believe in Karr's truth contract with her readers. Her fidelity and loyalty is only to story. She believes it is the writer's obligation to shape the work as literature, not as reportage, and if that means making fudge, then she'll make fudge, and if Mary Karr is niggled by it and calls her the "f" word (fabricator), so be it.

Serial memoirist Sandra Tsing Loh also plays for Team Loosey Goosey. She writes, "In my work, there is always a disclaimer that says up front, this is not witnessing, not a documentary; it's a composite. Whatever you want to reveal about yourself is up to the writer. You have to shape your material. If you need a character to say a particular thing, invent a character and have him or her say that." In her book *Writing for Your Life*, Deena Metzger concurs: "Sometimes we have to override accuracy to create verisimilitude. And sometimes we have to 'invent' details to communicate the story fully. In the privacy of our writing studio, we can honestly determine whether we are fabricating to reveal or to conceal." It's not a question of whether we fabricate, but *why* we fabricate.

I think it's useful for beginning memoirists to pick a team and write down their rules for the game. I'd suggest, however, if you're playing for Team Tighty Whitey, you hold those rules lightly. Remember Andrew Hudgins' righteous vow never to lie in writing about his past, and when he actually began writing, how he broke every rule. I find that when my students cling too tightly to writing only what they remember, their writing is often quite dull, their storytelling rather flat. Can you tell us what your teacher looked like? I'll ask. *I don't remember.* Can you tell us something about your bedroom so we can imagine you there? *I don't remember.* What were some of those delicious meals your mother cooked? *I don't remember.*

You get the point. These writers want to be faithful to the truth. These writers want to be faithful to memory. But these writers need help.

Let's call imagination onto the field.

Imagination Joins the Game

What all the team players above share, despite their differences about what it means to be faithful to truth and memory, is a commitment to be faithful to art. We heard it in Andrew Hudgins' work—a willingness to lie in order to be true to experience and feeling and to create something aesthetically pleasing. Mary Karr acknowledges the aesthetic nature of memoir writing right there in her book's title, *The Art of Memoir*; Judith Barrington does the same in her book's title, *Writing the Memoir: From Truth to Art*. Michael Steinberg, author of the memoir *Still Pitching*, writes:

> If a memoir is crafted with careful attention to language, detail, and form, it's striving to become a literary work rather than a direct confession or retelling of one's own personal story. Whether a piece of creative nonfiction succeeds or fails has a great deal to do with the writer's skill and ability to shape his or her experience into a satisfying artistic whole.

And how do we do that? How do we take the raw material of our memories, faulty as they are, and shape them into a satisfying artistic whole? We lean into imagination. Steinberg calls memoir a hybrid genre "which means that the narrator's personal story—which evolves out of memory and imagination—and the research and reportage—are both, in one way or another, the necessary raw materials that the writer still has to organize and craft into a coherent narrative." If we understand memoir as a hybrid genre that couples memory with imagination, perhaps we'd be less obsessed with delineating truth from untruth. In *I Could Tell You Stories*, Patricia Hampl agrees. "Memoir rightly does belong to the imaginative world . . . once writers and readers make their peace with this fact there will be less argument over the ethical question about the memoir's relation to 'facts' and 'truth.'"

This relationship between memory and imagination is also an archetypal relationship, taking us back into Greek mythology. The goddess of memory, Mnemosyne, gives birth to nine daughters, the nine muses of all the imaginative arts. Memory and imagination, a mother-daughter relationship, are inherently connected to each other.

Mark Doty speaks to that connection in writing his coming-of-age memoir, *Firebird*. "My recollections had a kind of intensity which betrayed the way that imagination and memory had fused, which is what happens, with our earliest memories." Maureen Murdock also speaks of this fusion in her book *Unreliable Truth*: "But because these events are not happening in present time, we have to use our imagination to reclaim them. So we can never separate the remembered event from our imagination. They stick together."

Judith Barrington gives us permission to play in the intersection of memory and imagination. "It is up to you to decide how imaginatively you transform the known facts—exactly how far you allow yourself to go to fill in the memory gaps. While imagination certainly plays a role in both kinds of writing, the application of it in memoir is circumscribed by the facts, while in fiction, it is circumscribed by what the reader will believe." It's a good distinction—memoir is circumscribed by facts, but not constrained by them.

Patricia Hampl's essay "Memory and Imagination" explores the curious nature of this intersection. She tells the story of sitting down to write the story of her first piano lesson. After she wrote it, she realized that she had told "a number of lies." She thought she was setting out to transcribe a memory, but she realized: "Clearly the work of writing a personal narrative caused me to do something very different from transcription. I am forced to admit that memory is not a warehouse of finished stories, not a gallery of framed pictures. I must admit that I invented." In particular, she focuses on a red Thompson piano book she had in the story—one she realizes after she emerges from her first draft that she never actually had, but longed for desperately. So why in her memory did the book appear so clearly? "Here," she writes, "memory impulsively reaches out and embraces imagination. That is the resort to invention. It isn't a lie, but an act of necessity, as the innate urge to locate truth always is." The piano book becomes a symbol, "palpable evidence" of her "childhood longing and disappointment."

Unless we have a photographic memory, childhood and coming-of-age memoirs may be the place where we need to "resort to invention" the most, especially if we're writing them as older adults, given the memory problem of transience. Michael Steinberg write of his childhood memoir:

> We know that memory is an unreliable narrator. We also know that imagination alters, even rearranges, the way we remember things. In my memoir, I wasn't trying for a literal rendering of my childhood. I was trying to reflect on what it *felt* like to be me growing up in New York in the 1950s. To accomplish that, I needed to get inside the mind and heart of the narrator as a young boy. In other words, I had to imagine (as opposed to remember or invent) things like: what did that boy think and how did he feel about all the things that were happening to him?

I'm not sure I agree with his distinction here, that imagining is opposed to inventing. Imagination is a great inventor. Memory too is a great inventor, as we saw in Schacter's work. In his memoir *Retablos: Stories From a Life Lived Along the Border*, Octavio Solis writes, "Every memory has a patina of invention on it. That patina thickens every time we revisit those moments in our past, until they seem more like stories and myths of our formation, more dreamlike and yet more real than what really happened to us. So where is the fact of what actually

happened? It's still there, lost inside of and enhanced by fiction."
Hampl's imagination invented a red Thompson piano book, a patently
false fiction that revealed an emotional truth from her childhood. "All
right," Hampl acquiesces. "Invention is inevitable. But why write memoir? Why not call it fiction and be done with it?"

Genre Troubles

Hampl's question points to an interesting idea that perhaps it's not
memory or truth that's troublesome but genre itself. Perhaps we fall into
these binary positions because we only have two choices, nonfiction or
fiction. Nonfiction claims the truth and facts, and fiction claims the lie
and imagination, when in fact, as we've seen with memoir, it's much
messier than that.

But here's the thing. Even with fiction, it's much messier than that.
French philosopher and author Albert Camus wrote, "Fiction is the lie
through which we tell the truth." I think he's getting at emotional truth
here, at psychological truth—that we invent fictional characters and
events to tell something true about the nature of human beings. But I
want to press in even more on this. Writers of fiction often lie about just
how non-fictive their work is, how "based on true events" it really is. If
memoirists fabricate when they borrow tools from fiction to tell a great
story, so do fiction writers fabricate when they borrow from nonfiction
to tell a great story. Just as no memoir is 100% truth, so too is no work
of fiction 100% a lie. I often wonder, if Mary Karr is "niggled" when she
doesn't know what the memoirist fudged in her book, is she equally niggled when she doesn't know what the fiction writer borrowed from real
life?

Take the fracas over James Frey and his memoir, *A Million Little
Pieces*, where Frey served up some gooey fudgy lies disguised as the
truth. This was not misremembering, just plain outright lying. He had a
root canal without a numbing agent while in rehab—that's a whopper.
He was in jail for a month for a DUI, when in actuality he was there for a
few hours—that's beyond exaggeration. Mary Karr is so niggled by him
that she discusses him in her chapter in *The Art of Memoir*, "Hucksters,
the Deluded, and Big Fat Liars." Frey had initially tried to publish the
book as fiction precisely because he had reasonably overstepped

memoir's limitations with his big fat lies, but when he couldn't sell the book, he was encouraged to switch genres and call the book a memoir, and it got snapped up instantly and became a runaway best seller. But when the truth of his lies came out, readers were furious—his upbraiding on television by Oprah, who had originally championed the book, shows the depth of her betrayal, along with much of the critical world and the reading public. It's hard to imagine the opposite being true— had the book been published as fiction, would readers have felt so absolutely betrayed? Would Oprah have had Frey back on her show and berated him for not letting us know that 95% of the supposed fiction was actually nonfiction?

No. This is not imaginable, because we allow, even expect, that fiction writers will draw material from real life and combine it with their creative imagination. So should we apply the same standard to nonfiction, allowing, even expecting, that memoirists will draw material from real life and combine it with their creative imagination? And what's the tipping point, percentage-wise? If 95% of *A Million Little Pieces* is true but it contains 5% of either made-up stories or imaginative exaggerations, we call it a lie, but wouldn't it be equally true that if 95% of the material is true and only 5% is imagined, it's a lie to call the book fiction?

It's this kind of genre double standard that causes memoir writers such grief. It's what makes the words of author Erica Jong make so much sense: "I've always thought the idea of genre was a blot on the soul of literature. Categories like novel, memoir, biography have no value when you're writing—however much value they have to librarians or bookstores. A book is a book is a book. I suspect that the idea of genre has silenced more writers than it has liberated." This happened to author Rachel Cusk. When she told the truth about her maternal ambivalence and the end of her marriage in the genre of memoir, she was slammed by readers who attacked her personally, something she experienced as a "creative death" that pushed her "into total silence." When she wrote about similar topics in fiction, her personal life was set aside and her work garnered praise.

It's also what makes many writers turn toward imagining a new genre, or rather, a genre that more adequately reflects what's being written. "Literary nonfiction" or "creative nonfiction" tries to do just that, to acknowledge that writers of nonfiction are using literary or creative elements to shape their texts. Michael Steinberg notes:

> Right now, creative nonfiction is a hotly debated genre. In fact, I believe we're in the middle of the first serious genre conversation since the advent of the novel in the 18th century. The novel, when new, was thought of as a "popular" genre, which means that many critics and writers looked upon it as a less-than-legitimate literary form. In a similar way, the memoir has become the most controversial literary form of our time. Some of the arguments we're having today are, in fact, every bit as polarizing as were the contentious quarrels about the novel back then.

Would a genre name change help settle the controversy? Other names have arisen from the desire to include imaginative elements in memoir such as "speculative memoir" and "imagined memoir." The "autobiographical novel" is another cross-over term, as is the now popular "autofiction." All of these terms aim for specificity, to accurately name work that blends the genres of fiction and nonfiction.

The need for accurate naming is illustrated in the struggles to categorize Tim O'Brien's book *The Things They Carried*, about a character named Tim O'Brien's experience in the Vietnam War. The book has been referred to as fiction, metafictional narrative, nonfiction, a war autobiography, a writer's memoir, a series of linked short stories, and an invented form. When asked about the way he blurs genre, O'Brien responded:

> I set out to write a book with the feel of utter and absolute reality, a work of fiction that would read like nonfiction and adhere to the conventions of a memoir: dedicating the book to the characters, using my name, drawing on my own life. This was a technical challenge. My goal was to compose a fiction with the texture, sound and authentic-seeming weight of nonfiction.

But really, when you read the book and read about the book and see how many of O'Brien's memories are in the story, it feels to me like he was writing memoir but giving himself radical permission with, in his term, "story truth," in order to tell a truer truth about his experience of war. He writes, "I wanted to explore multiple planes of 'reality' and multiple planes of 'truth.' Yes, there is a real war going, with real casualties and real horror, but at the same time those realities are being processed in a mix of memory and imagination. Which is how we shape experience."

In the book, the "fictional" narrator Tim O'Brien tells us,

> I want you to feel what I felt. I want you to know why story-truth is truer sometimes than happening-truth. Here is the happening-truth. I was once a soldier. There were many bodies, real bodies with real faces, but I was young then and I was afraid to look. . . . What stories can do, I guess, is make things present. I can look at things I never looked at. I can attach faces to grief and love and pity and God. I can be brave. I can make myself feel again.

The fictional Tim O'Brien and the real Tim O'Brien seem to coalesce in this quote. The latter needed to partly fictionalize himself in order to tell a truer truth, and he chose the genre of fiction to do so. The Vietnamese-American poet and author Ocean Vuong's novel made a similar choice, but for different reasons. His book *On Earth We're Briefly Gorgeous* is also categorized as fiction. Vuong, like O'Brien, has a first-person narrator with his same name. He also uses family members with their same names. He also uses his own memories and historically truthful autobiographical details. He makes this distinction between memoir and fiction. Memoir's goal "is to arrive at truth," while "the novel begins with truth and is realized by the imagination." He's an artist, and for him, writing his memories as a novel preserves his agency as an artist—not a journalist, not a historian, but an inventor.

But now I can hear a cacophony of memoirists' voices arguing with Vuong, asserting that memoir too begins with truth and is realized by the imagination. There's no way out of this, friends. We're going to have to be okay with ambiguity.

I'll give the last word to Brooke Warner, publisher of She Writes Press and a self-described "champion of memoir." Trying to deal with ambiguity by turning to a term like autofiction is of course a writer's prerogative, she says, though she notes that ultimately it makes no difference to a publishing world mired in the binary categories of fiction or nonfiction. She cautions:

> The term autofiction serves a purpose when it is applied in its original meaning—to describe a novel that draws from real life— but autofiction is not and has never been a genre. You will not find autofiction as a category on Amazon, nor does it exist as a subject heading in the industry's BISAC categorization system, which exists to help booksellers know where to shelve books. If an author has written a work of autofiction, the book can only be labeled as a novel, and as such it's sold in the fiction section with fiction categories and fiction BISACs.

But her concern with embracing the term autofiction goes beyond the practicalities of book publishing and selling. She worries "about what happens when the silencing that [Rachel] Cusk spoke of starts to become an exodus of would-be memoirists to autofiction, and what we might lose when authors don't claim their truth." Memoir, she writes, "insists that the author own their truth" while a category like fiction or autofiction "only distances the author from their personal lived experience of truth." And isn't that why we come to memoir in the first place, to read about the author's personal lived experience of the truth? If we just wanted to read a good story, there's a million trillion works of fiction we can turn to.

No, we come to memoir for the truth. And while this whole chapter is a big messy handwringing treatise on the nature of truth when viewed through the lens of memory, and while it comes to no easy conclusions on this existential matter, I can definitely suggest two simple paths for finding our way out of this thorny briar patch—offer a prefatory statement or an author's note, and use the occasional qualifying word, phrase, or sentence.

Prefatory Statements and Author's Notes

It's become fairly standard practice for memoirists to include some kind of prefatory statement that establishes the terms of the truth contract with the reader, or "the truth covenant," as Annie Dillard calls it. Robert

Root writes, "Nonfiction depends upon a tacit agreement between writer and reader where the writer will play fair with the facts in exchange for the reader's trust that the writer is sincerely trying to discern and depict truth." The writer and reader "are linked by the assumption of an honest effort at verification where possible and a clear signal of uncertainty or imaginative rendering when corroboration is impractical." But that sort of tacit agreement and assumption has been shaken to the core by the memoirists who got called out on their fabrications, so now many authors spell out the terms of the agreement so the reader doesn't have to assume.

Add to this "fake news" and "deep fakes" and "reality TV" that is anything but, and bots and all the trouble coming our way from artificial intelligence, and we definitely have trust issues. In his 2008 blog post, "Are Memoirs True?" Jerry Waxler seems downright innocent in his trust. In writing about Harry Bernstein's memoir *The Dream*, where Bernstein writes of events that took place 80 years earlier, Waxler writes, "So how can I trust Harry Bernstein's memory? It's simple. I set aside my doubts, and enter the book 'as if' it's true. Here's the contract I mentally construct with him. 'He's doing his best to capture the fluttering essence of Truth and I am doing my best to believe it. Together we walk through this particular rendition of the dream of life.'" Waxler, in writing his memoir, hopes to "balance memory on the razor's edge of Truth." If a prefatory statement helps capture and define that fluttering essence and razor's edginess of Truth, it seems to me we should use them liberally.

Prefatory statements go by numerous names, like "note," "author's note," and "disclaimer." The latter highlights the legalistic reason to write such a statement: to protect the author and publisher from lawsuits. Helen Sedwick, a business lawyer and author of *Self-Publisher's Legal Handbook,* suggests, "Legal disclaimers are like chicken soup when you have a cold. They can't hurt and might help. While they are unlikely to stop a lawsuit, they may put an obstacle in the way."

Sometimes disclaimers or author's notes are done for craft reasons, to give cover to the author who wishes to tell a good story and knows they've had to bend or even break the truth in order to do so. Writing teacher and editor Jenna Kalinsky notes:

One of the major critiques of the disclaimer is that it may give the memoirist a false feeling of security in employing creative license, which nudges the memoir away from its expected truth-telling and into fiction ("reality fiction"). While this is a concern to memoir purists, it's also an invitation to expand our relationship to the form and an opportunity to invite emotional attachment and feelings of intimacy in other ways.

That feeling of intimacy is created in Richard Hoffman's brief note that follows his dedication and acknowledgment page in his memoir about childhood sexual abuse, *Half the House*. He tells us he's taking no creative license: "This is not a work of fiction. It contains no composite characters, no invented scenes. I have, in most instances, altered the names of persons outside my family." And then, the final line: "In one instance, on principle, I have not." He gives the real name of his abuser, a decision he made right before publication.

In a craft essay titled "'I Didn't Ask to Be in Your Memoir': When Real Names Matter and When They Don't," Hoffman explains his choice: his abuser "was simply undeserving of protection, and I determined that I did not owe him silence, did not have to keep his secret." He calls this not a disclaimer but a "reclaimer, since it was my purpose to reclaim all manner of lost things in the narrative." Because his abuser had been arrested twice before for molesting young boys, his publisher agreed to keep the name in (though requiring Hoffman to indemnify them). As a result of the publication of the book, 400 boys and men came forward saying they were molested by the same coach. Hoffman's decision to write his "reclaimer," followed by Louise DeSalvo's introduction to the 20th-anniversary edition of the book where she recounts the repercussions of that one line, creates an instant intimacy and attachment to this courageous author.

Helen Sedwick notes that we form our relationship with the reader right there in our prefatory material, as Hoffman did, and, she adds, we can use them to highlight our literary voice. Don't get me wrong—plenty of these sorts of notes are quite bland and read like they were drafted by the legal department, as we'll see in some of the following examples, but the ones that mirror the author's voice serve as our first "Hello, it's me" moment of introduction to the author. Recall Andy Rooney's prefatory statement: "This is a memoir, not a history book, but in an effort to make it accurate, I've tried to check my memory against the facts. It is distressing for me to note how infrequently the facts concur with my memory of what happened. I assume, in cases like this, that the facts are wrong." Classic wry Andy Rooney, true to form.

Where these kind of statements are placed can vary. Sometimes they appear on the copyright page, or the page right after. Sometimes they appear in a preface or introduction. In the case of Jenny Lawson's memoir, *Let's Pretend This Never Happened: A Mostly True Memoir*, the disclaimer is right there in the title. Sometimes authors use an epigraph to convey the rules of the game, as Judith Moore did in *Fat Girl*, borrowing a line from Kurt Vonnegut: "All this happened, more or less." Rarely will it come at the end of the book, in an afterword or acknowledgments page, because by then it's too late to establish a truth contract and too risky to break it.

Sometimes the statements speak to the author's subjectivity, claiming the memories as "mine and mine alone," allowing that others may have experienced the same events differently, and may have different truths. Jemela S. Macer opens her memoir *Between Two Worlds: An Armenian-American Woman's Journey Home* with an author's note that reads in part:

> All the thoughts and feelings explored here are mine and mine alone, born of my particular psychological makeup and ways of experiencing life. Those raised in the same home or the same culture and under similar circumstances may well remember or view these experiences differently. I have done my best to stay as close to my emotional truth as possible in recounting events and experiences.

You can see the sort of protective shield a statement like this offers a writer, especially one like Macer who is sharing her intimate experience of biculturality, wanting to be careful not to claim or name the truth of anyone else's experience but hers.

Memoir geek that I am, I collect prefatory statements like others collect snow globes or Pez dispensers. I share these with you so you don't have to open every memoir book on your shelf to find examples. What follows is an attempt at categorization, though like any attempt at such things, there are inevitable overlaps.

The Very Basic

Some of the names, locations, and details of events in this book have been changed to protect the privacy of the people involved.

~Jesmyn Ward
Men We Reaped

This is a work of nonfiction, however, the names of some individuals have been changed in order to disguise their identities. Any resulting resemblance to persons living or dead is entirely coincidental and unintentional.

~Gail Caldwell
Let's Take the Long Way Home: A Memoir of Friendship

Then Again is a work of nonfiction. Some names and identifying details have been changed.

~Diane Keaton
Then, Again

Most individuals' names and many identifying details have been changed. Some individuals are composites.

~Kiese Laymon
Heavy: An American Memoir

Brief, and to the point. There's not much character here, zero intimacy, and certainly there's no literary voice. One imagines these are written by the legal department and foisted upon their authors (it's hard to imagine that Diane Keaton's statement is the best she can write!), and for that reason, they often appear on the copyright page. Notice these are written in passive voice–there's no "I" here.

The Extended Basic

These statements are written in both active and passive voice, and add a little more contractual detail.

> This work is a memoir. It reflects the author's present recollections of his experiences over a period of years. Certain names, locations, and identifying characteristics have been changed, and certain individuals are composites. Dialogue and events have been recreated from memory and, in some cases, have been compressed to convey the substance of what was said or what occurred.
>
> ~Nic Sheff
> *Tweaked: Growing Up on Methamphetamines*

> This is a work of creative nonfiction. In it, I describe experiences that had a profound emotional impact on me. The events in this book are true to the best of my recollection. For readability, in some cases I altered the order of or compressed sequences of events. I do not pretend that I am capable of remembering everything that took place exactly or offering everyone's perspective. This is my story and I write about what struck me personally. To protect the privacy of real individuals, I have changed or left out many names and identifying details, or used composite characters, and in some cases omitted people from the story.
>
> ~Gina Frangello
> *Blow the House Down:*
> *A Story of Marriage, Family, and Treason*

I have changed the names (except my own), and other details of persons in this book. I have not changed the name of a certain dog, which suited the animal and my story perfectly. Sometimes real life surprises fiction even in the details. I have, on a few oc-casions, changed the order of events, where those changes ben-efit narrative flow without altering a factual telling of the story. Otherwise, all dialogue and events took place as I remember and recount them in these pages.

~Julie Metz
Perfection: A Memoir of Betrayal and Renewal

To the Reader: Lord knows I've tried my best to tell the truth here, even when it would have been simpler to fabricate. While all of the incidents in this essay collection happened, I have changed the names of people, businesses, and institutions when it felt right. In a few cases I even nudged a fact slightly, but no more than necessary and only to avoid identifying somebody I love. I'm writing from memory most of the time, so be forgiving, gentle reader. I went to college in the seventies.

~Melissa Delbridge
Family Bible

The Humorous/Irreverent

Melissa Delbridge ends her author's statement on a humorous note, showing us something of her character. Using a humorous or irreverent author's note is a great way to highlight your literary voice. Of course, the tone must match the content of the book—you wouldn't expect to see one of these in a memoir that takes its subject matter very seriously.

Disclaimer: The author acknowledges that he is not Bob Wood-ward. Mr. Woodward is scrupulous with names and dates. This author is not. Mr. Woodward would never suggest that some-thing happened in October when, in fact, it occurred in April. This author would. Mr. Woodward recounts conversations as they actually occurred. This author would like to do that, but alas, he does not excel at penmanship and he cannot read his notes. However, the author has an excellent memory. You can trust him.

~J. Maarten Troost
Getting Stoned with Savages:
A Trip Through the Islands of Fiji and Vanuatu

The tales you are about to read are the truth, practically the truth, and nothing less than a half-truth....

~Nick Trout
Tell Me Where It Hurts: A Day of Humor,
Healing, and Hope in My Life as an Animal Surgeon

The names of the men in this book have been changed because most of them are named Dave."

~Ophira Eisenberg
Screw Everyone: Sleeping My Way to Monogamy

Everything in this book is mostly true but some details have been changed to protect the guilty. I know it's usually about 'protecting the innocent' but why would they need protection? *They're innocent.* And they're also not nearly as fun to write about as the guilty, who always have more fascinating stories and who make you feel better about yourself by comparison.

~Jenny Lawson
Furiously Happy: A Funny Book About Horrible Things

These are my recollections. If you remember things differently, send me your version—but only if it's funnier.

~Debbie Reynolds
Unsinkable

The Craft-Forward Focus

In these statements, authors highlight their intention to tell a good story or create a compelling work of art, and claim some measure of creative license to do so.

Everything here is true, but it may not be entirely factual. In some cases I have compressed events; in others I have made two people into one. I have occasionally embroidered. I learned early that the most important thing in life is a good story.

~Ruth Reichl
Tender at the Bone: Growing Up at the Table

I have changed the names of certain people, places, and businesses in order to protect those mentioned in the book and to safeguard my privacy and that of my family. On occasion, composite characters enter and exit the page, mainly because at times when I do remember faces or voices, I cannot remember names, or vice versa. In some chapters, time lapses serve the purpose of evading the superfluous. What I meant to do here was to create a mix of memory, research, and reporting told in a lyrical register reminiscent of other art forms I had previously studied: music, art history, architecture, and dance.

~Cinelle Barnes
Monsoon Mansion: A Memoir

This is the story of my Texas life. And while (essentially) true to my experience, I must warn that it often reads better (as in funnier, or happier) than it was lived. This service I've performed not merely for the sake of your sensibilities, but also for my art.

~Robert Leleux
The Memoirs of a Beautiful Boy

My childhood continues to amaze me as a constant reference point for who I've been, who I am, and who I will be. It feels concrete and accessible but, on some level, also elusive and fractured. As such, these pages are emotionally true, though not necessarily factual. Certainly, I've compressed events; changed the names of people, places, and things; and imagined dialogue. At times I have collaged two (or three) people into one, embroidered memories, or borrowed them. I've bent time and space in the way that the art of memory demands. My poet's soul believes that the emotional truth of these pages trumps everything Read as you would read my poems, trusting that what is here is real, beyond what is real—that truer truth which we come to call a life.

~Richard Blanco
The Prince of Los Cocuyos

The Specific

While many author's notes are relatively vague, there's no reason they have to be. It may serve your readers to be more specific, to pull back the curtain on your process, as David Carr does in his statement, or to assure your readers (and those you are writing about) that you've protected certain people, as Michael Greenberg does in his.

The following book is based on sixty interviews conducted over three years, most of which were recorded on video and/or audio and then transcribed by a third party. The events represented are primarily the product of mutual recollection and discussion. Hundreds of medical files, legal documents, journals, and published reports were used as source material in reconstructing personal history. Every effort was made to corroborate memory with fact and in significant instances where that was not possible, it is noted in the text. (Go to nightofthegun.com for more information concerning methodology.) All of which is not to say that every word of this book is true—all human stories are subject to errors of omission, fact, or interpretation regardless of intent—only that it is as true as I could make it.

~David Carr
The Night of the Gun

To protect their privacy, names and identifying details of medical staff, patients, and their families have been changed. In a few minor instances, the chronology of events during Sally's hospitalization have been slightly altered.

~Michael Greenberg
Hurry Down Sunshine: A Father's Story of Love and Madness

I have been corrected on some points, mostly of chronology. Also my mother claims that a dog I describe as ugly was actually quite handsome. I've allowed some of these points to stand, because this is a book of memory, and memory has its own story to tell. But I have done my best to make it tell a truthful story.

~Tobias Wolfe
This Boy's Life

All the names in this book have been changed except for those of Lupe and her children, to whom this book is dedicated.

~Mary Morris
Nothing to Declare: Memoirs of a Woman Traveling Alone

Using Qualifiers

An author's note or disclaimer is a one-time statement set apart from the actual text of the memoir that qualifies the truth within, but there are also ways to use qualifiers throughout the text proper. Mary Karr advocates for the liberal use of qualifiers to keep the reader's trust, to fulfill the truth contract between memoirist and reader, by either skipping "over the half-remembered scene or to replicate [your] own psychic uncertainty—'This part is blurry.' Any decent comp teacher schools you to work in the realms of maybe and perhaps. The great memoirist enacts recall's fuzzy form. That's why we trust her."

The realms of maybe and perhaps is the realm of qualifiers, words or phrases that change how certain or absolute we are about our memories, that suggest a certain fuzziness. Here are some examples.

- **Qualifiers of *quantity*:** some, most, many, several, a handful, rarely, numerous, a few, etc.
- **Qualifiers of *time*:** occasionally, sometimes, now and again, usually, sporadic, hardly ever, etc.
- **Qualifiers of *certainty*:** I guess, I think, I'm not sure, I imagine, I suspect, I assume, I have a hunch, I estimate, I suppose, etc.
- **Qualifiers of *possibility*:** Could, maybe, might, perhaps, likely, possible, probable, plausible, reasonable, conceivable, etc.

Let me use the example of my stepfather's drinking. As I mentioned, I'm uncertain how often he was drunk, but in my memory, it feels like every weekend and sometimes during the week. "Sometimes" is already a qualifier, but "every" is an absolute, and after the conversation with my mother, I'm uncertain about that. Here's how I can use more qualifiers to underscore that uncertainty.

- My stepfather was **rarely** sober on weekends.
- My stepfather was drunk **most** weekends.
- **Usually** my stepfather drank through the weekend.
- There would be a sober weekend **now and then**, depending on how angry my mother was with him that week.
- **I think** he started drinking most Friday nights, and that bled over onto the weekend.
- **If I had to guess**, I'd say he got drunk at least half the weekends each month, maybe more.
- **Maybe** there were a few weekends when he drank less.

We can remind the reader we're in the land of memory here, with sentences like:

- From what I recall...
- This part is blurry...
- I seem to remember...
- From what I remember...
- Much of the memory is lost except for...

We can make it clear we're in the land of emotional truth, with sentences like:

- I can't say for certain, but it felt like...
- Maybe he didn't say exactly that, but what I heard was...
- I don't remember why exactly, but I got the impression that....
- It's hard to know how long it lasted, but the impact on me was clear...

Judy Blunt could have saved herself from her father-in-law ratting her out to *The New York Times* by using this strategy. Instead of writing that he killed her typewriter by taking a sledgehammer to it, which was literally untrue but emotionally true, she could have written, "The old man pulled the plug on the typewriter, but it felt like he took a sledge-hammer to it and killed it" or "The old man pulled the plug on the type-writer, but if there had been a sledgehammer in the room, I think he would have killed it."

If you want to use your imagination to fill in a memory gap, but you don't want to niggle Mary Karr, you can use a sentence starter such as:

- I don't remember what came next, but in my imagination, I see...
- My mind goes blank when I try to remember what caused her reaction, but my best guess is...
- I can't recall a thing I did that summer, but it was probably what I did most summers, which was...

- She never told me about that conversation, but from what I can piece together...
- If I were to reconstruct that scene, I'd place him...
- If there was a photograph of that day, I imagine I'd be wearing...
- This part is cloudy, but it might have gone something like this...

All of these strategies fall under what the author Lisa Knopp calls "perhapsing." When we come to a dead end in our remembering, "where we don't have access to the facts we need to tell our story or to sustain our reflection with depth and fullness," perhapsing allows us to add "richness, texture, and complexity . . . without crossing the line into fiction." It has the added benefit of suggesting a reliable narrator and reinforcing the truth covenant between writer and reader.

Qualifying Memory Itself

Just as truth is an archetype, so too is memory—it comes hardwired on this brain computer of ours, a process we all have access to, though of course it may fade over time and be entirely corrupted and disrupted by disease. Since memoir sits squarely on the archetype of memory, one of the ways we can qualify its relationship with truth and imagination is to muse upon memory itself—what we remember, what we wish we could remember but have forgotten, why we remember and why we forget, how memory distorts and contorts. We can make *memory itself* a point of focus in our memoir, sharing with our readers how we feel about it or engage with it, and how we trust it or distrust it. In doing so, we find a point of connection with our readers who have their own memory troubles and share similar struggles and questions about the nature of memory.

In his book *Half a Life*, Darin Strauss gives us a beautiful example of the vagaries of memory. He's writing about his memories of the accident in which his car hit and killed a schoolmate on her bicycle. "This moment has been, for all my life, a kind of shadowy giant. I'm able, tick by tick, to remember each second before it: radio; friends; thoughts of mini-golf, another thought of maybe just going to the beach; the distance between

the car and bicycle closing: anything could still happen. But I am powerless to see what comes next; the moment raises a shoulder, lowers its
head, and slumps away." It's a beautiful metaphor–a moment as a shadowy giant–and who doesn't relate to being powerless to remember the
contours of something or someone so important in the shape of our
lives?

In her memoir *Hiroshima in the Morning,* Rahna Reiko Rizzuto opens
her prologue by musing about memory. "I can tell you the story but it
won't be true. It won't be the facts as they happened exactly each day
each footstep each breath. Time elides, events shift; sometimes we shift
them on purpose and forget that we did. Memory is just how we choose
to remember it. We choose." A paragraph break, and she moves into
story, the story of how she's making a list in preparation for leaving for
a six-month grant to do research in Japan. Then she slips back out of
story, sharing with us, "I will come to believe, months from now, that life
is a narrative. That who we are, what roles we choose–that these are deliberate characters we create to explain what we did and find a way to
face tomorrow. That memory is not history. That we rewrite ourselves
with every heartbeat." Her prologue not only sets the stage for her story,
but it tells us how to read it–not as fixed history or fact, but as something
shifty, a story crafted by a character who is making choices, who is re-
writing herself in this memoir, and it offers us a chance for reflection–do
we agree that memory is just how we choose to remember it? Can we
rewrite ourselves by remembering differently?

In another example of memory itself being part of the story, in an
essay on his childhood in *Getting Personal,* Phillip Lopate writes, "My
mother was seeing another man. His name was Willy. It may have been
childish confusion–I was eight years old at the time–or a trick memory
plays on us, but I seem to remember the jeep he drove was also a Willys.
This car has disappeared from modern life. I am unable even to picture
it. But at the time it colored all my thinking about the affair." Then he
goes on to draw comparisons between the two Willys. Childish confusion? A trick memory plays on us? Yes, we've all experienced this.
Lopate could have easily done some research, googled "Jeep Willys"
like I did, bring the vehicle to life, describe it to us, but he's making a
bigger point here about the nature of our childhood memories, and

he's qualifying for us how to read his particular memories, through memory's tricks and confusions.

Mark Doty makes a similar point about the writing of his childhood memoir, *Firebird*. There's a scene where he wonders why his sister wore a beige wedding dress, and a copyeditor wrote in the margin, "Why don't you just ask her?" She was, after all, still alive. Doty writes, "Then I wondered why it had never occurred to me to ask her, and immediately I understood that it simply wasn't that sort of book; my inquiry was into memory, not history: how it was to be that child, as that child re-arises in the mind, imaginatively reconstructed, reinhabited. Which is how the past goes on and on in us, changing, developing, its look and meanings built and rebuilt over time."

Doty would agree with the author Toni Morrison's reflection on memory: "Memory (the deliberate act of remembering) is a form of willed creation. It is not an effort to find out the way it really was—that is research. The point is to dwell on the way it appeared and why it appeared in that particular way." Doty's book is a masterclass on dwelling on memory—he's just as curious and concerned with *how* he remembers and *why* he remembers as *what* he remembers, and he steps out of narrative and breaks the fourth wall by musing on memory, often parenthetically, often with question marks as qualifiers. As we ride shotgun in his childhood car, truth takes the backseat, and memory is the driver.

Conclusion

Writing *Firebird* and sojourning in the land of memory helped Mark Doty to see that "the past is not static, or ever truly complete; as we age we see from new positions, shifting angles." Memoirist Sue William Silverman agrees, writing, "Memory is not the history of what happened; memory is the history of our *story* of what happened." The stories we tell now may be very different from the stories we told 20 years ago, because we are a different self with different experiences than we were 20 years ago, and memory, as we've seen, has a troubled relationship with the truth. That's why I define memory as what is remembered about the past self and her experiences by the present self with her experiences.

I think of this often when I read a memoir by someone in the first third of life, like *The New York Times* bestsellers Tara Westover's *Uneducated*, or Michelle Zauner's *Crying in H Mart*, or Stephanie Foo's *What My Bones Know: A Memoir of Healing From Complex Trauma*. Come back to me when you're 60, I want to whisper to them. Tell me the story of your childhood then. I promise you, it won't be the same story.

But it will still be true.

THE ARCHETYPE OF IMAGE
Metaphor and Its Superpowers

In the field of depth psychology where my mind was cultivated, we often speak of "archetypal images." Let me explain what that means, and its implication for memoir writing.

Remember that archetypes are empty forms, ideas, or templates that we fill with content. An archetype needs representation, and we're wired to represent them in images. The image-making function of the psyche is so strong that we even make them at night when we're asleep, when we're literally unconscious. We may feel afraid in our waking life, and we sleep and have a dream about a giant brown bear chasing us down—our psyche produced an image that represented the universal emotion of fear. The image-making function of the psyche is so strong that our bodies are implicated—we may wake from such a dream with an emotional response—our heart racing, our brow sweaty, our limbs jittery. We have to calm ourselves down by telling ourselves, "It's only a dream," but what is a dream anyway but a series of animated images?

Images are so ubiquitous that C.G. Jung wrote, "Everything of which we are conscious is an image, and that image is psyche." My dream example suggests that everything of which we are *unconscious* is also an image, or can be represented by the psyche as an image. We may not be consciously aware that we're afraid until the image of that brown bear appears in our dream, which is why Sigmund Freud called dreams "the royal road" to the unconscious.

When we think of the word "image," we typically think of something we can see, but that limits an image to one sense, when in fact, the other senses are implicated in images as well. We can close our eyes and still see images. We hear snoring and associate it with the person beside us. We smell smoke and associate it with fire. We taste a carbonated beverage and associate it with a can of soda. We touch cool leather and associate it with a couch or chair. In this expansion of the word "image," even people born without sight experience images—hearing snoring produces an image of the body next to us, even if we've never seen the body and know it only through the other senses.

As we'll explore more below, it's fair to say that human beings (homo sapiens) are, at our very core, image-making beings (*homo imago*). Image-making, consciously or unconsciously, is something that connects us with all other human beings—by implication, memoir writers who want to connect with their readers can do so, not just through ideas, the subject of our last chapter, but through images.

I can hear you sighing right now, perhaps uttering the word "duh" under your breath. "Of course," you might be thinking. "That's the old adage, 'Show, don't tell.'" You're right. But even when we tell, we can tell in images. When Gail Caldwell wants to tell us what grief is like, grief over losing her best friend, she opens the first page of her memoir *Let's Take the Long Way Home* by telling us: "My life had made so much sense alongside hers: For years we had played the easy, daily game that intimate connection implies. One ball, two gloves, equal joy in the throw and the return. Now I was in the field without her: one glove, no game. Grief is what tells you who you are alone."

What a less impactful paragraph if Caldwell had written, "My life had made so much sense alongside hers. Grief is what tells you who you are alone." Telling, no showing. Nothing but abstractions there. Nothing concrete. Nothing haunting like this—an image of Caldwell standing alone in field, baseball glove on one hand, ball in another, turning slowly in circles, no friend in sight to throw the ball to. (Notice my image-making psyche added something to her image—Caldwell turning. We do this too, bring our imaginations to bear in further animating images.)

Let's scrap the "show, don't tell" adage into something that mimics what our brains naturally do—tell through showing. Tell through image. And in this case, tell through metaphor, a particular but wildly universal type of image-making.

What is a Metaphor? A Rose By Any Other Name

Homo sapiens literally translates into "wise human." Aristotle was a *homo sapiens*, known for being more sapiens than the average bear (my biggest challenge in this chapter will be to resist pointing out every time I use a metaphor). So let's look to him for some wisdom about metaphor-making. In *Poetics,* he states, "It is a great thing, indeed, to make proper use of the poetic forms. . . . But the greatest thing so far is to be a master of metaphor." Metaphor-making, he asserts, "is a sign of genius. For the right use of metaphor means an eye for resemblances." In *Rhetoric*, he extols his listeners to use metaphors to "help give your language impressiveness."

Aristotle defined metaphor as "giving the thing a name that belongs to something else." In the simplest mathematical representation, a metaphor is when we say A = B. Grief equals standing alone in a field with a glove on one hand and a ball in another, without your beloved best friend to play catch with. The masters of metaphor George Lakoff and Mark Johnson, in their seminal book (semen, a metaphor—*shh, Jennifer*) *Metaphors to Live By,* call A "the target" and B "the source." The target domain (in Caldwell's case, grief) is understood in terms of the source domain (a solitary game of catch). Lakoff and Johnson call metaphor "one of the most basic mechanisms we have for understanding our experience." For writers, it's also one of the most basic mechanisms we have for *conveying* our experience so the reader understands it.

Etymologically, the word "convey" means to carry, to transport, from the Latin *com*, meaning with or together, and *via*, meaning the road or the way. When we make a metaphor, we transport the "A" across the equal sign to the "B"—we send two dissimilar things to travel together on the road of language. In fact, it's also the etymology of the word "metaphor" in Greek—*meta* (over, across, or beyond) and *phor* (to carry). Metaphor means "to carry across." When writers are struggling to convey a difficult concept or a complex experience, they might ask themselves, "How do I get this across?" and what might arise, as it did for Caldwell in describing her grief, is a metaphorical image.

Metaphors work because of the pattern-recognition function of the brain, something we discussed in the introduction. Archetypes are patterns, and so too are metaphors—they say, "This pattern in A matches this pattern in B. This pattern carries over to that," leading Jung to assert confidently, "An archetypal content expresses itself, first and foremost, in metaphors." "Our brains are always prospecting for patterns," Geary writes in *I is an Other: The Secret Life of Metaphor and How It Shapes the Way We See the World*, making metaphor one way to mine for those patterns.

Metaphor-making is so hardwired into our species that children learn to make them from an early age. Geary writes, "Developmental research routinely finds that kids produce metaphors with alacrity and ease. . . . Young children are such prolific metaphor producers because their pattern recognition circuits, not yet confined by conventional categorizations, are working full blast." When they're young, their metaphors are primarily perceptual. Broccoli is a tree on their plate. Rain is the sky crying. Ducks are bird boats. Tell a six-year-old she's just putting a band-aid on her problem and she's likely to go running for the box. Conceptual metaphors come online around the ages of 10-12, research shows—children of that age will likely understand what it means that someone has a hard heart, that love is a roller coaster, or how jealousy stings, because their brains have developed to make more complex conceptual connections.

At its heart, that's what a metaphor is—a connection—and a language genius can make them and make them original (more on originality to come). Metaphor-making is one way to put the word "creative" in front of the word "writer," because, as the tech genius Steve Jobs said, "Creativity is just connecting things." Dance genius Twyla Tharp agrees, writing, "Creativity is more about taking the facts, fictions, and feelings we store away and finding new ways to connect them. What we're talking about here is metaphor. Metaphor is the lifeblood of all art, if it is not art itself."

Not only is metaphor the metaphorical lifeblood of art, but the ability to make and understand metaphor may be the metaphorical lifeblood of cognition itself, the very way we know and think and understand.

Don't just take Aristotle's word for it. "To understand is to perceive patterns," the philosopher Isaiah Berlin stated. James Olney, in *Metaphors of Self*, simply states, "Metaphor is essentially a way of knowing." James Geary calls metaphorical thinking "our instinct not just for describing but for *comprehending* one thing in terms of another." Lakoff and Johnson write, "Our conceptual system is largely metaphorical . . . the way we think . . . is very much a matter of metaphor." They continue, "It is as though the ability to comprehend experience through metaphor were a sense, like seeing or touching or hearing, with metaphors providing the only ways to perceive and experience much of the world. Metaphor is as much a part of our functioning as our sense of touch, and as precious." Applying this sense to writing, the editor and critic Leon Wieseltier asserted that "the range of a writer's metaphor is a measure of the range of his cognition," which brings us back to Aristotle's idea that the genius writer is the writer of metaphor. Metaphors are not only artsy, but they're brainy. If intuition is our sixth sense, our sixth way of experiencing and knowing our world, then metaphor may be our seventh sense.

"This is Your Brain on Metaphors"

I want to stick with this discussion of the brain and metaphors a bit longer so we can apply it to the art of crafting metaphors in our memoirs. I borrow the title of this section from Robert Sapolsky's essay, "This is Your Brain on Metaphors." Sapolsky begins by showing how the typical human brain understands "symbols, metaphors, analogies, parables, synecdoche, figures of speech." I say typical, because atypical brains like those of people on the autism spectrum tend toward literal language and often can't comprehend metaphor. But in the neurotypical brain, as Sapolsky shows, not only can we understand symbols, metaphors, analogies, etc., but scientific studies prove that the brain cannot distinguish between metaphor and reality—the reasoning, conscious part of us can, but the biological and unconscious part of us responds very much the same way to metaphor and reality.

Hang in there with me—this is really important to us writers.

Now Sapolsky doesn't use the term the "unconscious brain," but I want to use it here. Because of course, if you tell me, "Hey Jennifer, I found a heavyweight champion for the job opening," consciously I don't expect the candidate to be heavy or overweight, or be a boxing champion. Consciously I understand the metaphor to mean the person is a serious, stand-out candidate, perhaps even overqualified, and we'd be lucky to hire them. But unconsciously, my brain is affected by the metaphor.

Sapolsky cites a study where the same resume for a candidate was attached to a light clipboard versus a heavy clipboard. The participants in the study who had the heavier clipboard assessed the candidate as more serious—a weightier candidate, so to speak. In another study, when researchers asked participants to recall something dirty or immoral they had done, they were more likely to wash their hands after the study than the participants who recalled a moral act. In other words, the brain responds literally to metaphor, and often unconsciously. I'm sure no participant said they favored the candidate because the clipboard was heavier, or they washed their hands because they felt psychologically dirty.

Kinda trippy, right? Let's trip some more.

In an essay by Michael Chorost, "Your Brain on Metaphors," he cites recent fMRI studies on the brain and language—researchers spying on the brain have discovered that the same part of the brain lights up when we read or hear a metaphor as when we do a similar action. For instance, if you read the sentence, "The player kicked the ball," your brain reacts the same way as if your body really kicked the ball. Okay, that's fascinating enough, but there's more. If you read the sentence, "The patient kicked the habit," the action part of the brain still lights up as if it were kicking, in a way that it doesn't if you read the sentence sans metaphor, "The patient stopped using drugs." Metaphors light up our brains in a way that conceptual language doesn't. Studies have shown that metaphor and imagery light up both the left and the right hemisphere of the brain (ala the patient kicked the habit), while concrete language tends to light up just the left hemisphere (ala the patient stopped using drugs).

An article in Science News titled "Readers Build Vivid Mental Simulations Of Narrative Situations" discusses the implications for the process of reading. These brain imaging studies shed light on "what it means to 'get lost in a good book'—suggesting that readers create vivid mental simulations of the sounds, sights, tastes and movements described in a textual narrative while simultaneously activating brain regions used to process similar experiences in real life." When reading a good memoir, if we feel like we're right there with the author in her world, that what's happening to her is happening to us, it's because, in the brain's biology, it literally is.

And, in another important finding for us writers, our reader's brain gets more bang for the buck, more stimulation, when the metaphors are original. Trite metaphors like "she smells like a rose" or overused idioms or clichés like "it's raining cats and dogs" don't stimulate the brain in the same way, which makes sense. Been there, heard that before, the brain says. No reason to light up here.

Michael Chorost writes, "For centuries, metaphor was just the place where poets went to show off" (they got Aristotle's message!) Not any longer. Science is showing us the power of metaphor and vivid imagery, and as writers, encouraging and inspiring us to make more use of metaphor and image in order to stimulate the whole brain of our readers.

The Pleasures of Metaphor

Not only do we light up the brains of our readers, but we also bring them pleasure, a wonderful hit of feel-good chemicals when encountering a good and rich metaphor. As a writing teacher, I know this well—when one of my memoir students lands a perfectly original metaphor, showing me a pattern between two things I had never connected before, my metaphorical—and sometimes literal—breath is taken away.

James Geary's wonderful book on metaphor is full of the work of contemporary neuroscientists and the words of more ancient philosophers. He quotes the Italian philosopher Giambattista Vico who wrote that the pleasure of metaphor lies in the hidden link between the source and the target, a connection Vico called the *ligamen*, from the Latin word *ligare*, meaning "to bind." He also quotes the Roman statesman Marcus Tullius Cicero: "Metaphorical terms give people much more pleasure, if the metaphor is a good one." That's the pleasure I'm referring to, the pleasure I experience when my memoir students write a good metaphor, binding a source and a target together in a unique way.

Geary believes part of that pleasure comes from working to "get" the connection—"Metaphors are so entertaining because of the pleasure we get from figuring them out." In fact, he points to research showing that "the greater the cognitive exertion" and "the more distant the source, the more surprising and delightful the metaphor" results in "greater the subsequent positive feelings." Friendship between two middle-aged women, death, grief—and the source is a game of catch in a field with a ball and a glove? Surprising and delightful (if you enjoy having your heart yanked out of your chest). Caldwell threw that metaphor to us and we catch it. Look at me—I've been holding onto that metaphor from her book for years, and now I throw it to you in this book. In this way, the writer and the reader become, in Geary's words, "accomplices; the one unpacks what the other presents." The metaphor itself *is* the ligament that binds the two of us together.

Geary offers a caveat to the "cognitive exertion" research: "But there has to be a conceptual tie that binds source to target. Otherwise, the result is mere surrealism." In other words, the writer has to make the ligament clear—the metaphor's meaning cannot be mysterious. Had Caldwell just written "Grief is a game of catch," the metaphor wouldn't work at all. We might scratch our stumped heads as we try to make any connection, blaming ourselves for not "getting" it or judging Caldwell as a poor writer.

What we're going for in writing metaphors is the good kind of mystery, the "I didn't see that coming but now that it's here, it makes perfect sense" kind of mystery. We're going for what novelist and literary critic John Gardner calls "the mysterious rightness of a good metaphor." To further the good mystery metaphor, the psychologist Amos Tversky states, "A good metaphor is like a good detective story. The solution should not be apparent in advance to maintain the reader's interest, yet it should seem plausible after the fact to maintain coherence of the story."

How Metaphor Travels

We've already seen that metaphor travels from A to B, from target to source, but it moves in other distinct directions that are useful for our craft as writers. James Geary discusses synesthetic metaphors, metaphors that travel across the senses—you might call the look on someone's face sweet (from sight to taste), you might call a voice smooth (from sound to touch), you might call an odor melodious (from smell to sound)—in synthetic metaphors, we borrow from the vocabulary of one sense and apply it to another (fun fact, the Arabic word for metaphor is isti'ara or "loan").

Metaphors also borrow from the concrete to amplify the abstract. Geary writes, "Metaphorical thinking usually travels one way, appropriating concrete language—the words we use for everyday experiences and physical things and sensations—to describe abstractions like thoughts, feelings, emotions, and ideas." Grief is abstract. A game of catch in a field where there's only one player is concrete, appealing to the sense of sight.

Cicero thought the sight was the superior source for metaphors, implying that when a writer is trying to "get something across," he can ask himself, what does it look like? Let's take the sentence, "The building was tall." Blah. The word "tall" is abstract and is really only meaningful in terms of its surroundings—a tall building in downtown Chicago may suggest something different from a tall building in the Kansas plains.

So the writer asks himself, what does the building look like? Maybe he writes, "The building looks like it's 60 feet tall." Okay, while that may give me a more accurate sense of the building's height, my brain isn't lighting up with excitement over that either—that's reporting, not storytelling. Try again, writer. Find a more original source for your target. What does the building look like? He looks around the room, sees an old football trophy on his shelves, and inspiration strikes! He writes, "Take eight NFL linebackers stacked on each other's shoulders, and add a petite cheerleader on top—that was about the size of the building." Now I'm loving it! I have a fun image in my brain, and not only can I see how tall that building is, but I also get the sense of how sturdy it is, something I didn't get when he wrote that the building was 60 feet tall. My brain is also lighting up because the image is novel—it's an unusual way to describe the height of a building, so it grabs my attention, slowing my reading down as I delight in the image. He could strengthen his verb choice here and instead of writing "add a petite cheerleader on top," he could write "boost a petite cheerleader to the top," and anyone who's seen cheerleading can visualize the act of boosting—and our brains will light up as if we're being boosted ourselves. This metaphor moves us from abstract to concrete using the sense of sight, and delights in its originality.

Let's look at another example, this time adding a metaphor that travels from abstract to concrete through the senses *and* travels across the senses. "She smelled wonderful." Nothing to light our brains up about that—just left-brain abstract words, no right-brain concrete image. Let's add a synesthetic metaphor, and travel from smell to sight. "She smelled like she had rolled in a bed of fabric softener sheets." Here we have a metaphor (a simile, to name the exact kind of metaphor, one that uses the linking word "like") that draws on two sight images—a bed and fabric softener sheets—and the touch image that comes with the texture of a fabric softener sheet.

But let's make it even more specific. Let's call it a king-sized bed, because that gives her much more room to roll and sharpens the sight image, and let's name the scent of the fabric softener sheets, because like every other basic consumer good in this country I live in, there are dozens of derivations, so perhaps lavender fabric softener sheets if I want to suggest femininity, or outdoor fresh fabric softener sheets if I want to suggest she's an active woman, or maybe I just name a brand like Snuggle fabric softener sheets if I want to make her a cuddly teddy bear of a woman—now we've both sharpened the scent image and added some character description. I could even throw in a qualifier like, "She smelled like she had rolled all morning. . ." to suggest just how strong her scent was, and to add to the dimension of time.

"She smelled like she had rolled all morning in a king-sized bed of Downy April Fresh fabric softener sheets." Look how far that metaphor traveled away from its original abstract adjective "wonderful."

The Archetypal Domains of Metaphors

If we want to strike a connection with our readers through our metaphors, it makes sense to draw on sources for our targets that are most universally shared and understood, and thus most resonant. That's why the five senses are so effective as metaphor sources, given that they come from the one thing all readers share with all writers—the body.

Somatic metaphors are popular for that reason. When we want to say what something's like to us, we can say what something's like in our bodies, or what something's like using any number of body-based comparisons. Our language is full of somatic metaphors: we say someone is thin-skinned; they have a hard heart; they have to muscle up to perform a task; they have their fingerprints all over it; they are itching to find out the truth; they strong-armed their competition; they sniffed out the culprit; they barely dipped their toes into the job, etc.

Another common domain we all share is nature. Though the nature we share may be very different (Australians experience Christmas in summer—Christmas songs like "I'm Dreaming of a White Christmas" and "Winter Wonderland" make no sense there), our exposure to other cultures through media, including books, help us understand specific nature metaphors regardless. We're also exposed to nature through our education, so even if we've never held a starfish in our hands or seen a live one with our eyes, most of us know starfish can survive if they have one of their five limbs removed, and thus we understand Gail Caldwell's other fantastic metaphor for grief—"Like a starfish, the heart endures its amputations." This metaphor takes as its source both the body and nature, as well as the senses of sight and touch.

Psychologist Solomon Asch tells us, "When we describe the workings of emotions, ideas, or trends of character, we almost invariably employ terms that also denote properties and processes observable in the world of nature." We come into the world as a body, through a body, and the world we come into is the world of nature. We swim in the sea of the womb. We take a watery ride down a canal and shoot into the atmosphere like a star. As very young beings, we are so fascinated by the sensual world around us that we want to put it all in our mouths, to taste the very dirt of life along with its sweeter offerings. We are all awe and wonder, delighting in the feeling of the blades of grass between our uncalloused toes, or the sound of the crunch of autumn leaves when we squeeze them with our ungraceful small and stubby hands.

Another domain we share in common with our fellow human beings is the world of animals. Some of the first sounds we learn to make are the sounds of animals. As I write this, my 14-month-old grand-niece has only a few clear words in her vocabulary—more, yes, no, Momma, Poppa, her sister's name (not mine yet, unfortunately, but I'm working on it), but she has a host of vocalizations for the sounds animals make. Animal sounds are some of our first sounds, the material our parents quiz us on, our first lessons, our first learned language. *What does the chicken say? Cluck, cluck. What does the cow say? Moo, moo.* Not, *what does the blow dryer say? Whooooosssshhhhhh, whooooosssshhhhhh.* Not, *what does the car ignition say? Beep, beep.*

And animals surround us as children—the ones that are stuffed and sleep in our beds with us, the ones on the front of our onesies, the ones in all our books, the lion kings and the shaggy dogs and the flying elephants that Disney entertains us with. Baby's first trip to the zoo is enchanting, a million photos snapped. Baby's first trip to Walmart, not so much. Animals are the principal players in nursery rhymes—the spider that scares Miss Muffett away, the baa baa black sheep and their wool, those three little kittens who lost their mittens (so careless!) Animals make up the cast of fairy tales—the big bad wolf in the woods, Puss in her boots, the golden goose (oh, those eggs!) Animals are some of the stars of mythology—Pegasus the flying horse, the phoenix rising from the ashes, the Sphinx and her riddle (what a mystery!).

We personify animals, it's true, giving them human traits even though we can never truly inhabit their worlds. But it's just as true that we "animalize" ourselves—we use animal metaphors to describe human states of being. When we're depressed, we want to hibernate like a bear. When we're manic, we're running around like a chicken with its head cut off. We're as loyal as dogs, as fickle as cats, as flighty as birds, as prickly as porcupines and sometimes we stink like a skunk.

It doesn't get any more archetypal than the body, nature, and animals. Our bodies *are* nature, *are* animals. We fart and wind escapes us. We have a fever and we're on fire. We twinkle like stars. We shed our skin cells like a snake. We have soft bellies and often want to hide in shells like a hermit crab. We coo like a dove in the presence of a baby. Because nature and animals are our kin, because we are *akin*, when we evoke nature and animal metaphors, we have the potential to provoke a powerful sympathetic response in our readers, evoking patterns they recognize.

Besides the body, nature, and animals, a few other shared human domains include music, food, home, buildings/structures, politics, common objects (let me *comb* through the details; she *raked* me over the coals). We also share common experiences—growing up, coming of age, aging, education, religion, culture, relationships, and work. We can mine any of these communal rivers for metaphorical gold and trust that the vast majority of our readers will appreciate the nuggets we discover there and place like prospectors on the page.

Metaphors and the Memoirist

Of course, metaphor-making crosses all genres of writing and is a must-have in all writers' toolboxes as another way to make our storytelling more vivid and our ideas more understandable. So why does memoir writer and teacher Maureen Murdock say, "The deepest memoir is full of metaphor"? What in particular about metaphor is useful to the memoirist? What in particular about memoir makes metaphor-making so important?

I want to offer two answers to these questions. The first answer gets to the heart of this book's project—the deepest memoirs are those that forge the deepest connection between memoirists and their readers by evoking archetypal patterns that stir resonance and stoke recognition. Memoirs at their best are intimate looks into the internal lives of their writers, showing us how they think, how they feel, what it's like to be them, what they value, how they experience someone or something, and what meaning they make of it. When we are taken into the inner life of the memoirist, we are engaging and connecting. Not just with our brains, but our hearts.

"I want to know not just *what* you see but also *how* you see, in every line that you call memoir," Beth Kephart writes. But how do we show someone how we see? How do we show someone how we experience? How do we bring someone into the private chambers of our hearts and the enclosed blob of our brains and show them how we feel and think? How do I share my self with you? James Olney articulates my answer: "The self expresses itself by the metaphors it creates and projects, and we know it by those metaphors." Maureen Murdock articulates my answer: "The metaphors we choose in the writing of memoir take us to a deeper level of knowing the self. The self is not an entity already formed, but an awareness in process. The metaphor we use to tease that awareness into consciousness is what makes the narrative interesting." We are "selves becoming," recalling the archetype of transition, and we can use metaphor to show who we have been and who we have become or are becoming as a result of the events and experiences inside our memoir. We can tell people what it's like to be us by showing them through metaphor's images.

Let's look at a few examples. In Gina Frangello's memoir *Blow Your House Down: A Memoir of Family, Feminism, and Treason*, Frangello turns to metaphor to tell us what it's like for her to have committed treason, betraying her husband and breaking up her family.

> This is what it is to have bitten the apple, and to understand for the first time why female desire and knowledge are the most feared and demonized forces in history. This is what it's like to be a destroyer of worlds: that woman, that apple, that serpent, all at once. Even if your Eden was partially imaginary, this is what it's like to watch the dream of it fade forever into the mist and to want to turn back the clock, to want to return, but also to never want to return, to ache to keep running. This is what it's like to have feared your entire life becoming your martyr of a mother, and to instead have become the monster under your children's bed. This is what it's like to choose love.

Frangello stacks her metaphors, her "this is what it's like" to flesh out her experience—betrayal is Eve, the apple, the serpent, all destroying the Garden of Eden. Betrayal is a contradiction—the desire to return to Eden (and the embedded metaphor of turning back the clock), and the desire to keep running away from it toward love. Betrayal is like being a monster under your children's bed, the exact opposite of a protective mother. She draws on multiple archetypal domains—she draws on the senses (the sound of the clock, the taste of an apple), she draws on the body (the ache of running), she draws on animals (the serpent), she draws on nature (the garden of Eden). I understand how fraught betrayal is for Frangello, how complex, how loaded, as she loads on the metaphors. Betrayal is not an abstraction. And although I've never betrayed partner or family like this, I get it. Because Frangello took the time to tell me what it's like for her, I can imagine into what it would be like

for me as well. Frangello's contribution to the human instruction manual–betrayal is the beastiest beast.

In her memoir *An American Childhood*, Annie Dillard uses metaphor to describe something incredibly abstract–how a child comes into
consciousness.

> I woke in bits, like all children, piecemeal over the years. I discov-
> ered myself and the world, and forgot them, and discovered
> them again. I woke at intervals until, by that September when Fa-
> ther went down the river, the intervals of waking tipped the
> scales, and I was more often awake than not. I noticed this pro-
> cess of waking, and predicted with terrifying logic that one of
> these years not far away I would be awake continuously and
> never slip back, and never be free of myself again.

The target of Dillard's metaphor is consciousness, such an elusive
concept, and the source of her metaphor is waking up, a universal experience. She takes her time with the metaphor, using the word "awake"
in its various forms five times in that paragraph. To show how once we
come into consciousness, we can't go back again, she turns to the visual
image of the scale, where piece by piece her consciousness is placed
until it reaches the tipping point, and by the end, we feel that scale
weighed all the way down by adult consciousness, something she fears
she'll never be free of again. There's melancholy in the metaphor, and
as a reader, I think back to my childhood and what was lost in coming
into consciousness–I feel weighed down and I miss my freer self alongside Dillard.

One last example. Beth Kephart wants to take us inside what's usually a very private experience–what it's like to read, specifically to read
memoir–and she uses a couple of different metaphors to do so.

> Reading is equally about exiting and entering, about going away
> and going nowhere. Reading early in the morning is like having
> one more dream, like lolling just a bit longer in the strange,
> sweet gauze of sleep. If I were to draw myself in the morning
> reading, I would draw my head as a cloud–edgeless and capa-
> cious and shape-shifting and unbound, hovering near but never

tethered to the bones and muscles of my body. I read, I am saying, and without moving anywhere I go—into the deep, wild,
sometimes contradicting, mostly illuminating language and
landscape of memoir.

The first metaphors she uses travel from abstract to more concrete
without using any senses. Reading is like exiting and entering, like going
away and going nowhere—she evokes a sense of the body in motion
here. Those metaphors still stay in the realm of telling what it's like, as
does comparing reading to dreaming. But then she gets more concrete,
giving us a verb we can visualize (lolling), a taste image (sweet), and a
touch image (gauzy). She follows that with a visual image of a drawing,
illustrating what her experience of reading looks like. And this metaphor
again connects the writer with her reader as we ask ourselves, does that
image capture my experience of reading too? If not, what might my
drawing look like?

In *Metaphors of the Self*, James Olney writes, "By their metaphors
shall you know them." We know something about Frangello through her
metaphors about betrayal; we know something about Dillard through
her metaphors about consciousness; we know something about
Kephart through her metaphors about reading. Olney continues, "And,
what is more surprising perhaps, by the same metaphors, if they are
used by an artist, shall you know yourselves." Sitting in the school of
their metaphors, I learn something about these writers, and I learn
something about myself.

Let me offer a second answer about why metaphor is so important
to a memoirist. To do so, I want to twist the Olney quote, "By their metaphors, shall you know them" into, "By our metaphors, shall we know
ourselves." Metaphors are not only a way to convey ourselves to our
readers, to make ourselves understandable—before that, they are a way
for us to discover ourselves, to make ourselves understandable to ourselves. In the first answer above, I wrote, "We can tell people what it's
like to be us by showing them through metaphor's images." In this answer, I'm asserting that images can tell us what it's like to be us when we
find the metaphor in them.

Let's unabstract this twisty tie of an idea with two concrete examples.
In the prologue to her memoir *Untamed*, Glennon Doyle opens with a

story that frames the premise of the entire book and gives it its name. On a visit to the zoo with her family, they go to a cheetah run. The cheetah in this case was named Tabitha, and she was born and raised at the zoo with a Labrador named Minnie whose job it was to help tame her. Tabitha, the zookeeper explained, wanted to do everything Minnie did.

With Tabitha watching, Minnie chased a dirty pink bunny on a rope down the expanse of the cheetah run. Then Tabitha was set free to do the same thing, only obviously much faster, and with a nice steak waiting at the end of the run.

Afterward, her zookeeper returned Tabitha to the small fenced field where she began stalking the periphery. Doyle's oldest daughter caught the look on Tabitha's face and whispered, "Mommy. She turned wild again." Then Doyle imagines what Tabitha would say if she could talk. How she feels restless, like something's off in her life, like there's something more beautiful out there. But then Doyle imagines Tabitha looking back at her cage with a sigh, and telling herself, "I should be grateful. I have a good enough life here. It's crazy to long for what doesn't even exist." To which Doyle wants to respond, "Tabitha. You are not crazy. You're a goddamn cheetah."

Then she opens the first chapter of her book with the metaphor she's discovered that helps explain herself to herself. When her now-wife Abby Wambach asks Doyle's parents for their blessing to propose marriage, her mother tells Wambach, "I have not seen my daughter this alive since she was ten years old." This statement sends Doyle into a time of deep reflection on what happened to her at 10, how she lost herself then. She learns that research points to the age of 10 as the time children start to hide themselves in order to become what the world expects of them. That's just what she did, becoming a good girl, becoming small, making herself fit in, and making herself sick and crazy as a result. And then she lands the metaphor. "I understand myself differently now. I was just a caged girl made for wide-open skies. I wasn't crazy. I was a goddamn cheetah."

The discovery of the metaphor—*I am a goddamn cheetah*—gives birth to the book. It gives *Untamed* its name and it gives the book its structure and its arc—an opening section called "Caged," a middle section called "Keys" for unlocking the cage, and a closing section called "Free." And because there are millions of women who can relate to the pattern—woman (cheetah) has been domesticated and forgets her wild and needs someone to remind her she's a goddamn cheetah and how to unlock her cage and set herself free—the book was a runaway bestseller, with over two million copies sold and still selling. Doyle discovered a truth about herself when she turned the image of the cheetah into a metaphor, and that truth set her free. When her book was released into the wild, it came with the promise that it would set its readers free as well.

The second example comes from David Payne who wrote the memoir *Barefoot to Avalon: A Brother's Story* about his relationship with his younger brother who he calls George A. He tells the story of the book's genesis, which began when he heard a voice whisper, 31 years after his brother's death, "It's time to write about George A." The voice gave him the subject of the book, but not the content, the what to write about George A. Then, the first thing that came to Payne's mind was the memory of being 20 years old, his brother 17, and training together every day running four miles. Payne usually finished first, but on this particular day, when he moved into the home stretch, his brother kicked into gear and the race was on. George A. beat him to the finish line. This memory became the first scene Payne wrote.

> It was at least a year and maybe two or three before I realized this was more than just a specific scene about a specific race we ran one summer; it was a metaphor for our whole lives as brothers, a lifelong race we ran that had love and camaraderie and esprit de corps and mutual assistance in it, together with ferocious competition and the will to win. I didn't choose the metaphor or craft those meanings into it; it came to me from some place beyond my conscious awareness and intention with the meanings already baked in. The metaphor, in a sense, knew more about me and about my relationship with my brother than I knew about myself or us, and my job as a writer was to pay attention to it until it revealed its hidden truth. By paying attention, I came to a better understanding of my relationship with my brother, got a through-line for my book, and, eventually, a title.

What Doyle and Payne show us is that we don't just make metaphors to convey our experience and understanding—sometimes we discover the metaphor in our images and memories. John Gardner notes, "The understanding which comes through the discovery of right metaphors can lead the writer to much deeper discoveries, discoveries of the kind made by interpreters of dreams—discoveries, that is, of how one dark metaphor relates to another, giving clues to the landscape of the writer's unconscious." Doyle connects a cheetah with her mother's observation and comes to understand something about the landscape of her unconscious, what she buried in herself at 10 years old. Beyond Payne's conscious awareness, a memory image becomes a metaphor that reveals a hidden truth about his entire relationship with his brother. They didn't go out to find a metaphor—their metaphors found them, and in turn, they found themselves in the metaphor.

This is the power of metaphor—they can help us both discover and convey the patterns in our lives. Metaphors are both consciousness-raising and consciousness-revealing.

Positioning Your Metaphors—Seven Suggestions and One Caveat

For both Doyle and Payne, discovering their metaphors gave them the title of their books and their thematic throughlines—woman as cheetah in need of untaming, brotherhood as a lifelong race. I call this a wraparound metaphor, and it's a powerful strategy to give cohesion to a memoir. I'll say more about that below, but let me build up to it by offering seven suggestions for placing your metaphors, arranging them from simple to more sophisticated.

1. The Single-Word Metaphor

Sometimes all we need is a single word in a single sentence to evoke a comparison.

- He was a bear to live with.
- She was thorny.
- A thundercloud entered the room.

Single-word metaphors work especially well when the writer can assume the reader's familiarity with the source, or trust they'll understand it in the surrounding context. For example, there are many qualities of a bear that the first sentence might allude to, and "a thundercloud entered the room" may refer to a person or to an atmospheric change, depending on context.

2. The Sentence-Length Metaphor

Expanding on the single-word metaphor, we can add in more comparative terms.

- He **lumbered** into his room like a **bear**, and I sensed it would be a long **hibernation** this time.
- Sure, she had **thorns,** but what **rose** doesn't?
- A **thundercloud blew** over the room, her eyes **spilled over** with tears, and I knew we were in for quite a **rainstorm.**

In the first and third examples, note that the verbs lumbered and blew and spilled over are specific to the metaphor itself and add another layer. "He went into his room like a bear" or "A thundercloud entered the room" do nothing to reinforce the metaphor and thus miss a layer of delight.

3. The Paragraph-Length Metaphor

A third way to position a metaphor is to extend it into a full paragraph, to keep playing with it, to keep evoking its power, to let the reader linger for longer in the metaphor's world.

- He **lumbered** into his room like a **bear**, and I sensed it would be a long **hibernation** this time. It hurt me to see him like this, my normally **fierce** and **strong cub**, but he was a **solitary animal** and his room, which I fondly called his **den**, was his **territory**, no mothers allowed, when he was depressed. I'd let him **winter** in there for a while, **luring** him out like I often did with the smell of his favorite food, freshly baked double chocolate chip cookies.

- Sure, she had **thorns**, but what **rose** doesn't? What mattered was this: that she was **lovely to look at.** That her **fragrance** was divine. That her skin was **petal-soft.** Does this make me shallow, that I wanted **to cut her from the bush** that was her family, and **put her in a vase** where only I could admire her?
- A **dark cloud** blew over the room, her eyes **spilled over** with tears, and I knew we were in for quite a **rainstorm**. I tucked under the blanket like an **umbrella**, determined this time to escape the **deluge** of guilt that her crying inevitably provoked in me. *Stay dry, stay dry, stay dry,* I repeated to myself. This **storm** will pass, I reminded myself. Don't increase the **atmospheric pressure** of the room with your **thundering** defensiveness. **Weather the storm**. It will **pass**. It always **passes**.

You have to be a bit careful here or you risk being too clever or clunky, especially if you try to shoe-horn something in that strains the comparison. And, it's memoir, so we have to stick closely to truth. Bears don't eat double-chocolate chip cookies in the wild (unless some unlucky camper leaves them out, and then, what bear could resist?), but if that's your son's favorite food, you can't lure him out with a raw mammal instead.

Mary Oliver has a fun paragraph-length metaphor in the afterword of *Blue Pastures*. "Writing this book has been like bathing the dog—with every go-around it has come out a little cleaner. Still, there's a time when the dog is in danger of becoming too clean, and losing his dogginess altogether. Just so, in similar fear of washing too much away—for I hope some bits of the actual world, chaff and grit, will cling to these pages—I put down the towel and call the book done." Try telling that to your editor when she wants yet another round of edits on your memoir—"I would, but I don't want it to lose its dogginess."

4. The Chapter or Section-Length Metaphor

The fourth way to position metaphors is to keep extending them beyond words or sentences or paragraphs and into entire chapters or sections.

Carmen Maria Machado does this masterfully in her memoir, *In the Dream House*, which chronicles how she got into, and out of, an abusive relationship. The Dream House is her name for the house where she lived with her abusive lover who was quite dreamy for a while, until she became verbally and physically abusive, and then it turned into a nightmare house. Most chapters are quite short and derive their titles and content from literary tropes, and some are metaphors, such as:

- *Dream House as* Shipwreck
- *Dream House as* the Apocalypse
- *Dream House as* the Pool of Tears
- *Dream House as* Newton's Apple
- *Dream House as* Vaccine

Lest we be tempted to read the Dream House as only a metaphor, she has an early chapter called *"Dream House as* Not a Metaphor." But, of course, it is and it isn't. It's a physical house (she tells us she could give us the address if she wanted, and we could drive there in our own car "and sit in front of that Dream House and try to imagine the things that have happened inside. I wouldn't recommend it. But you could.") If she didn't want to evoke the metaphor of the dream (and the nightmare), she could have just called her book *The House*.

In my chapter on structure, I mentioned Joy Harjo's *Crazy Brave*, which is organized into four sections based on the four directions. These directions are meant to be metaphors for the content within each section, though if you reach the end of one section and go back to the direction's description, not everything quite fits, but again, because it's memoir, Harjo can't change the events of her life to match her metaphor, and anyway, a metaphor is a comparison, and belongs to the realm of figurative, not literal, language.

5. The Title Plus Metaphor

Many memoirs contain metaphors in their titles that are explained and expanded upon somewhere in the book—they're in the title plus in the dedication, an epigraph, a prologue, a scene, a chapter, etc. The expansion can be brief, a one-and-done that's not referenced again, making the metaphor run in the background versus in the foreground like the wrap-around metaphor I'll discuss next.

One example comes from Maya Angelou's memoir, *I Know Why the Caged Bird Sings*. The title of the book comes from a line in the poem "Sympathy" by one of Angelou's literary heroes, Paul Laurence Dunbar, though the poem is not used in the book. In fact, the only reference to the metaphor in the title is in the dedication: "The book is dedicated to MY SON, GUY JOHNSON, and all the strong black birds of promise who defy the odds and gods and sing their songs." Still, we hear the metaphor echoing in the background when we read of Angelou's five years of silence after being raped as a child, and all the ways racism and sexism cage Angelou and her community of black birds in the Jim Crow south.

Caroline Knapp's memoir *Drinking: A Love Story* separates the metaphor's target and source in the title with a colon. In her first chapter, "Love," she explains the metaphor. At the height of her alcoholism, drinking was simply "the single most important relationship in my life." She writes, "Yes, this is a love story. It's about passion, sensual pleasure, deep pulls, lust, fears, yearning, hungers. It's about needs so strong they're crippling. It's about saying goodbye to something you can't fathom living without." While drinking wasn't love at first sight—she doesn't even remember when they first met—their relationship went from "general affection and enthusiasm for a lover to outright obsession." After Knapp lays out the central metaphor in that opening chapter, she can move on with telling the story of her addiction and recovery—she doesn't need to keep jackhammering the language of love because she's told us how to read the memoir through that metaphor.

An example of a more extensive rendering of the metaphor in the title comes from Mark Doty's *Firebird*. The inspiration to write his memoir, he tells us, "began with an odd memory—a wonderfully liberating experience of improvisational dance, in 1962, when my fourth-grade teacher in Tucson, Arizona, put Stravinsky's Firebird Suite on our classroom phonograph and said to the class, 'Now children, *move*.' I danced with abandon, without self-consciousness, and my teacher loved it." This story ends up in a chapter called "Firebird" about a quarter of the way into the memoir. Doty dances as the firebird, "swelling, taking form, the real body, triumphant boy, the bird in the fullness of its light, larger, empowered. Isn't it fire itself, the fact of burning, which enables the bird to dance?" The firebird is then referenced three other times in the book, and only briefly, but because of the power of the metaphor, we know Doty sees himself as a phoenix who rose from the ashes of a most difficult childhood through performance and art, something he discusses more fully in his essay about the book and its reception, "Return to Sender: Memory, Betrayal, and Memoir."

These three memoirs offer examples of how metaphors can explain what it's like to be us to our readers. Here's what it was like for me to be raped and trapped in a cage of silence, but eventually sing. Here's what it was like for me to be addicted to alcohol. Here's what it was like for me to both lose and gain myself in performance. Knapp's "Love" chapter is exemplary here—even if we've never struggled with addiction, even if we can't understand it as a patterned behavior, we can understand falling in love, a ubiquitous human experience, and staying in a relationship that no longer serves us—all the stuff that keeps therapists in business.

6. The Wrap-Around Metaphor

Glennon Doyle, David Payne, and Carmen Maria Machado all provide us with examples of what I call a wrap-around metaphor, one which takes its central metaphor as its title, its throughline, and its opening and/or closing. While the "title plus" metaphor may stay primarily in the background, as it does in I Know Why the Caged Bird Sings, or be so well-fleshed out in the beginning that it doesn't need to be revisited, as it does in Drinking: A Love Story, the wrap-around metaphor is in the foreground, inescapable and iterative.

Machado quite obviously uses the Dream House as a throughline, since every chapter is named "Dream House As," and the words "Dream House" occur constantly in the chapters themselves. The Dream House is evoked in the book's first and last chapters—both discuss the house and her time living in it.

In Untamed, Doyle opens with the cheetah story which quickly becomes metaphor, and the throughline runs from sections titled "Caged," "Keys," and "Free." In the book's last chapter, she tells the story of how she and a friend had both stayed in yoga rooms that made them uncomfortable and sick rather than taking care of their bodies. And now she gets it. Now she says she'll never stay "in a room or conversation or relationship or institution that requires me to abandon myself" the way Tabitha had to abandon her wildness and stay caged. If that happens again, she tells us, she'll pick up her mat and walk out. In her final line, she declares her freedom: "Because I have just remembered that the sun is shining, the breeze is cool, and these doors, they're not even locked." She's traveled far on the transformational arc from caged to untamed.

Payne wraps his memoir *Racing to Avalon* around the metaphor he discovered a few years into writing the memoir—the lifelong race between him and his brother. He references the title in Chapter 1, in a scene that will end with his brother's death: "The fundamental image of him I still carried in my heart was of the boy who'd run beside me barefoot to the pier. . . ." He tells us his brother was sick—his bipolar disorder had gotten the better of him, and Payne extends the race metaphor by saying that he found it hard to accept that his little brother "had run as long and hard and far as he was able and was going to and the race was over, there was never going to be another, better chapter." In Chapter 3, he places the literal race I referenced above, the first memory that returned to him when the voice whispered to him, "It's time to write about George A." And in his last words in the epilogue, addressing his brother in whatever world he's entered in death, he writes, "As dark falls, I see you at the border of a world that isn't this world anymore, not on this side, but on the far one, having crossed the finish line before me. Now you raise your hand and go. Go on, little brother, it's time. I'll see you when I get there."

There's something immensely satisfying about the wrap-around metaphor, spotlighting an author clearly in thoughtful control of their craft.

7. The Structure Metaphor

There's a seventh kind of metaphor that isn't necessarily more sophisticated than the wrap-around metaphor, but I place it last because it's different from the others—it doesn't refer to the content of the memoir, but to its structure.

We explored five examples of metaphor as structure in Chapter II, so let me just remind you of them in brief here. Eve Ensler names the controlling metaphor of her cancer memoir *In the Body of the World* as a CAT scan, writing, "Somehow scanning was the only way I could tell this story." For bell hooks in *Bone Black*, it is the metaphor of the hope chest that provides her structure; for Lydia Yuknavitch in *The Chronology of Water*, it is water; for Marilyn Schiwy in *Gypsy Fugue*, it is music; for Elizabeth Gilbert in *Eat, Pray, Love*, it is the 108 beads of the japa mala necklace. In my experience as a memoir teacher, structure is one of the hardest nuts to crack, so grabbing hold of a good metaphor can be a nutcracker par excellence for writers and their readers both.

The Caveat

Though I'm obviously advocating for metaphor-making in your memoir, there is such a thing as too much of a good thing. Let's call this "metaphor oversaturation." This almost invariably happens to my students after I teach metaphor. All of a sudden their writing is flooded with them. This has the effect of water-logging my brain, and it can be exhausting to stay above water and try to keep the shore in mind, the scene or story that the metaphor is there to serve.

See, I'm risking doing just that with my water metaphor above, making that paragraph too soggy. But at least there's consistency—I'm sticking with water. What I notice with my students is that instead of extending the metaphor, they'll lay three or four different metaphors side-by-side in the same paragraph. The effect is image-overload, making my brain fire left and right as I work to understand each target, each source, each pattern, and try to make sense of how they all fit together.

Let's look at an example from Mary Karr's *The Liar's Club*.

In the fields of gator grass, you could see the ghostly outline of oil rigs bucking in slow motion. They always reminded me of rodeo riders, or of some huge servant creatures rising up and bowing down to nothing in particular. In the distance, giant towers rose from each refinery, with flames that turned every night's sky an odd, acid-green color. The first time I saw a glow-in-the-dark rosary, it reminded me of those five-story torches that circled the town at night. Then there were the white oil-storage tanks, miles of them, like the abandoned eggs of some terrible prehistoric insect.

Let me list all the images in that paragraph:

- Fields of gator grass
- Ghostly outline of oil rigs
- Rodeo rider
- Huge servant creatures
- Giant refinery towers
- Flames
- Acid-green sky
- Glow-in-the-dark rosary
- Five-story torches that circle the town
- Miles of white oil-storage tanks
- Abandoned eggs of a prehistoric insect

In addition to the images themselves, there's a dizzying amount of movement in the paragraph. There's bucking, rising up, bowing down, towers rising, sky turning, a town encircled, miles of tanks, so much horizontal and vertical movement. Each time she adds a new metaphor, I have to stop and try to conjure it in my mind's eye. What does a "huge servant creature rising up and bowing down to nothing in particular" look like? How big would the "abandoned eggs of some terrible prehistoric insect" be? What would a prehistoric insect even look like?

Each sentence requires a slow conjuring of the landscape's tableau, and one of two things happens to me when I encounter an oversaturated paragraph or description: either I skim over it and let none of it land, or I read it repeatedly until I can make sense of it. In the former case, I'm impatient, and in the latter, I'm often irritated. I can admire the writer's precision with craft and appreciate each sentence for its images and metaphors. They're good things—they're just too much of a good thing when scrunched all together like that. If I were Mary Karr's teacher for that paragraph, I would have given her an A+ for cleverness, but a much lower grade for execution. If I wanted to be a tad snarky, I might remind her of Michael Chorost's line that metaphor is a place poets go to show off (Mary Karr was a poet long before she wrote memoir).

Craft Tips for Metaphoring

Let's use that caveat as a springboard to dive into talking about craft, now that I have my red pen out. Aristotle thought that metaphor-making was a sign of genius that couldn't be taught, but I disagree with him there (Mary Karr, you're in good company—I just took down Aristotle on the same page—my red pen runneth over). Maybe metaphor-making isn't your go-to craft tool in the box, but everyone with a working brain is capable of seeing patterns. And even if you don't naturally see them, you can go out looking for them, which will be craft tip number one.

Tip #1 – What Is It Like?

When we're trying to evoke a quality of a person, place, or experience for the reader, we can ask the question that leads us to a metaphor—what is it like? What is my mother's smile like? What was our summer cabin like? What was the experience of hearing those words like? Ask, then listen for a comparison to arise. The first comparisons might not be tight enough, so keep asking—the searchlight is now turned on, and you're likely to spot another one soon enough.

When Debra Marquart was writing *The Horizontal World: Growing Up in the Middle of Nowhere*, she was pressed to find a way to honor the land that her family had farmed for generations, to explain to us what that land was like, what it meant to her and the family. She did so in metaphor. "This is Logan County. While it may be just another patch of flat horizon to someone driving through, to the people of my family it's the navel of the earth, the place from which all things flow and to which all things return in time." What was Logan County like? The navel of the earth. The motherland. The place that nourished. The center of the world. So many associations flow from that simple yet elegant metaphor.

Tip #2 – Consider Archetypal Domains

If nothing comes to mind when you play the "What is it like?" game, then try to seed the source for your target in one of the archetypal domains we discussed above: the body, nature, animals, food, home, buildings/structures, common objects, and common experiences like growing up, coming of age, aging, education, politics, religion, culture, relationships, and work.

Debra Marquart found the source (the navel) for her target (Logan County) in the archetypal domain of the body. I don't know her process, but let's use her as an example here. She could have asked herself, if Logan County was an animal, what kind of animal would it be? If Logan County was in school, what kind of student would it be? If Logan County was an object, what would it most resemble? You won't hit pay dirt with each question, but it's a good way to coax out a reluctant metaphor, to give the hermit crab a shell to crawl into.

Tip #3 – Draw on the Senses

In this variation of "What is it like?" we draw upon each of the five senses as the source of our metaphors. What does it look like? What does it feel like? What does it taste like? If my target was an odor, what would it smell like? If my target was a sound, what would we hear?

You can use the same sense for your target and your source, like Mary Karr uses one visual metaphor (terrible abandoned prehistoric insect eggs) to describe her target (white oil-storage tanks). But consider too the synesthetic metaphor, those metaphors that cross senses. If you're trying to describe a sound, what would that sound taste like? If you're trying to describe a scent, what would that scent look like? If Logan County was a song, what would that song sound like? If Logan County was a food, what would it taste like?

Tip #4 – Personify

Personification is the friend who somehow always shows up looking just like you. If you just got your hair cut below your ears, so did she. If you decided to wear all black that day, low and behold, so did she. "We're just alike," she squeals with enthusiasm, as you order your double latte with almond milk. "Oh my gosh, that's exactly what I felt like having today," she exclaims, adding, "Make that two!" "One for me, one for you" is her motto, along with "same same, but sometimes different," though she'd rather focus on the same same. Personification has a knack for accents and impersonations and could have been a vocal coach in Hollywood, if she ever left the Twin Cities. When she was a young girl, her favorite Halloween costume was to dress up as a mirror. When you hurled an insult at her, she was always quick to reply, "I know you are, but what am I?" She never said it to be mean, but to let you know that we're really not so different after all.

Now isn't that definition a lot more fun than saying personification is *the attribution of a personal nature or human characteristics to something nonhuman or the representation of an abstract quality in human form*?

Maybe someday artificial intelligence bots will read and enjoy your memoir, but for now, remember you're writing as a person, to a person. Personhood is something we all share. So use personification to describe something nonhuman. Ask, if Logan County was a person, what kind of person would they be?

And then have fun! How would Logan County dress? What kind of shoes would Logan County wear? What would Logan County's voice sound like? How would Logan County walk? What would make Logan County happy? What would Logan County's first thoughts be upon waking in the morning? What does Logan County value the most? What would Logan County want for Christmas? Not the people in the county, but the county-as-a-person. The people in the county might want a new mayor, but the county-as-a-person might want a day of being pampered at the beauty parlor while a babysitter watches the kids.

You can take any noun you're writing about and turn it into a person. For example, a wedding ring.

The wedding ring nagged me day in and day out. She wagged her finger at me when I even so much as looked at another woman. She squeezed her grip on me when I went out to the bar for drinks with friends after work. She clinked against my scotch glass to get my attention—'Not another one, or you may lose control,' she warned me. She had 360-degree vision, and could spot a threat to my fidelity before it was even on my radar.

Or, a couch.

The couch slumped like an old man in a nursing home, and smelled like it hadn't been changed out of its clothes in months. Its leathery skin was wrinkled and thin, and if it hadn't already been brown, you might have thought you would bruise it just by sitting on it. I wanted to wheel it down the hallway and take it out into the street for a cup of coffee and some fresh air. Instead, I felt its despair, and sunk into it myself.

Personification is a great way to make abstractions (ideas, concepts, values, qualities) more specific and more relatable. One of my favorite little books is *The Book of Qualities* by J. Ruth Gendler. Gendler takes abstractions like integrity, greed, ambivalence, harmony, and clarity and turns them into people. Here are two examples.

Intensity's shirts are burgundy, and deep brown, and indigo. It's easy for him to forget about the paler tones. Sometimes, he seems to live as if the moon were always full; yet, he knows her dark side well. He rarely eats regular meals. He may be celibate for years at a time or spend weeks in bed with his beloved.

Anger sharpens kitchen knives at the local supermarket on the last Wednesday of the month. His face is scarred from adolescent battles. He has never been very popular. As soon as my son hears his footsteps, he is running for shelter underneath the twin bed in the guest room.

Consider casting your abstractions as people as well. If you're writing about someone's love or panic or courage or perseverance, turn it into a character with a few choice details that will help us understand it, while lighting up our brains with the delight of novelty.

Tip #5 – Make a List

Once you light upon a source you think is likely to be productive, it's time to make a list. I imagine Caroline Knapp doing this in *Drinking: A Love Story*. What are all the qualities of love I can think of? What are the common stages of love? What does being in love feel like? How do people commonly leave love affairs? What words are associated with love?

If you're a non-linear person, you could certainly do this as a word cloud, with love in the middle of the page and all your associations branching off from there. But the advantage of a list is that you can create a second column where you make your connections. If Knapp listed obsession as a quality of love in the left-hand column, she could note the equivalent in the right-hand column, how her addiction was obsessive. If she listed divorce in the left column, she could write about how getting sober was like divorcing the great love of her life in the right column.

Working backward from source to target is a great way to make new discoveries and find ways to deepen and broaden the metaphor.

Tip #6 – Don't Be Afraid to Be Contrary

It's perfectly okay, even desirable sometimes, to point out how the metaphor fails, where the pattern does not hold. Knapp does this when she writes that with drinking, it wasn't love at first sight. That allows her to talk about the beginning of her love affair with drinking–how she really doesn't remember how they met–while still staying inside the metaphor's world.

Debra Marquart could have done this with the navel metaphor. If she had made a list of navel associations, she might have considered childbirth, how we were once tethered to our mother through our navels. But this is a temporary state, just nine months of connection to the watery womb-land of our mothers before we are literally cut off. Marquart's family stayed in Logan County for generations–they did not leave the motherland. Exploring where the metaphor fails might prove very fruitful. It raises an interesting (though quite creepy) question–what would our lives be like if we remained connected to our mother's navel?

Is there a parallel there in a family staying on the motherland for generations?

When you make your list, you might discover a quality of your source is contrary to its target. You can include the "it's not like that" along with your "it is like this." In doing so, you may beat your readers to the punch, countering their yea-buts before they even form them.

Tip #7 – Research

Let's imagine that you're writing about a previous boss who made you completely uncomfortable with his lecherous eye. So you ask yourself, "What animal is he like?" and into your head pops the ostrich with its big ole eyes. But what else do you know about ostriches? You start to make a list and get stymied a few qualities in—you realize you know very little about ostriches. Now is the time for research.

You discover a few choice details that are interesting. An ostrich's eye is bigger than its brain—that'll work—your boss wasn't terribly smart. You find out a weird fact that ostriches have three stomachs—is there a comparison there? Maybe your boss eats so much that you suspect he might as well. Or you learn that ostriches can kill humans or other predators with a forward kick of their deceptively powerful legs—maybe you got fired by that same lecherous boss, and it felt like a forward kick out the door and into your future. You find out ostriches are the world's largest birds, but in fact, your boss is rather diminutive. Humm. Maybe you can write, "Unlike the ostrich, the world's largest bird, my boss was small and petty in body and spirit." Naming what something's *not* like gives you another opportunity to say what it *is* like.

Tip #8 – Explain/Educate as Needed

When we use a trite metaphor—an idiom or a cliché—we don't need to explain them to our readers. We can assume they'll understand them. "He was as hard as nails" or "She was as cool as a cucumber" don't need explaining if you grew up in a culture with these sayings (though now that I think about it, why are cucumbers cool? Have you ever taken one right off the vine on a summer day? They're actually quite warm).

But do consider whether your readers will understand your metaphor as is, or if it needs some context, some explaining and educating of said reader.

Joan Didion does this in *Blue Nights*, her grief memoir about the life and death of her daughter. It's also an extended meditation on aging and Didion's difficulties coming to terms with it. It is, indeed, a very blue book.

I understood blue nights as a metaphor the moment I picked up the book, but I thought of it just as blue as in the blues, as in nights when you are down and out. I thought it was a color metaphor, but it turns out it's far more interesting than that. Didion spends the first two pages of her book educating us on what blue nights are, beginning with the first sentence: "In certain latitudes there comes a span of time approaching and following the summer solstice, some weeks in all, when the twilights turn long and blue." After further describing the phenomenon, she ends that opening chapter by explaining:

> This book is called "Blue Nights" because at the time I began it I found my mind turning increasingly to illness, to the end of promise, the dwindling of the days, the inevitability of the fading, the dying of the brightness. Blue nights are the opposite of the dying of brightness, but they are also its warning.

And thus we are warned too—this book will chart the dying of brightness in Didion's life, her inevitable fading.

Metaphors that use cultural or historical references can be delightful—if you are an insider and recognize the reference. If not, they can frustrate or exclude your reader. You'll want to consider whether to stop and explain, or offer contextual clues to a reader on the outside of your metaphor's source.

Take, for example, this metaphor. "Our love was an intricate drawing on an Etch A Sketch that took years to painstakingly create, but in an instant, she took the red frame and shook it and just like that, erased our entire relationship." For readers who know what an Etch A Sketch is, this metaphor is vivid, sure to evoke all sorts of memories and associations. But there will be readers who have never seen an Etch A Sketch. Recognizing this, you have two options. First, you could try to explain it, but how to do so quickly, so you don't lose the momentum of your story? Second, you could leave it alone, knowing the reader can Google it if they're interested.

In this case, there's nothing really lost if a reader doesn't know what an Etch A Sketch is because the point is clear contextually—a relationship was quickly erased. The Etch A Sketch adds a visual metaphor that appeals to the insider without excluding the outsider from understanding your meaning. But if you simply wrote, "She shook our relationship like an Etch A Sketch," the meaning of the metaphor would be lost to the outsider.

Tip #9 – Consult Your Thesaurus

To further hone your metaphors, look for the words associated with your target. A thesaurus is very helpful here, as is an online dictionary that gives you idioms or usage examples. Maybe you're trying to write a metaphor about being angry, but you want a more precise word, or perhaps a word or phrase that gets to something concrete. You look it up and find the associated term "seeing red," itself a metaphor, and find you can make use of that.

You can also just type into a search engine "words associated with x" or visit a website like relatedwords.org. Another good resource is reversedictionary.org, where you can type in a definition and it will give you words. I typed in "I was so angry" and one phrase it gave me was "hopping mad," which is sure to light up the brain more than "I was so angry," since it implicates the body as well as the emotion.

Tip #10 – Extend Your Metaphors

In the revision process, one suggestion I offer my students is to look for metaphors they've already written, and see if they can extend them. Extending a metaphor consists of doing what I've suggested above, except we don't ask "What is it like?" because we already have a metaphor for that. Instead, we ask, "How else is it like that? And how else? And how else?" until we exhaust our imaginations. Then we can turn to the other tips like doing some research and consulting a thesaurus to see what other "how elses" we can generate.

I'm a huge fan of the extended metaphor, and take delight in them when I read them—remember the research that our brains are evolved pattern-makers and recognizers, and we experience pleasure when we encounter them. Extended metaphors allow me to stay in the world the writer has created where A=B, and opens up my imagination as well. I may never have noticed the pattern before, and when a writer extends the metaphor past a word or a sentence, it not only helps to deepen my connection to the metaphor but also to the author of the metaphor, who I kindly thank for taking the time to really craft that comparison.

Again with the caveat, don't overextend the metaphor's welcome!

Tip #11 – Call Back the Metaphor

A call-back is when a writer returns to a previous metaphor or an image— it may be to extend it into a different context, or to deepen it through new associations—and I find these equally delightful. As I mentioned, Mark Doty has an entire chapter devoted to the firebird metaphor, but he calls it back by name three times later in the book, and each one pings a pleasure center, a moment of recognition—"Oh yea, the firebird again!" In one example, he presents a scene where he's giving another performance, this time tap dancing at a school recital, which he is doing "with chemically induced enthusiasm," since he and his mother are high on amphetamines from their diet pills. He's intoxicated by the applause when he finishes, and writes, "My dance feels timeless to me, as if I'm weightless, an astronaut in a space capsule; I can float in the air over the darkened recital hall, over the spotlight in which my body executes, without a hitch, the timed and clattering steps of the dance. This is what becomes of the firebird, drugged and trained: everyone adores him."

The call-back is like the Easter eggs in movies and television, those hidden images that once you spot them, you think, "How clever!" and you feel kindly toward the person who hid it there for you to find. Call-backs aren't hidden, but they're equally clever and will predispose your reader to think kindly of you and appreciate your care with craft.

Aristotle would be proud.

Tip #12 – Replace

Recall the research I mentioned earlier in this chapter that brains don't light up over metaphors if they are clichés or idioms. Briefly, to define and distinguish those two terms, a cliché simply means an overused phrase. like "it was a piece of cake" to mean it was easy. But what does that even mean, it was a piece of cake? Clichés are both meaningless *and* meaningful, meaning we can be taught the meaning to attach to them, even if they're nonsensical.

Clichés can be both literal and figurative. A literal cliché is something like, "Everything happens for a reason." Nothing imagistic or metaphoric in that. A figurative cliché is something like, "It's raining cats and dogs." And this is where an idiom and a cliché overlap. Idioms are figurative clichés. "It's raining cats and dogs" is also an idiom. So is "she had cold feet on her wedding day." These are both clichés and idioms.

If your eyes are glossing over trying to grasp the distinction here between idiom and cliché, no worries. Just categorize them both as overused and unoriginal expressions that have lost their ability to stimulate the brain.

Can you use these in your writing? Of course. Salvador Dalí said, "The first man to compare the cheeks of a young woman to a rose was obviously a poet; the first to repeat it was possibly an idiot," but that's taking it a bit too far. Clichés and idioms are a kind of shorthand, and they can be useful–I've used some of them in this very book. They especially work in dialogue, because people speak in clichés and idiomatic phrases all the time. They can convey something about the person whose mouth you put them in. Maybe you once had the world's most boring coworker. Put clichés in his dialogue, and you'll convey something about his blandness.

But outside of dialogue, when you spot an idiom or cliché in your writing, consider replacing it with something more novel. And if you can't figure out how to replace the entire idiom or cliché, or you're rather attached to it, you can put your creative thumbprint on it and make it more novel. Subvert our expectations and light our brains up with a twist. Take a cliché like "it's raining cats and dogs" and try "it's raining kittens and teacup Yorkies" instead and you might buzz your reader's brain. Take "when life gives you lemons, make lemonade" and twist it into "I learned from my mother that when life gives you lemons, make a lemon drop martini, no doubt a factor in my burgeoning alcoholism" and your reader may smile before they sigh. Take "the writing was on the wall" and extend it to "the writing was on the wall. The problem is, the writing was ancient Egyptian cuneiform, and I had no idea how to decode it," and you've totally owned that idiom.

More than anything, I hope you'll have fun with these 12 tips. Einstein coined the term "combinatory play" for when we take two unrelated things and put them together to create something new. Just as readers find pleasure and delight when they read a novel metaphor, we can find pleasure and delight in writing them, in finding a tight and just right combination, the novel image sources whose pattern matches our target.

Conclusion

In his book *Metaphors of Self*, James Olney writes that the memoirist "who draws out of the flux of events a coherent pattern, or who creates a sufficient metaphor for experience, discovers in the particular, and reveals to us the universal." This is metaphor's superpower, aligning it exactly with the archetypal approach to memoir writing that I'm championing in this book. Let's break it into two parts.

The memoirist discovers in the particular. In *Metaphors We Live By*, George Lakoff and Mark Johnson write that "in self-understanding we are always searching for what unifies our own diverse experiences in order to give coherence to our lives." To do so, "we seek out *personal* metaphors to highlight and make coherent our own pasts, our present activities, and our dreams, hopes, and goals as well. A large part of self-understanding is the search for appropriate personal metaphors that make sense of our lives." This is what memoirists do—they search out those metaphors and key images that make personal and particular sense of their lives.

But metaphors are never only personal and particular to the memoirist because they draw on archetypal patterns that belong to all of us. "Mine" is never just "mine." "Mine" is also "ours," just as "I" is also an "us," a member of the 10-fingered human race. The fingerprint is particular, but the fingers are universal. Thus, **the memoirist reveals to us the**

universal, the finger behind the fingerprint, the pattern in the particular, the "us" in the "me."

The psychologist Thomas Moore wrote, "By being the curator of our images, we care for our souls." In sharing the curation of our metaphors in our memoir, we take our readers into the museums of our personal pasts, pointing out images that say, "This is what it's like to be me." An inclusive memoir, a memoir tuned for archetypal resonance, asks either overtly or invites the question in its subtext, "Is this also what it's like to be you?" And if the answer is no, an archetypal memoir encourages others to curate their own images, prospect and mine their own metaphors, and deepen their self-understanding while doing so, caring for their own souls as we have cared for ours through writing deep memoir.

THE ARCHETYPE OF TRANSFORMATION
The Alchemy Of Memoir Writing And Its Potential For Healing

"Thinking the event is the story is the biggest mistake
of student writers of memoir.
The transformation of the self is the story."

~Claire Dederer, in Theo Pauline Nestor's *Writing is My Drink*

In Chapter I, I made the case that the majority of memoirs are built around the archetype of transition, chronicling some sort of change the memoirist experienced. Transition is a process, I argued, whose end product may be transformation, or not. Let's look more closely at these two words to understand the distinction.

Etymologically, transition is a Latin word meaning "a going across or over." I connected the word "transition" to the word "journey" in Chapter III—journey is an Anglo-French word meaning to "travel from one place to another." Both of these words suggest movement, suggest a change in place, such as the transition from 10th grade to 11th grade, or the journey from California to New York.

But neither a transition nor a journey necessarily requires or inspires transformation. The etymological definition of the Latin word "transform" is "a change in shape, metamorphose." When we look up metamorphose, its definition is "to change into a different form, alter or modify the shape or character of." Therefore, a transformation requires a psychological change, a change in our character, a change in the shape of our soul, we might say. You can transition from 10th to 11th grade without any psychological change, any metamorphosis; you can journey from California to New York without any change in the shape of your character. Bottom line: transitions and journeys can happen without transformation.

Transformation can also happen without any literal transition or journey. I may be laying still as a stone on my sofa reading a book when I come across a passage that lands like an epiphany, setting in motion an earth-shaking psychological metamorphosis. I may be sitting in a movie theater mindlessly tossing back over-salted buttered popcorn when I experience a scene so moving that I know I must make a change in my life. In these examples, a transition may result *from* transformation; a journey may happen *after* transformation, but transitions and journeys are not necessarily precursors *of* transformation.

What are the implications of these distinctions? Yes, we may come to memoir with the desire to write about a transition we went through or a journey we took. For example, we may simply have a great travel story full of riveting adventures that we want to share with our readers. But you already know my bias—the deepest memoirs are those that make meaning through reflection, and the psychologically deepest memoirs will explore not just the transition or journey but the author's transformation, the way the experiences they had fundamentally altered them into the person they are now. Virginia Woolf wrote about the "I then" and the "I now" in memoir writing—the deepest memoirs show the transformational arc from I then to I now.

I turn this belief about the richness of the archetype of transformation into a brainstorming activity with my memoir students. Make a list of events that occurred in your life that changed you, I suggest. The big ones, of course, like deaths and illnesses and accidents; rites of passage like graduations and marriages and becoming a parent; fortuitous experiences like winning the lottery or landing a dream job or meeting the love of your life. The smaller ones too, the ones particular to your life story, like an embarrassing or shameful moment that taught you an important life lesson, or a chance encounter with a stranger that somehow changed your trajectory. Make a list of all events and experiences big and small that changed you, and then write about *how* they changed you, which may be explored in a simple formula: *before "y" happened, I was "x," and after "y" happened, I was "z."* This formula gives you the psychological arc of your story, from "x" to "y" to "z."

Writing about these kind of transformations in our pasts is a way to process them, to metabolize them, and in the language of this chapter, to alchemize them. We become metaphorical cows, so to speak, chewing on our cud—we had the experience once in the past, and we re-experience it in the present through writing about it, allowing us to digest it more fully and extract more nutrients from it.

But there's something else that happens in memoir writing, something that catches many a memoir student of mine unawares. They think they're coming into my course to write about a transformation that occurred in the past, but the process of writing about the past becomes transformative *in the present*. Stated a different way, they move from reporting about the past and how *it changed them then* to discovering that writing about the past *is changing them now*. We have to stir in a new letter to our alphabet soup—writing about how *before "y" happened, I was "x," and after "y" happened, I was "z" is changing me into "a."* This is especially true when we're writing about the tough stuff. Writing about a past trauma offers the potential for healing to occur in the present. Even if we think we come to the writing to report about how we were wounded and how we've healed, we may discover all new levels of healing that occur through the writing process.

In this way, we're not just writing about an alchemical process we've experienced, but we're also experiencing an alchemical process through writing.

Writing as an Alchemical Process

Alchemy is an ancient science where the practitioner attempted to turn base materials like lead into gold. In the metaphor of memoir writing as alchemy, we imagine the base material of lead to be our trauma or our wounds, and through the writing process, we turn that lead into gold, into the healing elixir. We turn our brokenness into wholeness through writing about it. We break what happened to us down by writing it down, and in doing so, we pull ourselves up from the page and put ourselves back together again.

In my field of depth psychology, scholars, most famously C.G. Jung, have been taken with the stages of the alchemical process as a metaphor for the individuation journey, the journey toward wholeness. Different scholars point to a different number of stages or a different number of alchemical processes, but for simplicity's sake, let's narrow them down to the three that encapsulate the heart of the process, and then see how these apply to memoir writing.

The first stage is the *nigredo*, the Latin word for dark. In the words of St. John of the Cross, it's the time of the dark night of the soul, or in the words of Pema Chödrön, it's the time when things fall apart. This is the underworld we discussed in Chapter II, the time of suffering and trauma, of depression and darkness, of emptiness and despair, of confusion and disorientation, of loss and grief. In life, it might come upon you as a sudden trauma such as an unexpected cancer diagnosis, a car accident, or a sexual assault, where you immediately find yourself plunged into the underworld. Or it might creep up on you, such as a series of health challenges that cause your decline, a relationship that worsens over time, or a chronic situation like childhood abuse or neglect.

The second stage is called the *albedo*, the Latin word for light or white. In this stage, the misery of the nigredo lessens its hold on us, and we can begin to see the metaphorical light, by which I mean we develop some consciousness and some clarity—we can see something we couldn't necessarily see in the nigredo when everything is dark and confusing. Imagine in the nigredo that you're at the bottom of a very deep well, your head hung low, your eyes shut, surrounded by absolute darkness, and you're unconscious of any way up from the well. Then imagine that you open your eyes, you lift your head, and you see light pouring down from the top of the well, illuminating a ladder that you can use for your ascent. That's the albedo.

The third stage is the *rubedo*, which is Latin for reddening. The rubedo is the stage when our blood quickens, and we experience a renewal of the life force within—the will to live, the will to climb out of the well up the ladder and into the glorious red-hot sunlight. Psychologically, it's the stage where we are self-actualizing, we're individuating, we're coming to know our highest self and that self's expression. We feel expansive, powerful, and purposeful, and if not healed, then at least more whole.

Before we turn to look at how memoirists experience and describe these three stages, let's look at a poetic rendering of them from "The Alchemy of Writing" by author Leslie Caplan.

> Writing is healing. It allows us to stream out, pour out, fall-on-our-ass-out, stumble our scrawl, or weave into the fibers, our silken fluidity. The page has no agenda. Only to be there for us. To hold us. To support us. To listen to every word we sing, scream, or stutter across it. . . .
>
> And when you do, alchemy happens. Emotions release, then metabolize. And what is revealed is pure and undiluted wisdom flowing from the marrow of bone, into the river of vein, and out the fingertips of your expression.
>
> There is something holy about this. Gritty and holy. Like life. Like humanity. Like a scar that has healed.
>
> And so it is, a lifetime of writing has been, and is, a continual current of discovery. A healed inner child. A woman swimming in the pool of her own cultivated wisdom. I owe this to writing. And to the chamber of ink, oh faithful friend. And to the page that never failed to open wide and say, "Write on me. Give me everything you've got. I can take it."
>
> And it did. It took my rage, my angst, my despair, my trauma, and churned that shit into fertilizer to grow myself whole in. Like a lotus. Growing out of the thickest muck and sludge with petals abounding, stalk strong and solid, and kissing the light of the morning sun every time it rises.
>
> And deep in the roots of that, I found myself. And find myself. Over and over again. Every time I pick up a pen, I no longer write. Instead, I am . . . written.

I love the line, "churned that shit into fertilizer to grow myself whole in." It's another way of saying I turned the lead of my life into gold. And you can hear the alchemical stages in that whole paragraph. The shit of the trauma and the muck and sludge as the nigredo. The stalk rising out of the muck and sledge as the lightening of the albedo. The lotus petals abounding, kissing the light of the morning sun, as the rubedo. Writing is not always that to me, but when it is, it's an undeniable blessing.

Caplan points to the promise of writing: "a healed inner child" and "a woman swimming in the pool of her own cultivated wisdom." The promise of healing a scar. The promise of finding oneself. And in her last line, she arrives at the same destination I'm driving toward here—in writing memoir, we are written, and in most cases, written more whole.

I use the term "more whole" because I want to temper the claim that you can become whole through writing. This stems from my belief that psychological healing is a process, that we are always healing and never completely and categorically healed. So we don't become whole through writing about and through our broken places, but *more whole* or, if you'll allow me two neologisms, *wholer* or *wholerish*.

Louise DeSalvo, who has written the seminal book *Writing as a Way of Healing*, stakes the claim that you can, in fact, write yourself whole. She raises a question that serves as a premise of her book: "What if writing were a simple, significant, yet necessary way to achieve spiritual, emotional, and psychic wholeness?" Yes, it is that, she promises. Imagine if I used that as marketing text for my memoir course—take this course and achieve spiritual, emotional, and psychic wholeness! Oh my. On the upside, there would be a very long waitlist for the course, and on the downside, a lot of very unhappy people at the end of the course. But it is true that the majority of memoir writers I know, especially those writing about wounding and traumatic life experiences, do end up feeling wholer or wholerish as a result of the writing process—they do testify that memoir writing is a powerful vehicle that takes them to surprising places off the map from which they began, and often drops them off closer to the wholeness station than they were before.

But first, it's gonna hurt.

The Nigredo Phase

In order to get the most bang for our alchemical buck, in order to move from still kinda broken to wholerish, we have to enter into the brokenness. Many published memoir writers talk about re-entering the nigredo when writing about the nigredo. They share their process of entering the darkness, being confused and unclear about what they are writing and why they are writing, while re-experiencing loss, grief, and despair. They discuss the emotional toll revisiting these memories takes on them.

David Sheff, author of *Beautiful Boy: A Father's Journey Through His Son's Addiction*, shares, "Writing felt like slitting my wrist with a razor, bloodletting. It was visceral." A.M. Homes, author of *The Mistress's Daughter*, also uses the physical comparison of a self-inflicted wound: "Writing my memoir was unpleasant, like being a doctor examining myself: Does it hurt here? Which part hurts the most? Oops! I made you bleed again. There were many points at which I thought, I don't really want to be doing this. I want to stop." Allison Hedge Coke, author of *Rock, Ghost, Willow, Deer*, shares, "The writing of it, the self-assessing and self-involvement, felt suicidal. Going there was wickedly rough. Each visualization opened doors to sure wounding."

For Kate Bornstein, writing her memoir *A Queer and Pleasant Danger* didn't just cause a metaphorical wound. "I got terribly sick while writing it, all kinds of intestinal stuff—diverticulitis—and they had to take out close to a foot of intestine. You know, it gets you right in your gut, and that's what writing this book was doing, and masochist that I am, I took that as a sign that I was on the right track." Writing her memoir took a toll on her mental health as well. She wasn't eating or sleeping much, and her partner helped her see that writing was triggering Bornstein's borderline personality disorder and suggested she get therapy, which made all the difference.

In *The Right to Write*, Julia Cameron talks about writing as a form of medicine, "a medicine all of us can make and administer to ourselves." But in the nigredo phase, writing is also a form of wounding ourselves, or rather, re-wounding ourselves. And while we might anticipate that writing about past trauma is going to be difficult, we often have no idea exactly how difficult, which is why a number of published memoirists, while they don't outright say they regret writing their memoir, do say if they had it to do over again, they probably wouldn't. Or they wouldn't write another one.

Jesmyn Ward falls into that category. She shares, "Writing *Men We Reaped* broke me in different ways at different spots in the drafting process." The first draft was particularly difficult because she was just getting the memories of the five young men who died in her life onto the page, and the memories were so painful, especially, she notes, "recounting the events when my brother died." In hindsight, "The process of writing the first one was so awful, I don't know if I could do it again." David Sheff, even though he admits that writing his memoir was ultimately healing, said he won't write another one either.

Carmen Maria Machado, who wrote *In the Dream House* about the experience of intimate partner abuse, comes the closest to admitting regret. When asked if she would go back again and write that memoir, her answer was probably not. When asked if it was worth it for her, her answer was the same—probably not. It came at too high a cost for her own mental health, which is ongoing. Since the publication of the book in 2020, the attention it received means that she's constantly speaking about it and answering questions about it, which makes the memory of the abuse "inescapable." She also notes a common experience for my memoir writers when engaging with trauma: "Things are going to get worse before they get better." She made the mistake of stopping therapy when she went away on a retreat to write the book, leading her to "a slow breakdown in the middle of the wilderness." She suggests all memoir writers engaging with trauma either continue or start therapy: "I cannot emphasize enough that you should be thinking about that as one of your lines of defense."

Machado believes it's a common misperception that writing memoir is therapeutic, though she doesn't dismiss that some writers find it to be. Stephanie Foo, who chronicles her healing journey from complex PTSD in *What My Bones Know*, is in her camp. She didn't find writing her memoir either healing or cathartic—it was the therapy she had already done before writing the book that was the most cathartic.

But Machado and Foo are exceptions—most memoir writers dealing with trauma do report that the experience was therapeutic, even if entering into the nigredo was initially re-wounding. Edwidge Danticat said of her memoir *Brother, I'm Dying*, whose major tragedy is the death of her father and her beloved uncle within five months of each other, "Writing that book was therapeutic in a way that writing no other book has ever been for me." Richard Blanco, who wrote about painful and grief-filled times in his life in *The Prince of Los Cocuyos*, says, "Even therapy can't compare to writing a memoir. One memoir is about ten years' worth of therapy." Jesmyn Ward called the process of writing *Brother, I'm Dying* therapeutic, saying, "The therapeutic work I did, writing the memoir, was exactly the kind of work I needed to do," and David Strauss noted that even though he had been in therapy, that he came to understand the impact of accidentally killing a classmate much more deeply as a result of writing *Half a Life*.

The Albedo Stage

In the albedo, the whitening stage of memoir writing, we're standing in the bottom of that dark well and looking up toward the light. We are beginning to understand our past and how it has affected the present in new ways, and we may begin to feel a lightening. It's similar to the process of therapy, only we are the ones aiming the flashlight at ourselves in order to see ourselves more clearly. In the albedo stage, we experience memoir's healing potential through the insight it provides us as we write. And in this stage, many writers speak about the importance of vulnerable and honest introspection.

David Sheff writes of memoir, "It's a powerful form that involved deep and continuous and often painful introspection, copping to stuff that I didn't want to admit to myself, and wrestling with things about myself that I didn't want to acknowledge or accept." And yet, because he was able to do so, he called writing *Beautiful Boy* a healing experience.

Abigail Thomas also speaks of the importance of honesty to a memoir writer. In *A Three Dog Life*, she writes of her husband's car accident and subsequent traumatic brain injury. She comes to realize she can't care for him at home, and she makes the decision to place him in an institution, a decision that leaves her full of guilt. She says, "If you write a memoir, you are bound to discover things that you wish weren't true. These feelings are part of who I am. You really have to be honest and face the parts of yourself you'd might rather not look at. No matter how painful, it was part of my truth." By holding those parts of herself up to the light in the albedo stage, she was able to forgive herself for her decision and the difficult feelings surrounding it.

One side effect of this honest and vulnerable backward glance is that we may see ourselves through more compassionate eyes. Many of my memoir students have told me this—they realized in the albedo just how hard and judgmental they had been on themselves for their decisions in the past. And yet, in writing their stories and having them witnessed by compassionate coursemates, they came to a new compassion for themselves as well. Jerald Walker had the same experience as he wrote his memoir *Street Shadow: A Memoir of Race, Rebellion, and Redemption*, which chronicles his "thug-life" in inner-city Chicago, and the wake-up call that transformed him into a man he could be proud of. He writes, "At some point I stopped seeing the 'I' as me, and I started seeing the 'I' as a character I was writing about. Often, I would feel so bad for the character Jerry in the book as a kid. . . . I felt so bad for the choices I'd made, just seeing them on the page. Many times I brought myself to tears, but I was crying for the character on the page, more than I was crying for me as a person."

It's worth noting that in memoir writing, the stages of alchemy don't always follow a straight line ascent from darkness into light into life-affirming. It's possible to have an insight in the albedo stage that sends you back into the nigredo—back into those tears that Walker references. Jesmyn Ward talks about a moment in writing one chapter when she realized how much her self-loathing and worthlessness were tied up in one particular incident in her childhood, and suddenly everything became very clear. After this moment in the albedo, she slipped right down the well again into the nigredo, writing, "It broke something in me to realize how helpless I was in the face of all that."

It's also possible to be in the nigredo and the albedo simultaneously. Joan Wickersham wrote *The Suicide Index* about her father's suicide and its aftermath. She tells us, "Even though it was incredibly painful, I was feeling this utter excitement. It was joyous. I knew that this writing was expressing what I needed to express." She held both the darkness and the light, as did Marianne Leone when she wrote *Jesse: A Mother's Story*, about the sudden death of her 17-year-old son. In an interview with Leone that Melanie Brooks shares in her book *Writing Hard Stories: Celebrated Memoirists Who Shaped Art From Trauma*, Brooks notes that people like Leone "understand exactly what it's like to tug threads of experience out of the darkness and find some glimmers of light." Leone had to remember all the painful parts of Jesse's life—and there was so much pain—but, she notes, "For me, the majority of the time spent was with good memories too. . . . That sustained me emotionally through some of the really hard parts of doing it." Like so many other people who write grief memoirs, writing about her son kept him close, as she felt his presence in the process of writing the book.

The Rubedo Stage

The rubedo stage is marked by the color red, which the early alchemists equated with what they called "the Philosopher's Stone," a symbol of the completion of the alchemical process. It's also the color of blood, a color associated with childbirth, the completion of the pregnancy process. In the rubedo stage, we give birth to our memoir, and we feel hopeful and positive about the potential of this new life we're offering the world. In Louise DeSalvo's language, the rubedo is the place of wholeness, the state of being healed, the gold standard; in my language, the rubedo is the place of feeling wholer, the feeling that healing has taken place. It is the rare memoirist, such as Carmen Maria Machado, who doesn't feel reborn in the process of birthing their memoir, who doesn't feel the possibilities of new life in the present as a result of completing something from the past.

Louise DeSalvo notes, "Through writing, suffering can be transmuted into art." For many memoirists, it's the alchemical process of turning the traumas of their lives into art that makes time spent in the nigredo worthwhile. Jerald Walker said of his memoir *Street Shadow: A Memoir of Race, Rebellion, and Redemption*:

> The process of having this book come about healed me in a way. I saw that my life had amounted to something that I could be pretty proud of. I had taken these things from my life that I had been so ashamed of [the "thug life"] and crafted them into art. Something important. Something valuable. . . . When the book was finished, I saw that those ten years were probably the most important ten years of my life, because they'd made me who I am and they'd also made me produce something that was ultimately valuable.

Richard Hoffman felt something similar upon finishing his memoir *Half the House*, which in part tells the story of his rape when he was 10 by a coach, the publication of which ultimately led to the man's conviction. "I felt elation," he reports. "I was able to say to myself that I had done something that I thought was extraordinary. I had taken the thing that was the deepest, darkest, foulest thing that was a part of me and turned it into art." Edwidge Danticat says that she had "accomplished something artful" in her memoir *Brother, I'm Dying*. And besides art, she felt she'd created a memorial through her memoir. "I feel like this is the most beautiful memorial I could have created for my uncle and father. They're extraordinary to me, but their lives might not have meant anything to a lot of people. This was a way to honor them. Even as it's published and it's out there and time goes away, it becomes another kind of grief site. A place I can always go."

Jessica Handler expressed the same thing about her experience of completing *Invisible Sisters*, a memoir about the childhood illnesses and ultimate deaths of her only two siblings. "[It felt] stunning. Not because, 'Oh, I wrote a book, I'm going to be famous' because I'm not. But I felt like I had done right by my sisters."

This is a common sentiment expressed by many memoirists who write of loss and grief—the idea of memorializing their loved ones, and for those who died tragically, of somehow righting their lives by writing of their lives. Mark Doty went deep into the nigredo when writing about his lover Wally's death from AIDS in *Heaven's Coast*: "It was like just pushing my way up this very tall, spirally staircase. I'd write and cry and write and cry and write and cry." But, he says, "I also felt exhilarated by its completion. . . . I felt like in that book, I had made something that stands where Wally and I were."

Kim Stafford notes the same thing about his experience of losing his brother to suicide, a story he chronicles in *100 Tricks Every Boy Can Do: How My Brother Disappeared*. Holding his published memoir in his hands for the first time, he had an epiphany.

Looking up at the curb in the shade, as I let the book fall closed in my hands, I realized something essential about my time on earth had changed. I had set down a difficult and awkward burden and could step forth along a new path. There was an opening ahead. The final resolutions of the book had released me. I now had the power to begin something new. . . . In this book, my brother's story is alive. As I stood up from the curb, and put this first copy into my backpack, something in me had grown younger.

All these memoir authors earned the blood of the rubedo with the sweat of the albedo and the tears of the nigredo. From the dark well of the nigredo, they have risen toward the light of the albedo and the sun of the rubedo like the mythological phoenix, itself an ancient alchemical symbol of the process of transformation. They know what Cheryl Strayed knows from her experience writing *Wild*: "The place of true healing is a fierce place. It's a giant place. It's a place of monstrous beauty [the rubedo] and endless dark [the nigredo] and glimmering light [the albedo]. And you have to work really, really, really hard to get there, but you can do it."

The Science Behind the Transformative Power of Writing

Alchemy is a medieval science that shares an archetypal resonance with the memoir writing process, but let's turn now to contemporary science to explore the relationship between writing, transformation, and healing. I've called upon science often in this book to support my assertions, a witness on the stand. I call science forth now because I want to take a stand—on behalf of you and all memoir writers who are writing about difficult experiences, I want to say don't just take my word for it, there is healing on the other side of the suffering you're doing on behalf of your art. Take heart. Keep writing.

In their book *Opening Up By Writing It Down: How Expressive Writing Improves Health and Eases Emotional Pain*, university professors James W. Pennebaker and Joshua M. Smyth summarize years of research and several hundred studies that show the positive effects of "expressive writing." As they define it, "Expressive writing is a technique where people typically write about an upsetting experience for 15 to 20 minutes a day for three or four days." It's certainly not the same thing as memoir writing where you may write for far longer a day, and for far more days, even years, but still, their conclusions are totally applicable to memoir writing, especially writing about traumatic or painful experiences. They summarize the results as follows: "This very simple exercise has been found to improve people's physical and mental health for weeks, months, and even years when compared to individuals who write about emotionally neutral topics (or other comparison groups)."

The research studies mentioned in the book are fascinating, and I highly recommend reading the book—not only do they discuss the studies in the chapters, but they also have 16 pages of references, making a compelling case for the transformative power of writing. I'll just summarize one here. College-age volunteers came to a lab and had what's called a "small punch biopsy," where a small chunk of flesh was removed from their arms (ouch!) Afterward, one group did expressive writing on traumas or emotional upheavals and another wrote about neutral topics. They tracked the healing of the punch wounds of both groups, and get this—the group who wrote about emotional upheavals healed much faster than the group who wrote about neutral topics. After the initial experiment was over, they tracked visitations to the health center over the following six months and found that the students who wrote about upheavals had half as many visits as the students who wrote about neutral subjects. The results of this study and the others in the book seem incredulous, but the sheer volume of them and their replicability are convincing. If this kind of healing is available after writing 15 to 20 minutes a day for three or four days, imagine what's possible for the writer of a full-length memoir who's writing about traumas or emotional upheavals!

In the first chapter of their book, "'Shh . . . It's a Secret': Beginning to Explore the Connection Between Confession and Health," they focus on expressive writing about secrets. They argue:

> Major secrets can be stressful. Like other stressors, keeping secrets from those close to us can affect our health, including our immune function, the action of our heart and vascular systems, and even the biochemical workings of our brain and nervous systems. In short, keeping back thoughts, feelings, and behaviors can place us at risk for both major and minor diseases.

They offer a formula: *a secret plus a confession equals catharsis*. This too follows the alchemical stages–the secret is the nigredo, held in darkness; the confession is the albedo, bringing the secret into the light; and catharsis is the rubedo, the warm sun of transformation and healing.

Now obviously, this can happen in therapy as well, or even in conversations between friends. Writing is just one way of activating this alchemical process. But here's a critical distinction. In Pennebaker and Smyth's writing experiments, they have people write not only about the trauma but also their thoughts and feelings about it 1) when they experienced it in the past, and 2) how they experience it in writing about it now. The critical elements here are *understanding* and *meaning-making*. Just venting about an experience doesn't produce the same results. In fact, they write, "A large number of good scientific studies conclude that the mere expression of emotion is usually not beneficial on its own. Rather, people typically must learn to recognize and identify their emotional reactions to events. Talking (and other forms of expression) is beneficial when it helps people make sense of their experiences." It's the reflection that matters, they argue, and that puts us squarely in the field of memoir writing. If I were to offer a parallel formula, I would say that *story plus reflection equals transformation*.

And this equation, too, is alchemical. Pennebaker and Smyth acknowledge that in their experiments with people writing about trauma, there was usually an increase in feelings of sadness and anxiety after a writing session. "Virtually no one felt excited, on top of the world, or cheerful immediately after writing about the worst experiences of their lives." This insight seems rather obvious–the alchemy apparently doesn't happen in 15 minutes! After writing about the nigredo, their participants were still in the nigredo. But *reflecting* upon the story, *understanding* it better, and *making meaning* from it led them from the nigredo into the albedo and ultimately into the rubedo where transformation occurs.

Pennebaker and Smyth's book explores many benefits of expressive writing, but I want to highlight just two more that are particularly applicable to memoir writing. They share, "The mere acknowledgment that the event occurred can be healing. Just labeling the actions and emotions starts to produce structure, and creates categories and order that makes sense from the writer's perspective." They continue, "Writing forces additional structure on the experience. A timeline is identified and possible causes and effects are explored." In this equation, *story plus organization equals transformation*. It's what Mark Doty bears witness to here:

> I wanted to tell the story of my life in order, once again, to take control of it, to shape some comprehensible element of cause-and-effect, because the instability and complexity of experience means that this sense of pattern is always slipping away from us. Memoir is a way of reclaiming, at least temporarily, the sense of shapeliness in a life.

We grow more whole, Rebecca Solnit writes, "as the fragments are gathered, the patterns found."

As we've discussed before, when we write memoir, we're not simply writing down our already-discovered meanings of the stories we tell, but we're also discovering or uncovering more meaning through the writing process. To quote the novelist Eudora Welty, "As we discover, we remember; remembering, we discover." Especially remembering on the page. Yes, transformation can happen when we are talking to a therapist or a friend, but when we write it down, we really externalize it, storing it in language that can be revisited again and again. We can read and re-read our own pages, versus when we talk (without a recording device) and our language evaporates in the air—we may lose the insight by the time we walk out of our therapist's door.

Pennebaker and Smyth make this exact point. "We can . . . construe the act of writing about a trauma as a method of externalizing a traumatic experience. Once it has been written down or told to another, the memory and value of it have been preserved. . . . With a more understandable or manageable story, there is less need to continue processing it." The equation here? *Story plus externalization equals transformation*.

Transformation's Four Equations

Let's take each of these four equations in turn, and see how our memoirist friends have experienced them.

Secrets Plus Confession Equals Catharsis

Pennebaker and Smyth argue that "when keeping a big secret, we don't translate the event into language. This can prevent us from understanding the event." And if we don't understand an event, we're unlikely to be able to release it, to achieve catharsis. What's more, keeping secrets takes a physiological toll on us—Pennebaker and Smyth share some of that research in their book. Jill Christman knows this from firsthand experience, having chosen to reveal secrets in her memoir, *Darkroom: A Family Exposure*. She writes:

> Because I'm a survivor of sexual abuse . . . I know the danger of a well-kept secret. The secrets of my childhood mutated, dividing and growing into malignant cells of shame and isolation, multiplying until I had the choice to cut them out or be consumed. Writing *Darkroom* was healing for me, and to a lesser degree for my entire family. I'm finished with secrets.

Sue William Silverman has written two memoirs that reveal secrets no one outside of her therapist and husband knew—*Because I Remember Terror, Father, I Remember You* and *Love Sick: One Woman's Journey Through Sexual Addiction*. She shares:

> Through writing, I've divulged that my father sexually molested me, that my mother didn't protect me, that my sister, to protect herself, abandoned her family as much as possible. In addition to childhood secrets, I've confessed adult secrets as well: unhappy marriages, divorces, infidelities, an eating disorder, and a sexual addiction.

Why would she do that? She asks and answers, "Because it's a relief to no longer hide behind a veil of secrets. . . . Now, after writing my secrets, the weight of life feels lighter. I step into the world more honestly. . . . After years of silence, I have a voice." To go from secrets and silence to confession to catharsis shows how writing those two memoirs was an alchemical journey for Silverman.

A difficult journey, for sure. Mark Matousek, in *Writing to Awaken*, shares:

> At first, it may be difficult to admit that your story is constructed from false information. Every life is a patchwork of secrets, half-truths, cover-ups, shames, and disguises. The most authentic among us have hidden compartments, shadowy corners, and contradictions we keep under wraps for fear of destroying our public image.

No one knows this better than Kathryn Harrison, whose public image was forever changed after she revealed the secret of her incestuous relationship with her father when she was a young woman in *The Kiss*. Despite the public shaming and blaming, she, too, found catharsis. She called her confession "a tremendous relief in many ways because my relationship with my father was one that I had kept secret for more than 15 years. That was costly to me. I don't think it is possible to keep such a large portion of your life or your heart secret without erecting a sort of general barrier inside yourself that has to be maintained at psychic cost. It's a relief to have spilled the beans."

Story Plus Reflection Equals Transformation

In arguing for writing down our secrets, Pennebaker and Smyth's research shows that "disclosing or confronting a trauma helps us understand and ultimately assimilate the event." The whole premise of expressive writing is that it's not enough to simply *narrate* the event—the healing power of writing comes through the efforts to *understand* the event. It's not simply telling our story, but the reflection upon our story that catalyzes transformation. As I said, this can be done with a therapist or trusted friend, but there's something about writing our story plus our reflections that's particularly transformative.

Kathryn Harrison shares:

> I have at times seen an analyst, but the work that I have done with a therapist has not been in any way separate from my writing life. It's more true about me to say that I discover who I am, that I

understand myself on the page first, and the therapeutic process can be something that precipitates that or provides some kind of lubricant to that process. But for me, the real exploration of self occurs through writing. It always has.

Serial memoirists Melissa Febos and Abigail Thomas share that experience. Febos says, "Writing has become for me a primary means of digesting and integrating my experiences and thereby reducing the pains of living, or if not, at least making them useful to myself and others. There is no pain in my life that has not been given value by the alchemy of creative attention." In *A Three Dog Life*, Abigail Thomas wrote through the pain of her husband's car accident that led to his traumatic brain injury and the end of her marriage as she knew it. "It wasn't so much a weight off my person, but I think we all need a way to express or make something out of experiences that otherwise have no meaning. . . . I'd made something that meant nothing mean something." She shares, "Writing is the way I try to understand. I'm hoping for clarity."

Elizabeth Gilbert, too, finds understanding and meaning through writing:

> There are certain events, incidents, and experiences in my life that I cannot glean the merit from until I have written about them. So, as it's happening to me, I'm aware that something very interesting and important is going on, but it's not getting into my bones until I sit down and craft it into a story. By the time that story is finished being written, that experience is sewn into the embroidery of my life in a way that it never could have been any other way.

Pennebaker and Smyth note that expressive writing allows us to expand our understanding of the events of our lives and make new connections, just as Gilbert notes. They write, "Multiple perspectives and additional complexities of the experience can be added to the narrative. This can include tying the event to other relevant ones that may have occurred prior, during, or after the experience." Eve Ensler does this in her cancer memoir, *In the Body of the World*. In a chapter called "How'd I Get It?" Ensler lists 50 different questions that point to 50 different ways she might have gotten cancer, adding additional complexities to her story, different causes beyond her childhood exile from her parents. In the list, she ties in relevant events from her childhood, including the hair chemicals her mother used on her and the processed food she ate, and as an adult, other possibly relevant events that occurred prior to her diagnosis, including protesting at nuclear power plants and sleeping in radioactive dust.

Multiple perspectives and additional complexities can also occur as we're writing about significant people besides ourselves. When we see the people in our lives as characters on the page, it can lead us to get curious about them. Why *did* they do that? What motivated them to do this? We may slip into their perspective and see that perhaps the simple story we have been telling ourselves may, in truth, be much more complex, providing us with another opportunity to get wholerish. As Mark Doty writes, "What is healing, but a shift in perspective?" Louise DeSalvo agrees:

> We are the accumulation of the stories we tell ourselves about who we are. So changing our stories . . . can change our personal history, can change us. Through writing, we revisit our past and review and revise it. What we thought happened, what we believed happened to us, shifts and changes as we discover deeper and more complex truths.

This happened to Jesmyn Ward in working with her editor on *Men We Reaped*, a process she found therapeutic. She had written a story in the book about a cellar in the woods she would visit, and her editor encouraged her to dig deeper to understand what that cellar meant to her. In the revision process, she discovered what the cellar embodied:

> It symbolized all the dark things that had happened to me. . . . My ideas about sexuality, gender, romantic relationships—all my nebulous ideas about myself, and who I'd grow up to be, were all tied into that cellar. I didn't realize any of that until I was working on revisions.

She also realized how much she was influenced by her parents' experiences in life, "and what the culture at large thought I was worth. . . . in that moment of revision, suddenly everything became very clear to me." A simple cellar in the woods takes on such complexity, and explains something to Ward about herself, her family, her sexuality, gender, and culture. In digging deeper, she experienced what Carmen Maria Machado experienced—that memoir writing "gives you space to develop context for your experience."

Ward's process of digging deeper into her story and that key image of the cellar illustrates what author Hope Edelman notes.

> I'm reluctant to apply a blanket "healing" label to the process of memoir writing, though, because simply writing down one's story is not what helps an author come to new insights about the self. To achieve that kind of insight requires a level of engagement with the story that goes beyond an episodic accounting of events and involves a willingness to identify, explore, and reconsider some of the long-held beliefs about oneself and one's story.

It's all in the reflection upon events, not just the narration, the core research-proven principle of expressive writing.

Story Plus Organization Equals Transformation

Reflecting on our stories is an important element of the healing process, and as we reflect upon them, we begin to see patterns, to understand causes and effects, as Ward did when she came to understand how much she was affected not just by her parents, but by the culture she grew up in at large. Pennebaker and Smyth write, "Good narratives or stories, then, organize the seemingly infinite faces of overwhelming events." In fact, overwhelming events often shatter our sense of a world that makes sense; traumatic events often tear things asunder. The etymology of the word "coherence" is the "act or state of sticking or cleaving of one thing to another," and this is one effect of expressive writing, according to Pennebaker and Smyth: "Expressive writing pushed people to rearrange their thoughts about their traumatic experiences into more coherent stories."

The prolific author and memoirist Ariel Gore writes:

It's about integrating the enormity of everything. It's about taking the traumatic, disparate moments of life that are scattered around us and sewing them back together into something beautiful that maybe emboldens people who are going through the same thing—which we all are—because the "same thing" is life and it's hard and fucked up and delicious.

In doing the work of integration through organization, we create what Louise DeSalvo calls "a healing narrative," one that "tells a complete, complex, coherent story."

Edwinge Danticat created such a healing narrative in *Brother, I'm Dying*. Having her father and her uncle die at the same time she was pregnant with her first child created "this whirlwind of events and emotions" and writing through it "was the only way I could stay sane." At the end of the first chapter of her memoir, she writes, "This is an attempt at cohesiveness, and at re-creating a few wondrous and terrible months when their lives and mine intersected in startling ways, forcing me to look forward and back at the same time."

After the death of his beloved, Mark Doty wrote his way through his grief as well. At the end, *Heaven's Coast* in hand, he says, "I had done something that was really important to me, which was giving a form to that year." He shares, "It's a very satisfying thing to do to give shape to your story. To concretize it. To have something you can give people and say, 'I made this. This stands for me.' It's a joy." Julia Cameron calls this shaping "a way to move from passive to active. We may still be the victims of circumstance, but by our understanding those circumstances we place events within the ongoing context of our own life, that is, the life we 'own.'" This is my own story, Doty's book says. I was the victim of the circumstances of my beloved's diagnosis and eventual death, but I made something of it through writing. Doty took the scattered pieces of his love and loss and sewed them together into a healing narrative for himself—in the face of overwhelming loss, he organizes his memories into a coherent story and creates a healing narrative for his readers as well.

From her experience writing two memoirs, Sue William Silverman sees how "memoir writing, gathering words onto pieces of paper, helps me shape my life to a manageable size. By discovering plot, arc, theme, and metaphor, I offer my life an organization, a frame, which would be otherwise unseen, unknown." After framing her experience of 14 years of sexual abuse at her father's hands in *Because I Remember Terror, Father, I Remember You*, she says, "It felt really good. . . . I felt relieved. I had found my voice." She had spent 10 years trying to write about the abuse as a novel, and had in fact written six novels she calls "really awful" that also explored incest and abuse in various forms. But it wasn't until she was willing to reveal the secret of being abused by her father and to find a frame within which to tell that story that she found her voice, and found herself with a book "worthy of publication."

Darin Strauss is very clear about the healing power of telling that story in his memoir *Half a Life*. He took the overwhelming event of accidentally killing a high school classmate and he organized it, and in doing so, he understood himself and his own story better. He shares:

> When you write your own story you have to face it in order to make decisions about how you're going to tell it, what to emphasize, what's important. Those things that help us shape the story also help us shape our understanding of the events we're writing about. I found it very advantageous in dealing with them.

Even though David Sheff, author of *Beautiful Boy: A Father's Journey Through His Son's Addiction*, doesn't think he'll write another memoir because it was so difficult, still he found the writing process "revelatory sometimes. It was about trying to make sense of what was chaos in my brain and in our lives."

All these memoirists make it clear—taking a story from chaos to cohesion by organizing and shaping it can be revelatory and lead to transformation.

Story Plus Externalization Equals Transformation

After we've reflected upon our stories and organized them from chaos to coherence, memoir writing carries the promise of getting us unstuck in the past so we can move on with our lives. Sandra Scofield talks about her alchemical process of writing *Occasions of Sin*, a memoir, among other topics, about the loss of her mother as an adolescent. When she first started, she felt "angry, resentful, sad, lonely, confused, frustrated," but she kept writing. Her first draft was "unfocused and ill proportioned." But, she says, "With something down on paper, I could start chipping out of the narrative and building it into something cohesive." Doing so brought her into the albedo: "I could climb out of all the feelings into work." But then, she says, "What I hadn't figured on was the way that processing memory settles it. Mother standing in the window–a flitting, fragmentary, painful but cherished recollection–became a woman on a page, and I stopped 'seeing' her at all. In a very real sense, my book put her on the shelf." This is the rubedo, when we become untethered to our past pain and thus free to move into the present.

In her book on memoir writing, *Shimmering Images*, Lisa Dale Norton writes:

> Stories order the chaos of our lives. But if you do not write those stories, they may remain confused inside your body–a splatter of potent events on the map of your life, bugging the daylights out of you, year after year. If you don't line them up in some pattern (narrative) that offers grace for all involved and then eject that narrative from your body through the physical act of writing it down, you will never be able to get on to other things in your life.

This is what Scofield did–she built her narrative into something cohesive, then ejected the narrative from her body, and with her mother safely tucked into a bookshelf, she's able to move forward with her life.

When Scofield says she stopped seeing her mother in that memory, it echoes Pennebaker and Smyth's research that shows once our trauma stories have been expressed on the page, "There is now less of a reason to rehearse the event actively." Joan Wickersham's experience writing about her father's suicide in *The Suicide Index* bears this out:

> For me, it didn't haunt me in the same way. That desperate need to write about it got quenched. . . . I didn't have to dwell on the gory details in the same way. I wasn't responsible for remembering them anymore in the same way. I can remember my father without always thinking about the way he died, without always feeling it like a punch in the gut.

Through the process of externalization, Wickersham writes, "The obsession burns itself out." Her experience validates what Patricia Hampl shares in *I Could Tell You Stories: Sojourns in the Land of Memory*. "When a writer keeps things inside, it becomes a ball of tangled yarn. As each story is told, the ball becomes untangled. Writing from memory can help us to let go of those stories we tell over and over again. We may not even need to tell them again."

Edwinge Danticat has a message for memoir writers who tackle trauma: "It's doable. It's survivable. It's actually even helpful, because once you have the story wrapped up somewhere, you can dip in anytime. It's like a treasure chest with little pieces you can go in and look at, and step out." The book as the treasure chest holds the trauma, so you can think about it less, knowing it's preserved in there.

The pain never fully goes away, of course. Just because it's held in a treasure chest or on a bookshelf doesn't mean it's still not carried in the heart. Jessica Handler, who wrote about sister-loss in *Invisible Sisters*, shares, "I tell this to my students all the time when I'm teaching trauma writing. It doesn't mean that I don't miss my sisters. It doesn't mean that I don't love them. . . . You don't get rid of the story. Writing the book made the story something that I can integrate. . . . You take it out of yourself and look at it so that you can reintegrate it and move forward."

This echoes Maureen Murdock's assertion that "the fundamental premise of memoir writing is a belief in the restorative power of telling one's truth; once told, the writer can begin to move on with her life." That's been Sue Monk Kidd's experience as well: "When I write about myself, I find release and freedom in the end because I've managed to distill the experience into some sort of meaning that I can integrate into my life, and then move on without all the preoccupation and uncon-scious pull of it. It's the unexamined experience that seems to wreak the most havoc in my day-to-day world."

The Heart in the Art of Memoir Writing

Sue Monk Kidd believes in the transformational power of memoir writ-ing. She tells us, "Writing memoir not only has the ability to reveal me to myself, it also has the power to change me. I suspect writing memoir is partially about the need to bring about wholeness in myself. Maybe I'm trying to resolve something inside, heal a wound, redeem some part of myself that has been orphaned or lost, or give a voice to what has been silenced."

We discussed the importance of showing the reader how you've changed in the chapter on character, discussed how it's one way to evoke feeling in our readers, a heartfelt sense of connection. We read *Heaven's Coast* and we feel for Mark Doty; we feel for his loss, and we feel our own losses, and how powerless we are in the face of death, the biggest of all life changes. We read *Eat, Pray, Love* and we feel for Eliz-abeth Gilbert; we feel how devastated she was when her stale marriage crumbled into pieces, we feel how liberated she became when she al-lowed herself to leave home and become a seeker, and we feel the places in our lives where we are stale too, and wonder how we might change our lives.

Donald Maass writes, "We want to know that in spite of the difficulty we can all change." When we share our healing narratives with others, when we open the doors and windows of our houses of pain and invite readers inside, when we show them the sense we have made of the senseless and how we survived, and hopefully now thrive, we offer them possibilities for their own lives. What a gift our writing then becomes, offered from one heart and opened by another.

Author and memoirist Mark Matousek believes this is the magic of memoir.

> The magic comes from taking the raw materials of life, however confusing, painful, or shapeless, and creating something beau-tiful (and meaningful) to share with others. When you can make

a story out of loss or pain—or any mixed-up experience that comes with being human—there's a kind of redemption that happens. Nothing is wasted if you take time to write it. It's a way of transcending the limits of unexpressed pain. . . . When you tell the truth, your story changes; when your story changes, your life is transformed.

And when you offer that transformation to your readers in the human instruction manual that is your memoir, your work has the potential to transform their lives as well.

That's the magic, the medicine, and the alchemy of memoir writing. That's the heart in the art.

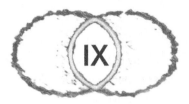

THE ARCHETYPE OF COMMUNITY
On the Value and Virtues of Memoir Writing Groups

I have been teaching memoir writing now for nearly a decade as I write this in 2023, and though I've taken on a few solo consulting clients, I've done the majority of my work in in-person and online communities, in groups ranging from six to 56. My shortest group was three months–most of them begin with nine months, and many continue for years (my longest group so far is at the six-year mark). But before I took this deep dive into memoir, I was always a classroom teacher, beginning back in 1988 as a high school English teacher. All this biography to say, I believe in the power of learning in community.

I believe in the power of community, full-stop. I believe we are social animals (even introverts–they just like their gatherings with fewer animals), and we need each other to thrive physically and psychologically. I won't cite all the research ranging from evolutionary biology to contemporary neuroscience–they all draw the same conclusions–community is archetypal and universal, of evolutionary and neuroscientific benefit, necessary for our health and well-being as individuals. I'm happy that our current surgeon general, Dr. Vivek Murphy, is calling attention to the public health crisis that is loneliness, isolation, and lack of connection. He states, "Our epidemic of loneliness and isolation has been an underappreciated public health crisis that has harmed individual and societal health. Our relationships are a source of healing and well-being hiding in plain sight—one that can help us live healthier, more fulfilled, and more productive lives."

I especially believe in the value of writing memoir in community. I believe the relationships we form with other memoir writers can also be a source of healing and well-being—I believe they can help us live healthier, more fulfilled, and more productive writing lives.

But they have to be the right kind of writing communities. It's just as easy to imagine that the relationships we form in the wrong kind of writing communities can be a source of wounding and psychological disease, and can destroy our writing lives.

Let me clarify what I mean by the "wrong" kind of writing community. I mean a writing community that is unconscious and unmindful. I mean a writing community that is based on hierarchy, where the better writers bludgeon the weaker writers until they leave their bloody pens behind. I mean a writing community that fosters unuseful comparison, envy, jealousy, resentment, embarrassment, righteousness, rigidity, unhealthy self-doubt, competitiveness, and fear.

You may work well in those kinds of communities. Some writers like to be whipped into shape, flogged into improvement, pummeled into progress. Some writers thrive on competition, on having someone to outpace. Some writers like knowing their place on the food chain, and reinforcing it by eating lesser writer-fish.

If you're not that kind of writer, stick around. I've got some ideas for you.

Why Join a Writing Group?

People join writing groups or take courses or degree programs for all kinds of reasons. Anne Lamott lists several in *Bird By Bird: Some Instructions on Writing and Life*.

- We want to learn to write better
- We want feedback
- We want encouragement
- We want to be in the company of other writers
- We want to hear how others craft their stories

- We want "benevolent pressure," which is another way of saying we want accountability

And yes, all of these reasons apply to the subset of writers called memoirists, but I want to take it deeper because memoirists *go* deeper. Memoirists spelunk into the caves of the past. Memoirists go down wells into the nigredo. Memoirists, if writing to heal, are both patient and doctor, both client and therapist. Memoirists are time-travelers in the uncertain terrain of memory. Memoirists open the closets of their past and risk what may jump out of there. Memoirists face criticisms of navel-gazing, self-indulgence, narcissism, sadomasochism, and the selfish betrayal of others. Memoirists face self-doubt, particularly of the "Who am I?" and "Who gives two shits about my story?" kind. Not to mention the competitiveness of the market, which means there's no guarantee that all your years of spelunking are going to result in a published book that anyone finds in today's glutted market where over three million books are published *each year*.

It's hard out there for a memoir writer. We need to huddle up.

The Archetype of the Critic

Most writers' groups and formal writing programs like MFAs operate under one main archetype: the archetype of the critic. There might be other benefits you get from the group, including accountability, but their main reason for existence is critique, defined by the Online Etymology Dictionary as a "critical examination or review of the merits of something." Though participants may be encouraged to share what's working in any given piece, it's assumed that you're going to get feedback on what's not working with the intention that such feedback will help you improve the piece. That's the meaning of "constructive feedback"—feedback that will help you construct something better than what you brought to the group. And while I think critique is necessary for a writer, I think the wrong kind of critique at the wrong time in the writing process can be destructive for a writer, even devastating.

This is especially true for the memoir writer, for two main reasons. First, your memoir is not something you made up. It's more than a story you imagined—*it's your life*—and all the messy choices that all of our lives contain. For a fiction writer, a critique of your pages may feel like a critique of your imagination or your craft skills, but for the memoir writer, a critique of your pages can feel like a critique of your life–why you acted the way you acted, why you felt what you felt, why you made the decisions you made.

I know some writing teachers advocate for calling the writer "the narrator" when they are giving feedback, as in, "The narrator's choice doesn't make sense here," but that's just a clever linguistic trick that does little to disguise the fact that someone just told you that a choice you made in your life didn't make sense. If someone is telling you that "the narrator" is harsh on her father or judgmental about her mother, it's hard not to feel an assault on your character.

Even if a writing teacher tells us to offer feedback just about the writing, not about the writer, it's often quite impossible for sensitive souls to feel the difference. If someone tells you the scene where you describe a date rape reads emotionally flat, it's hard not to hear that something is wrong with your emotional response to the rape. (This is part of the reason so many memoir writers turn to fiction for its protective layer of distance.)

The second reason the archetype of the critic is such a harsh one for memoir writers pertains to our subject matter. I don't know the statistics on this (or even if such statistics exist), but most of us who write memoir are writing about difficult times in our lives–painful events we've gone through, tragedies we've suffered, challenges we've faced, journeys through the underworld we've made. In one of my memoir groups, I have students writing about the following: the suicide of a beloved father; a mass shooting in the workplace; the end of a long-term relationship; the death of a husband; a cancer diagnosis; a mother with Alzheimer's; being expelled from the Church because of homosexuality; rape; a long-term incestuous relationship with a parent; the list goes on. I don't think I'm especially a tragedy magnet as a memoir teacher–I just think that when it comes to writing the human instruction manual, we need more instructions on how to survive life's challenges than on how to survive its joys. Our topics are vulnerable, which means we are vulnerable, and there's nothing like judgment to make our vulnerable selves curl up into a protective ball and roll away from writing altogether.

None of this may apply to memoir writers with "easier" topics. The occasional writers who come to me to tell humorous stories, fun family anecdotes, or light challenge memoirs (ala, the year I ate at all 66 Bob's Big Boy restaurants across the United States) seem to have an easier time of it. None of this may apply to memoir writers with thicker skins, like one of my students who told me he wanted me to kick his ass hard like the toughest football coach and spare him no criticism. But for most memoir writers, particularly those in the early stages of writing, the archetype of the critic is counterproductive.

Putting the Writer in the Driver's Seat

One problem with the critic is we never really know what they're going to strike, so it's hard to be prepared. This is especially true when a critique group is run via gag order, as many of them are, where the members of the group critique our pages as we're forced to sit quietly and listen without response. When we give someone our pages with a carte blanche invitation to critique them like that, it's like we move into the backseat of our own car, a child who should be seen and not heard, while our group acts like parents in the front seat, discussing our bad behavior as if we aren't there (and hopefully occasionally praising our good).

I was once in a screenwriting critique group that ran just like this. I had to turn in the first 10 pages of my screenplay without a word of explanation or context, and without any request for the kinds of feedback I might find useful at that stage. My screenplay was a comedy where a life-long lesbian suddenly finds herself attracted to men, something that had recently happened to me, so it was memoir-adjacent. I sat silently at a table while the cis-group obsessively and aggressively used the entirety of my critique time to tear down the premise of my story, dismissing it as something that could never happen. This was not useful because I knew it could happen and, in fact, was happening—I wanted to hear more about the comedic timing, the snappiness of the dialogue, any characters they thought might need more fleshing out. After the thrashing was over, I was allowed to say something brief in response (as is often the case in such gag-order groups). All I could say was, well, it did happen to me. They looked at me quizzically, like dogs cocking their heads when they hear something they don't quite understand, then moved on to the next writer.

So. Not. Useful.

My suggestion to combat this kind of car crash is to put the writer in the front seat, steering the feedback in a direction that they deem useful to them. When my writers turn in pages, they ask for specific feedback, usually between three to five questions they have or areas where they want us to focus our attention. But before they even do that, I have them provide any brief context for the pages (something that is often not allowed in writer's groups). They might turn in pages from the middle of a chapter or out of chronological order, and they want to tell us this. This allows them to beat us to the punch, making it unnecessary for us to say, "I feel like I was dropped into the middle of a scene and I don't know what's going on," which can read like a critique unless the writer tells us that's exactly what she's doing, and why.

After the context (if necessary), they ask their questions. I encourage them not to ask yes/no questions like, "Is the dialogue realistic?" or "Does this scene drag on too much?" but instead more specific questions that drive us into the text, like, "I'm really working on realistic dialogue. Please point out any lines that you think might be improved" or "I'm working on pacing in this scene, so could you show me any sentences you think might be removed to speed it along?" Knowing the writer's specific intentions is useful for the feedback giver, but it's also useful for the writer, reminding them that writing is an intentional craft, and making them more conscious of their choices.

I also allow my students to ask for areas of no feedback. I encourage them to let us know if they feel vulnerable about something and would prefer us not to comment on it. Perhaps they are really sensitive about a specific person in the piece—they may say something like, "In the part about my husband, I'm not ready for feedback quite yet." Maybe they know there's an area of weakness in the writing, and they might say something like, "I know I need to do more work with setting the scene, so there's no need to comment on that yet." This frees up the perfectionists in the group who might not turn in pages otherwise but feel inoculated against critique for their self-acknowledged "still drafty" areas. It also reminds all of us that our pages are always works-in-progress, and more work needs to be done—and a self-aware writer knows this.

No Teachers, No Therapists

Just as I tell my students they aren't in the archetypal role of the critic in my courses, they're also not in the archetypal roles of teacher or therapist. They don't use feedback to correct someone's grammar or teach them how to punctuate dialogue or point out their use of passive voice. There's a time and a place for that, but it's not in the early drafting stages, and that's a good job for an editor or editing software. No "red penning" is allowed in my courses—it can shut writers down and make them far too self-conscious at the wrong stage of the writing process, plus it creates a hierarchical relationship between peers when one takes on the role of a teacher.

Feedback is also not the place to step into the role of a therapist. Writing is not therapy, though it is therapeutic, and feedback is certainly not therapy, though it can be therapeutic as well. No commenting on someone's story, "I think you should see a somatic therapist. Sounds like your job is making you sick" or, "Maybe you could read about the five love languages because I think it would really help you understand your partner better." It's a writing group, and we're there to engage with the words on the page, not tinker with the psyche of the writer.

Of course, friendships do form in writing groups, and there have been times when one writer has noticed another writer is great at editing and really enjoys it, so they make an agreement between themselves to exchange pages offline with editing in mind. Similarly, a friendship might form where writers grab coffee together or chat on Zoom and they do share therapeutic suggestions or listen to each other's problems and comment on them. This is fine. It's just important to maintain boundaries inside the classroom container. Writing communities work best when everyone understands the agreements and is accountable for abiding by them.

One Teacher, One Therapist

Do writing groups need a teacher to lead them? Not always. Leaderless groups can form and govern by consensus, setting up their own rules, agreeing to accountability parameters.

But the problem with a leaderless group is the ole "nature abhors a vacuum" saying—in the absence of leadership, a group often falls into chaos or slowly slides into sloppiness regarding their own agreements, and someone steps in to enforce the rules and agreements. Opportunities for resentment can arise, and people may split off and grouse about one another. The most well-intentioned group can lose steam as energy wanes and members leave due to disappointment or frustration. If no one steps into leadership, the group is likely to dissolve as well.

For this reason, I see the value in having a teacher lead the group, and if the teacher is a therapist or has a therapeutic background, all the better, because memoir writing is certainly psychoactive! A teacher with therapeutic sensibilities can define the values the group will operate within (something I'll discuss next), make sure those values are upheld, and help mediate or resolve conflict between members of the group. A teacher with therapeutic sensibilities can set the tone for the group, and hold members responsible if they violate the group's values or tone. Knowing that there's a trusted teacher leading the group allows for group members to focus on the task at hand—writing their memoir, and supporting others to do the same—instead of worrying about group dynamics and reigning in errant members.

I'm sure it's my bias as a lifelong teacher, but I do believe delivering content to the group is useful as well. Obviously, the more we study the genre, the more nuanced writers we become, and the more time we spend reading exemplary memoirs, the more we absorb their lessons and work them into our writing. That's why in my writing groups, we have monthly "Memoir of the Month" Zooms where I pick a memoir that's a particularly good match with the content I'm delivering that month and I lead a discussion about it.

The good news is there's no shortage of memoir teachers out there, though that means the onus is on you to do your due diligence and make a careful and thoughtful selection. I hope the rest of this chapter provides you with some food for thought in choosing your chef. Allow me to throw out a few ingredients like the archetypal values and archetypal roles I've come to believe through experience serve up the most successful and satisfying memoir writing group experiences.

The Archetypal Value of Curiosity

While curiosity may have killed the cat, it can really invigorate a memoir writer. When someone leans into our story and becomes curious enough to ask questions about it, it can be a meaningful experience, even a healing one. So in addition to having the feedbacker answer the questions of the writer, I also suggest they ask their own questions about places where they find themselves curious.

I encourage my students to name those places where questions come up for them as a reader, or places where they'd like to know more. This often catalyzes the writer's process of discovery. Memoir writer and teacher Peter Gibb acknowledges the discovery aspect of writing. "Memoir writing, for me, is about discovery. I now understand my life in a way that I never did before. Sure, I knew the facts of my life, or at least the ones I could remember. But even though I'd had lots of therapy and thought of myself as an introspective, self-aware person, I had only a cursory understanding of my story."

Of course, we don't need a writing group in order to make discoveries about our lives. That will happen naturally enough just in the process of writing our memoir, as we've discussed in this book already. But time and time again, I've seen questions open writers up to discoveries they may not have made on their own.

I've been inspired to emphasize the value of questions by a Quaker process called a "clearness committee." In this small group process, one person brings a problem or a dilemma to the group that they would like to get clear on. After listening to the focus person describe their issue, the committee only has one job—to ask open, honest questions. That's it. Just pose open, honest questions.

The philosophy that undergirds this is that we all have an inner teacher or wisdom figure within. The questions are meant to activate that inner figure, to help the focus person come into more consciousness. So too, asking questions of a writer allows the writer to come to more clarity about their story, to see what they might be missing. Even a simple question like, "I'm curious about your dad's relationship with his father, and how that might play into his response here" may open an avenue of inquiry, and has the potential to lead to seismic discoveries that may shift the plates of how you understand your father and portray him on the page.

The questions I encourage my students to ask tend to fall into the following categories:

- ○ **Plot questions:** Often we're unaware of leaps we're making, of places where our reader might need some bridging information.
  Examples:
    - • I'm curious, what happened in between your husband's diagnosis and that call with his mother?
    - • I'm wondering, did your teacher ever apologize for that comment?
    - • This has me question, how close was your ex-boyfriend to your parents?

- ○ **Timeline questions**: In our heads, we're probably clear on the timeline, so we often fail to provide specific time markers to our readers.
  Examples:
    - • I wonder, how long did it take for you to broach that conversation?
    - • How much older you were when you had that realization?
    - • Here, I'm curious—how early in your marriage did you first feel that doubt?

- ○ **Emotional response questions**: I call these the "wait wait wait" questions. If we were sitting across from each other at a café and you were telling me this story, I might touch your hand and say, "Wait wait wait, how did you feel when he said that?"
  Examples:
    - • Here, do you think she was trying to anger you or was she just insensitive?
    - • In this scene, I'm curious, how did your father react?
    - • Before you move on, can you give us a sense of how that statement landed in your body?

- o **Reflection questions**: These questions get to the meaning we make of our experiences. While emotional response questions get to feelings, reflection questions get to thoughts.
    Examples:
    - I'm wondering, did you think forgiveness was possible here?
    - How did his suggestion dovetail with your hopes for your marriage?
    - If the priest had acted differently, do you think you'd still have lost your faith?

- o **"Say more" questions**: These questions act as encouragement for a writer to expand on a plot point, add backstory, or further a description or scene. They are some of my favorite questions because they show the writer what's interesting about their story, the places where we want to lean in and know more.
    Examples:
    - Can you give us some more examples of microaggressions at your job?
    - Was this your first health challenge, or were there others in the past?
    - Was there anything in his behavior up to this point that was a red flag?

Sometimes I don't ask direct questions if I feel like they may be too intrusive, but I'll just reflect my curiosity in a statement like, "I find myself curious here about x."

I believe the value of such curiosity cannot be overstated. Not only have I seen writers make amazing connections and discoveries through good questions and knowing what makes a reader curious, but I've also seen them come alive through the attention that curiosity offers and the encouragement of having a reader engage with their stories.

The Archetypal Value of Appreciation

In her book *Memoir as Medicine*, memoir teacher Nancy Slonim Aronie shares the one and only rule she has for participants in her Writing from the Heart workshops—"When someone finishes reading, *tell her what you loved.*" It's quite the opposite of what we've come to expect in writing groups, and I understand the point—if we show a writer her strengths, she'll continue to get stronger. While I still stand by my "ask and answer" model of feedback, I do encourage readers to offer their appreciation for what works in the piece, because, well, who doesn't value appreciation?

Here are some suggestions for areas we might shine some light and love on:

- A particularly strong word choice
- An evocative sentence
- Character details that are especially effective
- Stand-out metaphors
- Powerful imagery
- Rich description
- Places that are emotionally stirring ("I smiled here" or "This made me laugh out loud" or "I felt myself getting teary-eyed here" or "My shoulders are tensing up just reading this")
- Meaningful reflections

The playwright Thornton Wilder once wrote, "We can only be said to be alive in those moments when our hearts are conscious of our treasures." Telling a writer what we appreciate about their work, and showing them where their treasures lie, can help them come alive and encourage them to continue writing, despite its difficulties and challenges. In a quote attributed to Margaret Cousins, she says, "Appreciation can make a day, even change a life. Your willingness to put it all into words is all that is necessary."

The Archetypal Values of Safety and Vulnerability

In psychologist Abraham Maslow's famous hierarchy of needs, he counts safety and security as two basic human needs, only above the physiological needs for food, water, shelter, etc. Why is safety so critical? Because we're vulnerable as human beings to each other physically and psychologically. The Oxford English Dictionary definition of vulnerability is just that: "the quality or state of being exposed to the possibility of being attacked or harmed, either physically or emotionally."

Safety is particularly critical to a memoir writer. Like any artist, putting your work out in the world makes you vulnerable to the judgments of others. But as I've noted, when the work you are putting out in the world is *your life*, you're especially vulnerable.

And yet readers come to memoir, consciously or not, expecting vulnerability. They may call it authenticity instead—they want the memoirist to keep it real—but being authentic means being vulnerable, since vulnerability comes with the human condition.

We are most vulnerable when we are sharing stories about which we feel shame or guilt. In her book *Writing is My Drink*, Theo Pauline Nestor notes:

> These moments of shame that even the boldest memoirist can dread revealing are the very ones that memoir readers come to the page hungry for, not necessarily because they want to know every sordid detail of our lives, but because memoir readers crave the reader/author intimacy that occurs when we selectively share those moments which most of us wish to hide. Memoir readers, perhaps more than those of any other genre, seek authenticity. . . .

In order to be authentic and vulnerable, memoir writers need a safe container to trial-run their stories, to beta-test their ability to share their work. Sharing writing, *any writing*, can be vulnerable. Even if your story is not a difficult one to tell, writing is always difficult (of course, only writers know this—everyone else thinks it's easy, which is why the author Thomas Mann said, "A writer is a person for whom writing is more difficult than it is for other people"). I have a motto for my memoir courses—they are "a safe place to do dangerous work."

Safety is tantamount for memoir writers who are writing about difficult material. Memoir teachers Brooke Warner and Linda Joy Myers share, "We've encountered three s's that waylay writers on the way to writing their truths: secrets, silence, and shame." So let's add another "s"—the only antidote to these waylayers is safety. A memoir writing group needs to be a safe place to share secrets, to break silence, and to counteract shame. In AA, there's the saying that we're only as sick as our secrets, and if we want to be in a writing group that doesn't make us sick, then it's critical that we aren't silenced and shamed when we share our secrets. Warner and Myers continue: "Exposing one's full self is an exercise in extreme vulnerability, and even writers who come to the page with a take-no-prisoners attitude, who feel ready to risk everything for the truth and their art, encounter shame." The metaphor of exposing oneself is a good one. If you imagine yourself standing naked in the center of a room with a bunch of critics slinging arrows—well, enough said.

The Archetypal Values of Courage, Compassion, and Connection

"The deepest memories are stored in the heart, not the brain," Peter Gibb writes. Apply this metaphor to memoir writing—when we share our memoir pages, we share our hearts. This is how we connect with our readers. This is how we broaden our memoir's appeal. And I want us to come to that sharing with our whole hearts—to write from the heart, to write with heart, and to share our writing in ways that hearten us, not dishearten us, as premature critique can do (what Linda Joy Myers calls "critique trauma").

Here I find Brené Brown's definition of wholehearted living to be helpful. People who live wholeheartedly, she writes, cultivate the values of courage, compassion, and connection. Courage itself comes from the Latin word *cor*, meaning heart. Memoirists need to have brave hearts to muster the courage to write and to share that writing. When they know they're writing for an initial audience defined by their compassion—which etymologically means "to suffer with another" and a "feeling of sorrow or deep tenderness for one who is suffering"—courage comes easier, and writers become en-couraged to share even more deeply.

With courage and compassion in place, connection follows. Brown writes, "I define *connection* as *the energy that exists between people when they feel seen, heard, and valued; when they can give and receive without judgment; and when they derive sustenance and strength from the relationship.*" I believe this is why so many successful memoir writing groups stay together for years—when we feel witnessed with compassion by our peers, we feel connected to them and want to stay connected to them. I believe this is why so many memoirists mention their writing group members in the acknowledgments section of their published work—they derived sustenance and strength from their connection, and lord knows we need both sustenance and strength to sustain a writing project that can last years.

In *Writing the Memoir*, Judith Barrington worries that compassion "can invite critiquers to drop their standards when the story involves surviving great hardship . . . a critiquer's sympathy may well get in the way of honest feedback." Of course this can happen, but with guardrails put in place, such as offer honest answers to the questions posed by the writer, offer appreciation and praise, and lean into curiosity, I trust the humanity of the human beings in my courses to deliver useful feedback with kindness and care.

One way I suggest doing this is to distinguish between the story the writer is telling on the page and the way the story is written on the page. I will often lead with compassion for the writer. "I'm so sorry this happened to you," or "This story breaks my heart," or "How resilient you are to have survived this experience," and then, in a new paragraph, I'll pivot to the writing with a sentence like, "Now, let me turn to your pages," or "Now, let me address your questions." First and foremost, I'm a human being with a bleeding heart who is deeply touched by the stories I have the privilege to read; only second am I a teacher.

The Archetypal Roles of the Companion and the Witness

I argued earlier against the archetypal roles of the critic (too soon in the process), the teacher, and the therapist. The two most valuable roles I suggest memoir writing groups embrace, and the ones I lead with in my classes, are the companion and the witness.

Etymologically, the word "companion" is created from *com*—with, and *pane*, bread. A companion is someone you share bread with—or in our case as memoir writers, someone you share stories with. A companion is someone you travel with for a time, someone who accompanies you on a journey. And that's what we do for each other. We companion each other as we take this journey into the past, in order to create something in the present to offer to our readers in the future.

I like this definition of the companion archetype as defined by Stacy Couch.

> A companion is someone who travels through life with another person sharing his or her ups and downs. A companionship is a partnership, a pairing of two people with one supporting the dreams and motivations of the other. With a true companionship, there is no concern about who is first and who is second. Each person trusts that they have equal but different merit, power, intelligence, and creativity.

Sharing ups and downs? Check. Lots of ups and downs in memoir writing. Supporting the dreams and motivations of the other? Check. I have my students share their motivations for writing, and everyone shares the same ultimate dream—to be published, or to leave behind a completed story for their family and/or friends. Who is first and who is second? Check. We're all peers with our own writing gifts and challenges.

In *Writing As a Way of Healing*, Louise DeSalvo says, "When we share our writing, someone else knows what we've been through. Someone else cares. Someone else has heard our voice. Someone else understands. We learn that we are no longer alone and that we no longer need to be alone." This parallels what Arthur W. Frank writes in his book *The Wounded Storyteller*: "Suffering needs stories: to tell one's own story, a person needs others' stories. We were all, I realized, wounded storytellers."

This is what happens inside of the archetype of the companion in a memoir group—we realize we are part of a tribe, the tribe of wounded storytellers. And as he writes, "The wounded storyteller, ending silences, speaking truths, creating communities, becomes the wounded healer." Having our wounds witnessed, having companions on our journey toward wholeness, that in itself is healing. Rachel Naomi Remen writes, "My wound evokes your healer. Your wound evokes my healer. My wound enables me to find you with your wound where you have the illusion of having become lost." It's hard to get totally lost when you have a tribe of writing companions traveling with you, reaching out with compassion and encouraging you on.

For this reason, I have to disagree with Judith Barrington's decree that writers in groups do not "tell stories from your own experience that the work in question reminds you of (this is not about you)." Now on the one hand, I get it. We don't want to hijack someone's story by one-upping the story ("If you think your divorce was bad, wait until you hear about mine"), or using all our feedback time for the writer to tell our own story.

But on the other hand, sharing our stories in an appropriate time and place can make a writer feel less alone, knowing that others have traveled this path before, or have struggled with the same issues or asked the same questions. Sharing our stories makes us connected as a tribe, and, of course, in an archetypal approach to memoir writing, we remember that there's something universal in every individual story, so hearing from others about how they resonate or relate to what we've written only helps us better understand the universal thread in our own story.

So unlike Barrington, I suggest that in addition to answering all the writer's questions and asking questions of the writer, in addition to voicing appreciation for what's working well in the pages, the person giving feedback can, if they feel comfortable, tell the writer where they resonate with or relate to the story, using phrases or sentence-starters like, "This scene reminds me of a similar one I had with my son—so hard," or "I have reacted just like that in your situation," or "I remember a teacher who made me feel the same way." We share our stories with our companions, not to override or one-up them, but in the spirit of "Yes, me too, and though my story is different, I can really relate." And we follow that up with, "Tell me more about your story," being careful not to suggest that because we have our own similar story, we're not interested in hearing theirs. We're careful not to collapse our similar stories, thinking that theirs will follow the same trajectory as ours, and we stay attuned to the details of their particular story.

I once had a group of three students, two women and one man, who followed each other's work as companions for three years. In the beginning, there was little to suggest that they'd find common connections in their stories, but as time unfolded, they began to share their "me toos" until the connections reached the level of the uncanny. When they came to the end of their time together, one woman wrote to the others, "The mutual sharing of this space . . . that we were truly journeying together, supporting each other as we evolved, this was beyond the beyond of what I imagined I would experience in this container." She had done years of therapy across multiple modalities, but found this process of companioning each other to be just as powerful as anything she had done in therapy, particularly because it wasn't one-sided. This is why I have a problem with writer's groups and workshops where the writer is gagged, where the critic's voice is prioritized, and where no sharing of common stories is allowed (all these appear in Barrington's advice on writing groups in her book, *Writing the Memoir*).

This group had formed a beautiful connection as a tribe of wounded storytellers. Brené Brown states that connection is the energy between people *when they feel seen, heard, and valued*. In saying his goodbyes to the group, the man wrote, "You have a knack for seeing the invisible connections in my sometimes convoluted narratives that make me feel so seen!" This is the role of the archetypal witness—a person or a group who sees you, who hears you, and who values you.

This doesn't mean someone has to value your writing abilities, which is what the critic is there to judge. What it means instead is that they value you as a human being, and value your right to tell your story, and as you tell it, they assure you that you are seen and you are heard. Memoirist Eanlai Cronin writes, "There are things nudging against the skin of the storyteller, begging to be told." The witness is the one who hears and holds those skin-tight stories, who leans in with curiosity before you have to beg and says, "Tell me more."

In *Writing For Your Life*, Deanna Metzger notes, "When we've finished writing, we may not be aware of what we've written. That is why we need an audience, an interested and compassionate listener, one who reflects back to us, without judgment, the value of recording our lives." Louise DeSalvo also advocates for the role of compassionate listeners and witnesses, especially when we're writing about sites of woundedness. "Sharing with empathetic witnesses our work about the shocks we've survived is, for me, an essential part of the process of using writing as a way of healing. Writing our story and keeping it locked away where no one can read it repeats the lethal pattern of silencing and tyranny and shame that so often accompanies trauma."

Caroline Myss, the author of several books and a robust website on archetypes, writes, "The Witness role—indeed, the Witness archetype—is among the most powerful archetypes in the cosmos. We require the role of the witness in order to heal. We need our injuries and wounds to be witnessed by others. We need others to witness that we have been violated. Without the Witness, we cannot truly, fully heal." But even if we're not writing about our injuries and wounds, the witness is still someone who sees our story and sees its value. Even if we're writing the humorous memoir, we need a witness who can "see the funny in it" and reflect that back to us.

In every group I've taught, when people bring their wholeheartedness, and when they stand firmly in the archetypes of the witness and the companion, healing happens. So does love. We fall in love with our companions; we fall in love with those who see us and show us our value. We feel love from them and we feel love for them. This quote from Dani Shapiro on writing groups is on my syllabus for my second-year course:

This love is a strange alchemy of mutual recognition. We are, each one of us, wrestling with words, with our futile stabs at some kind of human eloquence. We are solitary by nature but we have chosen to come together because the page benefits from the eyes of others. Because we are unable to see our own work clearly. Because we have developed connections and metaphors that are unknowable to us until someone else switches the lights on. We come to the workshop table—even the most defensive and cynical among us—in an act of faith. *See me*, we are saying. *See beneath my words to the truer words that rush in a river beneath. Plunge your hands into this river. Show me what I have done.*

It's on the syllabus for the second-year course because no one would quite believe this magic at the beginning of the process. The vulnerability, tenderness, love, safety, companionship, witnessing—they have to be experienced to be believed. But by the second year when I hand this to my students, they get it. "Yep, this is what we've been up to," they affirm.

I like Shapiro's line, "Show me what I have done." This is the value of a witness, to show us what's on the page that we perhaps haven't even seen, or to show us what's not on the page that they would like to see. Often we come into memoir writing with our ideas fixed, pinned like a butterfly in a box. The right question, the astute observation, can remove the pin from the butterfly and allow it to fly.

I've seen time and time again my students shift their opinions about people in their lives—mostly for better, sometimes for worse. A student will come in with pages about her difficult mother to whom she is giving loads of compassion on the page. Someone raises the question, "Did you ever get angry with her?" The student steps back. Why isn't she angrier with her mother? She realizes that to survive her home life, she couldn't get angry. She was punished for expressing anger, and she learned to repress it, which is what she's still doing now.

Or the opposite happens—someone is writing about all the difficulties in their relationship with their mother, all the ways they were wronged. Their companions witness this, and one asks gently, "I wonder if you had good times with your mom sometimes too," and the butterfly is suddenly unpinned and memories begin to flutter. My students will often say something like, "The mother I came into this course with is different than my mother now." (The bad news for a writer—this means more revisions!)

The Wholehearted Writer

In Brené Brown's TED Talk "The Power of Vulnerability," she discusses three aspects of wholehearted living: love, belonging, and vulnerability. Writing groups, when done well, can cultivate all three. She writes, "We cultivate love when we allow our most vulnerable and powerful selves to be deeply seen and known, and when we honor the spiritual connection that grows from that offering with trust, respect, kindness and affection." (I could have written about the archetypal values of trust, respect, kindness, and affection in this chapter. I could have added any number of heart-values that make us better human beings. Bring all of those things to your writing groups as well.)

Writing groups offer a contrast to the image of the solitary writer alone at her desk, cat on her lap or dog at her feet, but essentially still alone. She is writing for invisible, future readers who may not read her work for a decade, if she's lucky enough to get published. Writing groups are a tonic to literary exile, the writer banished from the company of others, alone with his words. In *The Truth of Memoir*, Kerry Cohen writes, *"Exile is the most human of experiences. All human beings ache to be less alone, to be connected to others, and writers aim to do so through their work."*

In *Bird by Bird*, Anne Lamott offers a sweet anecdote that speaks to the opposite of exile—belonging. She shares the story of a group of four writers who met in her writing class and have continued to meet without her for four years. She runs into them occasionally, and sometimes they come to her writing classes. She writes, "They end up giving the new students rousing people talks about how great it is to be part of a writing group, how much they've come to care for one another, how it helps them get their work done. They've gone from being four tense, slightly conceited, lonely people who wanted to write to one of those weird little families we fashion out of whoever's around us." They have become a tribe of wounded storytellers, because aren't we all wounded?

Lamott continues, "They're very tender with each other. They all look a lot less slick and cool than they did when they were in my class, because helping each other has made their hearts bigger." Only one of them has been published at all during those four years, and it was just one article, Lamott tells us, "But you know what? They love each other. They still look forward to their meetings after all these years. They are better writers and better people because of their work with each other."

Love. Belonging. Vulnerability. Safety. Compassion. This is the promise of a thoughtfully considered and well-designed memoir writing group. We become not only better writers but better people because of our time spent companioning each other. Our hearts open, we experience meaningful connections, and we can't help but fall in love with each other—and fall a little more in love with ourselves through the soft gaze of compassionate witnesses.

EPILOGUE

Once upon a time, before we got so lonely and isolated, we were tribal people, deeply connected to each other.

I've read of tribes that gathered together around a fire in the morning upon waking. If someone had a dream, they were invited to share it, because it was assumed that although the dream came through one member of the tribe, it was for the whole tribe. There was no "my dream" or "your dream," there was only "our dream." Dreams were the human instruction manual, providing wisdom for all.

You holding this book in your hands, you have a dream. Your dream is your story, the one you have come to the fire to share with us because you know there's something in it for us, there's something in it that's our story too.

You have wisdom to share. You deserve a page in the human instruction manual.

Write it. Write your page. Write the deepest, most beautiful story you can. Write your heart onto every page, so when readers pick up your book, they'll lift it to their ear like a shell because they can hear the blood rushing through it.

Own it. Own it all, and give it all away.

My dream for this book—may it serve your dream.

May it serve our dream.

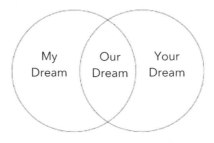

SUGGESTED READING

Memoirs Mentioned in This Book

Adiele, Faith. (2004). *Meeting Faith: The Forest Journals of a Black Buddhist Nun.*

Adiele, Faith. (2013). *The Nigerian-Nordic Girl's Guide to Lady Problems.*

Albom, Mitch. (2002). *Tuesdays with Morrie: An Old Man, a Young Man, and Life's Greatest Lesson (25th-Anniversary* Edition).

Alexander, Elizabeth. (2016). *The Light of the World: A Memoir.*

Alexie, Sherman. (2019). *You Don't Have to Say You Love Me: A Memoir.*

Allison, Dorothy. (1995). *Two or Three Things I Know For Sure.*

Anderson, Carol E. (2017). *You Can't Buy Love Like That: Growing Up Gay in the Sixties.*

Barnes, Cinelle. (2018). *Monsoon Mansion: A Memoir.*

Bauby, Jean-Dominique. (1998). *The Diving Bell and the Butterfly: A Memoir of Life in Death.*

Beah, Ismael. (2008). *A Long Way Gone: Memoirs of a Boy Soldier.*

Bechtel, Allison. (2007). *Fun Home: A Family Tragicomic.*

Bernstein, Harry. (2009). *The Dream: A Memoir.*

Black, Dustin Lance. (2019). *Mama's Boy: A Memoir.*

Blanco, Richard. (2015). *The Prince of Los Cocuyos: A Miami Childhood.*

Blunt, Judy. (2003). *Breaking Clean.*

Bornstein, Kate. (2013). *A Queer and Pleasant Danger: A Memoir*

Boylan, Jennifer Finney. (2013). *She's Not There: A Life in Two Genders.*

Branan, Karen. (2017). *The Family Tree: A Lynching in Georgia, a Legacy of Secrets, and My Search for the Truth.*

Broome, Brian. (2021). *Punch Me Up to the Gods: A Memoir.*

Burroughs, Augusten. (2013). *Dry: A Memoir (10th-Anniversary Edition)*

Caldwell, Gayle. (2011). *Let's Take the Long Way Home: A Memoir of Friendship.*

Carr, David. (2009). *The Night of the Gun.*

Christensen, Kate. (2013). *Blue Plate Special: An Autobiography of My Appetites.*

Christensen, Kate. (2016). *How to Cook a Moose: A Culinary Memoir.*

Christman, Jill. (2011). *Darkroom: A Family Exposure.*

Coke, Allison Hedge. (2004). *Rock, Ghost, Willow, Deer: A Story of Survival.*

Cook, Peggy. (2021). *Released: Walking From Blame and Shame Into Wholeness.*

Crooks, Cori. (2008). *Sweet Charlotte's Seventh Mistake.*

Danticat, Edwidge. (2008). *Brother, I'm Dying.*

Davis, Viola. (2023). *Finding Me.*

De Rossi, Portia. (2011). *Unbearable Lightness: A Memoir of Loss and Gain.*

Delbridge, Melissa J. (2010). *Family Bible.*

Didion, Joan. (2007). *The Year of Magical Thinking.*

Doty, Mark. (2000). *Firebird: A Memoir.*

Doty, Mark. (1996). *Heaven's Coast: A Memoir.*

Doyle, Glennon. (2013). *Carry On, Warrior: The Power of Embracing Your Messy, Beautiful Life.*

Doyle, Glennon. (2017). *Love Warrior: A Memoir.*

Doyle, Glennon. (2020). *Untamed.*

Eisenberg, Ophira. (2013). *Screw Everyone: Sleeping My Way to Monogamy.*

Ensler, Eve. (2014). *In the Body of the World: A Memoir of Cancer and Connection.*

Febos, Melissa. (2018). *Abandon Me: Memoirs.*

Febos, Melissa. (2022). *Girlhood.*

Febos, Melissa. (2011). *Whip Smart: The True Story of a Secret Life.*

Ferris, Amy, and Dexter, Hollye (Editors). (2012). *Dancing at the Shame Prom: Sharing the Stories That Keep Us Small.*

Foo, Stephanie. (2023). *What My Bones Know: A Memoir of Healing From Complex Trauma.*

Ford, Ashley C. (2022). *Somebody's Daughter: A Memoir.*

Frangello, Gina. (2022). *Blow Your House Down: A Story of Family, Feminism, and Treason.*

Frey, James. (2005). *A Million Little Pieces.*

Gardner, Rita M. (2014). *The Coconut Latitudes: Secrets, Storms, and Survival in the Caribbean.*

Gay, Roxane. (2017). *Hunger: A Memoir of (My) Body.*

Gilbert, Elizabeth. (2011). *Committed: A Love Story.*

Gilbert, Elizabeth. (2007). *Eat, Pray, Love: One Woman's Search for Everything Across Italy, India and Indonesia (10th-Anniversary Edition).*

Greenberg, Michael. (2018). *Hurry Down Sunshine: A Father's Memoir of Love and Madness.*

Hampl, Patricia. (2000). *I Could Tell You Stories: Sojourns in the Land of Memory.*

Handler, Jessica. (2020). *Invisible Sisters: A Memoir.*

Harjo, Joy. (2013). *Crazy Brave: A Memoir.*

Harrison, Kathryn. (2011). *The Kiss: A Memoir.*

Hoffman, Richard. (2018). *Half the House (20th-Anniversary Edition).*

Homes, A.M. (2008). *The Mistress's Daughter: A Memoir.*

hooks, bell. (1997). *Bone Black: Memories of Childhood.*

Hsu, Hua. (2023). *Stay True: A Memoir.*

Jacob, Mira. (2020). *Good Talk: A Memoir in Conversation.*

Jacques, Juliet. (2016). *Trans: A Memoir.*

Jamison, Leslie. (2019). *The Recovering: Intoxication and Its Aftermath.*

Jung, C.G. (1963). *Memories, Dreams, Reflections.*

Kalanithi, Paul. (2016). *When Breath Becomes Air.*

Karr, Mary. (2005). *The Liar's Club: A Memoir.*

Karr, Mary. (2010). *Lit: A Memoir.*

Keaton, Diane. (2012). *Then, Again.*

Kephart, Beth. (2000). *Into the Tangle of Friendship: A Memoir of the Things That Matter.*

Kidd, Sue Monk. (2016). *The Dance of the Dissident Daughter: A Woman's Journey From Christian Tradition to the Sacred Feminine (20th-Anniversary Edition).*

Knapp, Caroline. (1997). *Drinking: A Love Story.*

Kobabe, Maia. (2019). *Gender Queer: A Memoir.*

Krans, Kim. (2020). *Blossoms and Bones: Drawing a Life Back Together.*

Lawson, Jenny. (2017). *Furiously Happy: A Funny Book About Horrible Things.*

Lawson, Jenny. (2013). *Let's Pretend This Never Happened: A Mostly True Memoir.*

Laymon, Kiese. (2019). *Heavy: An American Memoir.*

Leleux, Robert. (2009). *The Memoirs of a Beautiful Boy.*

Leone, Marianne. (2011). *Jessie: A Mother's Story.*

Leve, Ariel. (2016). *An Abbreviated Life: A Memoir.*

Lopate, Phillip. (2003). *Getting Personal: Selected Essays.*

Macer, Jemela. (2023). *Between Two Worlds: An Armenian-American Woman's Journey Home.*

Machado, Carmen Maria. (2020). *The Dream House: A Memoir.*

Mann, Sally. (2016). *Still Life: A Memoir With Photographs.*

Marquart, Debra. (2007). *The Horizontal World: Growing Up in the Middle of Nowhere.*

McCourt, Frank. (1996). *Angela's Ashes: A Memoir.*

McGuire, Meg. (2017). *Blinded by Hope: One Mother's Journey Through Her Son's Bipolar Illness and Addiction.*

Metz, Julie. (2009). *Perfection: A Memoir of Betrayal and Renewal.*

Miller, Channel. (2019). *Know My Name: A Memoir.*

Moaveni, Azadeh. (2006). *Lipstick Jihad: A Memoir of Growing Up Iranian in America and American in Iran.*

Montgomery, Sy. (2018). *How to Be a Good Creature: A Memoir in Thirteen Animals.*

Myers, Linda Joy. (2017). *Song of the Plains: A Memoir of Family, Secrets, and Silence.*

Nelson, Maggie. (2016). *The Argonauts.*

Nestor, Theo Pauline. (2009). *How To Sleep Alone in a King-Size Bed: A Memoir of Starting Over.*

Nestor, Theo Pauline. (2013). *Writing is My Drink: A Writer's Story of Finding Her Voice (and a Guide to How You Can Too).*

Norris, Mary. (1989). *Nothing to Declare: Memoirs of a Woman Traveling Alone.*

O'Farrell, Maggie. (2018). *I Am, I Am, I Am: Seventeen Brushes with Death.*

Orr, Gregory. (2019). *The Blessing: A Memoir.*

Page, Elliot. (2023). *Pageboy: A Memoir.*

Payne, David. (2015). *Barefoot to Avalon: A Brother's Story.*

Pincus, Marsha Rosenzweig. (2022). *Holding Up the Moon: A Memoir in Haiku.*

Plank, Ronit. (2021). *When She Comes Back: A Memoir.*

Plante, David. (2009). *The Pure Lover: A Memoir of Grief.*

Rankin, Lissa. (2015). *The Anatomy of a Calling: A Doctor's Journey From the Head to the Heart and a Prescription for Finding Your Life's Purpose.*

Reichl, Ruth. (2010). *Tender at the Bone: Growing Up at the Table.*

Reynolds, Debbie. (2013). *Unsinkable: A Memoir.*

Rizzuto, Rahna Reiko. (2010). *Hiroshima in the Morning.*

Schiwy, Marilyn. (2018). *Gypsy Fugue: An Archetypal Memoir.*

Schulz, Kathryn. (2022). *Lost & Found: A Memoir.*

Scofield, Sandra. (2004). *Occasions of Sin: A Memoir.*

Sellers, Heather. (2011). *You Don't Look Like Anyone I Know: A True Story of Family, Face Blindness, and Forgiveness.*

Shah, Sejal. (2020). *This is One Way to Dance: Essays.*

Shapiro, Dani. (2017). *Hourglass: Time, Memory, Marriage.*

Shapiro, Dani. (2020). *Inheritance: A Memoir of Genealogy, Paternity, and Love.*

Shapiro, Maya. (2007). *Four Sublets: Becoming a Poet in New York.*

Sheff, David. (2009). *Beautiful Boy: A Father's Journey Through His Son's Addiction.*

Sheff, Nic. (2009). *Tweaked: Growing Up on Methamphetamines.*

Silverman, Sue William. (1999). *Because I Remember Terror, Father, I Remember You.*

Silverman, Sue William. (2008). *Love Sick: One Woman's Journey Through Sexual Addiction.*

Solis, Octavio. (2018). *Retablos: Stories From a Life Lived Along the Border.*

Stafford, Kim. (2012). *100 Tricks Every Boy Can Do: A Memoir.*

Steinberg, Michael. (2003). *Still Pitching: A Memoir.*

Strauss, Darin. (2011). *Half a Life: A Memoir.*

Strayed, Cheryl. (2013). *Wild: From Lost to Found on the Pacific Crest Trail.*

Taylor, Jill Bolte. (2009). *My Stroke of Genius: A Brain Scientist's Personal Journey.*

Thomas, Abigail. (2001). *Safekeeping: Some True Stories From a Life.*

Thomas, Abigail. (2007). *A Three Dog Life: A Memoir.*

Thomas, Abigail. (2016). *What Comes Next and How to Like It: A Memoir.*

Trethewey, Natasha. (2020). *Memoir Drive: A Daughter's Memoir.*

Troost, J. Maarten. (2006). *Getting Stoned with Savages: A Trip Through the Islands of Fiji and Vanuatu.*

Trout. Nick. (2009). *Tell Me Where It Hurts: A Day of Humor, Healing, and Hope in My Life as an Animal Surgeon.*

Vance, J.D. (2018). *Hillbilly Elegy: A Memoir of a Family and Culture in Crisis.*

Walker, Jerald. (2010). *Street Shadow: A Memoir of Race, Rebellion, and Redemption*

Ward, Jesmyn. (2014). *Men We've Reaped.*

Westover, Tara. (2022). *Uneducated: A Memoir.*

Wickersham, Joan. (2009). *The Suicide Index: Putting My Father's Death in Order.*

Winn, Rebecca. (2020). *One Hundred Daffodils: Finding Beauty, Grace, and Meaning When Things Fall Apart.*

Wolff, Tobias. (2019). *This Boy's Life (30th-Anniversary Edition).*

Yuknavitch, Lidia. (2011). *The Chronology of Water: A Memoir.*

Zailckas, Koren. (2005). *Smashed: Story of a Drunken Girlhood.*

Zauner, Michelle. (2021). *Crying in H-Mart: A Memoir.*

Memoir and Writing Craft Books

Aronie, Nancy Slonim. (2022). *Memoir as Medicine: The Healing Power of Writing Your Messy, Imperfect, Unruly (but Gorgeously Yours) Life Story.*

Barrington, Judith. (2002). *Writing the Memoir: From Truth to Art.*

Birkerts, Sven. (2007). *The Art of Time in Memoir: Then, Again.*

Brooks, Melanie. (2017). *Writing Hard Stories: Celebrated Memoirists Who Shaped Art From Trauma.*

Cameron, Julia. (1998). *The Right to Write: An Invitation and Initiation Into the Writing Life.*

Cohen, Kerry. (2014). *The Truth of Memoir: How to Write About Yourself and Others With Honesty, Emotion, and Integrity.*

Faulkner, Grant. (2023). *The Art of Brevity: Crafting the Very Short Story.*

Goldberg, Natalie. (2009). *Old Friend From Far Away: The Practice of Writing Memoir.*

Karr, Mary. (2016). *The Art of Memoir.*

Kephart, Beth. (2013). *Handling the Truth: On the Writing of Memoir.*

Lamott, Anne. (1995). *Bird by Bird: On Writing and Life.*

Larson, Thomas. (2017). *The Memoir and the Memoirist: Reading and Writing Personal Narrative.*

Maran, Meredith. (2016). *Why We Write About Ourselves: Twenty Memoirists On Why They Expose Themselves (and Others) in the Name of Literature.*

McAdams, Dan P. (1993). *The Stories We Live By: Personal Myths and the Making of the Self.*

Metzger, Deena. (1992). *Writing For Your Life: Discovering the Story of Your Life's Journey.*

Mark Matousek. (2107). *Writing to Awaken: A Journey of Truth, Transformation, and Self-Discovery.*

Murdock, Maureen. (2003). *Unreliable Truth: On Memoir and Memory.*

Nestor, Theo Pauline. (2013). *Writing is My Drink: A Writer's Story of Finding Her Voice (and a Guide to How You Can Too).*

Norton, Lisa Dale. (2008). *Shimmering Images: A Handy Little Guide to Writing Memoir.*

Root, Robert. (2008). *The Nonfictionist's Guide: On Reading and Writing Creative Nonfiction.*

Smith, Marion Roach. (2011). *The Memoir Project: A Thoroughly Non-Standardized Text for Writing & Life.*

Van Cleave, Ryan G. (2013). *Memoir Writing For Dummies.*

Warner, Brooke, and Myers, Linda Joy. (2015). *Breaking Ground On Your Memoir: Craft, Inspiration, and Motivation for Memoir Writers.*

Warner, Brooke, and Myers, Linda Joy. (2016). *The Magic of Memoir: Inspiration for the Writing Journey.*

Waxler, Jerry. (2013). *Memoir Revolution: A Social and Literary Shift That Uses Your Story to Heal, Connect and Inspire.*

Yagoda, Ben. (2010). *Memoir: A History.*

Zinsser, William (Editor). (1998). *Inventing the Truth: The Art and Craft of Memoir.*

Other Recommended Reading

Cron, Lisa. (2012). *Wired for Story: The Writer's Guide to Using Brain Science to Hook Readers From the Very First Sentence.*

Dodson, Daphne. (2017). *Imaginal Remembering: Our Soul's Journey Through Memory and Imagination.*

Edelman, Gerald M. (2006). *Second Nature: Brain Science and Human Knowledge.*

Geary, James. (2012). *I Is an Other: The Secret Life of Metaphor and How It Shapes the Way We See the World.*

Jung, C.G. (1969). *The Archetypes and the Collective Unconscious.*

Maass, Donald. (2016). *The Emotional Craft of Fiction: How to Write the Story Beneath the Surface.*

Marks, Dara. (2009). *Inside Story: The Power of the Transformational Arc.*

Olney, James. (2017). *Metaphors of Self: The Meaning of Autobiography.*

Pennebaker, James W. and Smyth, Joshua M. (2016). *Opening Up By Writing It Down: How Expressive Writing Improves Health and Eases Emotional Pain (Third Edition).*

Schacter, Daniel L. (2021). *The Seven Sins of Memory: How the Mind Forgets and Remembers (Updated Edition).*

ACKNOWLEDGMENTS

It takes a village to raise a memoir teacher.

To all the memoir teachers whose books have been instrumental in deepening my understanding and broadening my appreciation of the genre, it is an honor to sit on the shelves next to you now. Who would've thunk? Special thanks to Maureen Murdock, my teacher before she was my co-teacher. It's been an honor and a joy, a highlight of this decade of my life. To Daphne Dodson and Ruth Salmon, whom I also taught with, being a single parent is fine, but it was way more fun co-parenting with you.

To Dennis Patrick Slattery, thank you for your friendship and unconditional support. I honor and adore you more than all the words in this wordy book.

To Pacifica Graduate Institute and particularly David Odoriso, thank you for the opportunity to cut my memoir teaching teeth over the last decade. You've brought me the most amazing and inspiring students.

To those amazing and inspiring memoir students, just when I think I have nothing more to say about the genre, you call something forth. This book is for and because of you, my beloved community.

And to you reading this book, consider joining our writing community. Find my courses at my website, www.jenniferleighselig.com. You, no doubt, will amaze and inspire me, inspire us, as well.

ABOUT THE AUTHOR

Jennifer Leigh Selig has had a lifelong love affair with books, both reading and writing them. One of her favorite activities from childhood combined both—she would lay a piece of tracing paper over her favorite books, and copy the words to make a replica. Once she grew up a little and learned that copying other people's words was plagiarism, she started to write her own books. Now she is the author, editor, or contributor to over 20 books, and she's published more than 70 titles for others through her imprints Mandorla Books and Empress Publications. In addition, she has published dozens of newspaper articles, book reviews, journal articles, essays, and has written three unproduced (as of yet!) screenplays.

Her bachelor's degree in English and her master's degree in Multicultural Women's Literature served her well as she took her love of story into the high school classroom as a teacher for 16 years. During that time, she completed a Ph.D. in Depth Psychology at Pacifica Graduate Institute in Santa Barbara, California. Shortly after finishing her dissertation on Dr. Martin Luther King, Jr., which later became her book *Integration: The Psychology and Mythology of Martin Luther King, Jr. and His (Unfinished) Therapy With the Soul of America*, she joined the faculty at Pacifica, where she taught for another 12 years. During that time, she founded and chaired the Ph.D. program in Jungian and Archetypal Studies.

An archetypal approach informs everything Jennifer teaches, including three of her most popular courses. In *Deep Vocation: Finding and Following Your Life's Purpose and Passion*, she helps participants discern the archetypal patterns that comprise their unique character and calling. In *On Longing: A Pilgrimage Toward Our Heart's Deepest Desires*, Jennifer introduces 13 archetypal longings and empowers participants to fully embrace the longings woven deep in the fabric of their hearts and souls. In *Following the Sacred Thread: A Spiritual Writing Retreat*, participants explore their spiritual archetypes, temperament types, and archetypal metaphors of their spiritual journey. All courses are available on her website, www.jenniferleighselig.com, along with her memoir courses.

An archetypal approach also underpins Jennifer's writing prior to *Deep Memoir*, including her co-written book, *Deep Creativity: Seven Ways to Spark Your Creative Spirit* (with Deborah Anne Quibell and Dennis Patrick Slattery), and her book *Everyday Reverence: A Hundred Ways to Kneel and Kiss the Ground*, which looks at universal ways people connect with the sacred.

Jennifer is also the mastermind researcher behind the MoneyType Personality Test, offered by the financial editor at NBC's "Today" show, Jean Chatsky, and featured on her HerMoney website (www.moneytype.hermoney.com). This survey offers insight into the five archetypal roles that drive our relationship with money: the Producer, the Visionary, the Connoisseur, the Nurturer, and the Independent.

Jennifer resides in California where her family has lived for generations. When she's not spending time with family, she loves to combine her passion for teaching and travel by leading workshops and speaking at conferences all over the United States and internationally, including gigs in Brazil, Canada, Mexico, Australia, and the Philippines.

Made in the USA
Las Vegas, NV
21 March 2024

87533023R00174